Forces of Habit

Forces of Habit

DRUGS AND THE
MAKING OF THE
MODERN WORLD

DAVID T. COURTWRIGHT

HARVARD UNIVERSITY PRESS
Cambridge, Massachusetts, and London, England   2001

Library of Congress Cataloging-in-Publication Data
Courtwright, David T., 1952–
Forces of habit : drugs and the making of the modern world / David T. Courtwright.
p. cm.
Includes bibliographical references and index.
ISBN 0-674-00458-2 (alk. paper)
1. Substance abuse—History. 2. Psychotropic drugs—History.
3. Substance abuse—Economic aspects. 4. Substance abuse—Social aspects.
5. Substance abuse—Prevention. I. Title.

HV4997 .C68 2000
362.29—dc21   00-061466

To my brothers Chris and Mike,
historians in their own unique ways

Acknowledgments

TEN YEARS AGO, while killing time between flights in a duty-free shop, I found myself wondering why I was surrounded by drugs. Marlboro cartons loomed to my left, Drambuie bottles to my right, Belgian chocolates behind me, Kenyan coffee straight ahead—everywhere I looked, I saw imported psychoactive products. How did these things get here? And why could "here" be anywhere—why did duty-free shops all seem to be stocked with the same merchandise? (Indeed, I can no longer recall which airport I was passing through.) Though I had long been interested in the history of narcotic drugs, this book grew out of a broader curiosity about psychoactive commerce, a ubiquitous—and, I now believe, defining—feature of the modern world.

I could not have acted on that curiosity without a timely research leave from the University of North Florida and a fellowship from the National Endowment for the Humanities. The Francis C. Wood Institute for the History of Medicine supported my work at the College of Physicians of Philadelphia Library; the Sonnedecker Visiting Research Program financed a visit to the University of Wisconsin. Librarians there extended me every professional courtesy, as did those at the Universities of North Florida, Pennsylvania, and Kansas.

I am especially indebted to UNF's Alisa Craddock, who filled countless interlibrary loan requests, often cryptic and fiendishly obscure. Elaine Stroud, Greg Higby, and Glenn Sonnedecker offered assistance and advice during my stay in Madison. Charles Greifenstein, Marjorie Smink, Sophie Sereda, and Thomas Horrocks rendered similar services at the College of Physicians of Philadelphia. Deborah Franklin, editor of the College's *Transactions*, kindly granted permission to incorporate parts of my article, "Medicine's

Problem Children," vol. 21, ser. 5 (1999): 59–86, into Chapter 4 of this book. At Duke University, Ellen Gartrell, Elizabeth Dunn, and Gary Boye steered me to valuable holdings in the Special Collections Library. Mort Goren, Rosemary Russo, Lavonne Wienke, Daphne Joseph, and Nora Beecher assisted me at (and often escorted me to) the Drug Enforcement Administration Library in Arlington, Virginia.

The editors and staff of Harvard University Press—particularly Aïda Donald, Elizabeth Suttell, Mary Ellen Geer, Tim Jones, and Sheila Barrett— were helpful and accommodating at every stage of the book's development. Many scholars, colleagues, and students rendered assistance along the way. H. Wayne Morgan generously turned over research files to me. Dale Clifford, Jeffrey Kaimowitz, Bert Koegler, Kathryn Meyer, Debra Murphy, Shira Schwam-Baird, and John Tucker provided iconographic and translation advice. Rodney Brown, Andrew Courtwright, Janice Fluegel, Michael Hoffmann, Harold Hyman, Sam Kimball, William McAllister, Scott Martin and his seminar students, Shelby Miller, Stephen M. Miller, Ron Roizen, Wade Schemer, Susan Speaker, Kunisi Venkatasubban, and Linda Wilson read preliminary drafts of the manuscript, saving me from many errors and infelicities. Any that remain are stubbornly my own.

Contents

Introduction

THE PSYCHOACTIVE REVOLUTION

ON JULY 13, 1926, Anthony Colombo, a man of many habits, all of them bad, checked into the Philadelphia General Hospital. The staff assigned him to the drug ward—a good choice, considering that each day of his life he smoked a quarter-ounce of opium, puffed 80 cigarettes, drank two cups of coffee or tea, and downed a quart of whiskey. He got drunk nearly every day, he explained to an intern. He had begun smoking the opium to sober up.

But he didn't use the hard stuff. No cocaine. No barbiturates. "No narcotics other than opium"—a lie betrayed by his upper arms and thighs, pitted with the scars of hypodermic abscesses. Or perhaps it was a white lie. Opium smokers looked down on needle users in those days. Colombo had his pride to consider.

He was, after all, a working man. Addiction to opium had affected neither his will power, he boasted, nor his ability to work. He was in the liquor business, he said—a striking admission from the citizen of a country that did not, in 1926, officially have a liquor business.

The opium habit did not affect his appetite, the intern noted. Just 33 years of age, Colombo tipped the scales at 275 pounds. "The chest is immense," he wrote; "the abdomen is large and pendulous." Considering Colombo's weight, his "three to five meals daily," his opium, his four score cigarettes, his coffee, his tea, and his whiskey, some form of gratification must have been passing through his mouth practically every waking moment. Indeed,

Colombo led a life—probably not a long life—of such continuous and varied stimulation and psychoactive pleasure that no emperor, no despot, no potentate of the ancient world, however wealthy, determined, or decadent, could have matched it.[1]

Yet Anthony Colombo was a lowly man, a petty bootlegger of modest means. It was his luck, or misfortune, to live in the twentieth century, in an industrial city in an industrial nation that had, in its brief history, managed to refine and mass-market an impressive array of psychoactive pleasures. By the time Colombo checked into the hospital, millions of ordinary people throughout the world could lead, in neurochemical terms, a life-style unimaginable for even the wealthiest five hundred years earlier.

I call this development the psychoactive revolution. People everywhere have acquired progressively more, and more potent, means of altering their ordinary waking consciousness. One of the signal events of world history, this development had its roots in the transoceanic commerce and empire building of the early modern period—that is, the years from about 1500 to 1789. *Forces of Habit* describes how early modern merchants, planters, and other imperial elites succeeded in bringing about the confluence of the world's psychoactive resources and then explores why, despite enormous profits and tax revenues, their successors changed their minds and restricted or prohibited many—but not all—drugs.

The term "drugs" is an extremely problematic one, connoting such things as abuse and addiction. For all its baggage, the word has one great virtue. It is short. Indeed, one of the reasons its use persisted, over the objections of offended pharmacists, was that headline writers needed something pithier than "narcotic drugs." In this book I use "drugs" as a convenient and neutral term of reference for a long list of psychoactive substances, licit or illicit, mild or potent, deployed for medical and nonmedical purposes. Alcoholic and caffeinated beverages, cannabis, coca, cocaine, opium, morphine, and tobacco are all drugs in this sense, as are heroin, methamphetamine, and many other semisynthetic and synthetic substances. None is inherently evil. All can be abused. All are sources of profit. All have become, or at least have the potential to become, global commodities.[2]

This might not be apparent from a casual inspection of drug histories. Most scholarship deals with particular drugs or types of drugs in a particular setting: tea in Japan, vodka in Russia, narcotics in America, and so on. I have tried to connect these scholarly dots, linking the many separate histories in a big-picture narrative of the discovery, interchange, and exploitation of the planet's psychoactive resources. I aim to do for drugs what William McNeill did for diseases in *Plagues and Peoples* (1976), a world-historical study of the exchange of microorganisms and its impact on civilizations. Disease and drug exchanges have many close parallels. That imported alcohol, for example, acted as a deadly pathogen for indigenous peoples is more than a metaphor. But there are also important differences. McNeill's story was largely one of tragic happenstance. Invisible germs spread by human contact had lethal but usually unintended consequences. The spread of drug cultivation and manufacturing, however, was anything but accidental. It depended on conscious human enterprise, and only secondarily on unconscious biological processes.

The book's first section describes the confluence of the world's principal psychoactive resources, concentrating on alcoholic and caffeinated beverages, tobacco, opiates, cannabis, coca, cocaine, and sugar—the last a key ingredient in many drug products. These substances, once geographically confined, all entered the stream of global commerce, though at different times and from different places. Coffee, for example, spread from Ethiopia, where the bush was indigenous, to Arabia, and then throughout the Islamic lands and Christian Europe. Europeans took the taste and the beans to the Americas, which produced 70 percent of the world's coffee crop by the late nineteenth century.[3] European farmers and planters, employing indentured and slave labor, enjoyed great success cultivating drug crops in both hemispheres. Their collective efforts expanded world supply, drove down prices, and drew millions of less affluent purchasers into the market, democratizing drug consumption.

But not for all drugs. Embedded in the story of psychoactive commerce is a mystery, one that is often overlooked. A number of regionally popular plant drugs—kava, betel, qat, peyote—failed to become commodities in both hemispheres in the way that wine or opium did. Global drug commerce, propelled by European overseas expansion, was highly selective. For reasons that ranged from limited shelf life to cultural biases against their effects, Europeans chose to ignore or suppress many novel psychoactive plants. The ones they found useful and acceptable they traded and cultivated throughout the world, with social and environmental consequences that are still very much in evidence.

The second section, on drugs and commerce, deals with psychoactive substances as medical and recreational products. Drugs typically began their careers as expensive and rarefied medicines, touted for a variety of human and

animal ailments. Once their pleasurable and consciousness-altering properties became known, they escaped the therapeutic realm and entered that of
popular consumption. As they did so, their political status changed. Widespread nonmedical use of spirits, tobacco, amphetamines, and other psychoactive substances occasioned controversy, alarm, and official intervention.
All large-scale societies differentiated in some way between the medical use
and the nonmedical abuse of drugs, and eventually they made this distinction the moral and legal foundation for the international drug control
system.

Such a system was necessary because drugs were at once dangerous and lucrative products. The opposite of "durable goods," they were quickly consumed and had to be just as quickly replaced by those dependent on them.
Regular users needed larger doses to experience the original effect, which
meant that the volume of sales was likely to increase. Inventions such as improved stills, hypodermic syringes, and blended cigarettes made for more
efficient, speedier, and more profitable ways to get refined chemicals into
consumers' brains. Competition sparked further innovation and widespread
advertising, as manufacturers sought to cut their costs, increase market share,
and enhance the appeal of their products. As drugs became cheaper and
more seductive, they attracted millions of new users, generating profitable
opportunities in enterprises ranging from addiction treatment to Zippo lighters. Drug commerce and its externalities were manifestations of mature capitalism's limbic turn, its increasing focus on pleasure and emotional gratification, as opposed to consumers' material needs. Drug commerce, to
paraphrase the anthropologist Robert Ardrey, flourished in a world in which
the hungry psyche was replacing the hungry belly.[4]

The third section, which concerns drugs and power, shows how psychoactive trade benefited mercantile and imperial elites in ways that went beyond
ordinary commercial profits. These elites quickly discovered that they could
use drugs to control manual laborers and exploit indigenes. Opium, for instance, kept Chinese laborers in a state of debt and dependency. Alcohol induced native peoples to trade their furs, sell their captives into slavery, and
negotiate away their lands. Early modern political elites found drugs to be
dependable sources of revenue. Though rulers were often initially hostile to
novel drugs (tobacco struck them as an especially nasty foreign vice, provok-
ing sanctions from royal denunciations to ritual executions), they bowed to
the inevitable and imposed taxes or their equivalents, monopolies, on the expanding commerce. They prospered beyond their dreams. By 1885 taxes on

alcohol, tobacco, and tea accounted for close to half of the British government's gross income. Drug taxation was the fiscal cornerstone of the modern state, and the chief financial prop of European colonial empires.[5]

Political elites do not ordinarily kill the geese that lay their golden eggs. Yet, during the last hundred years, they have selectively abandoned a policy of taxed, legal commerce for one of greater restriction and prohibition, achieved by domestic legislation and international treaties. The final chapters explore the modernizing pressures, medical developments, and political maneuvers that prompted so many governments to reverse course, and why they did so for some drugs rather than others. The psychoactive counterrevolution was strikingly erratic. Its legacy is a world in which (for now) tobacco and liquor are easily and legally available, while drugs like cannabis or heroin are generally not.

Writing world history is like peering through a microscope with a low-powered lens. The observer can see a good deal of the specimen, but only by sacrificing detail. One way to avoid this problem, and the narrative monotony it entails, is to periodically zoom in on a particular episode or personality, and then back out to the larger picture. That, at any rate, is my narrative strategy. Generalizations culled from the historical, social scientific, and scientific literature are fleshed out with specific examples and—dialing up the power further—several case studies. Among these are the democratization of amphetamines, James Duke and the cigarette industry, alcohol taxation in India, and the failure of prohibition in the Soviet Union. Each of these cases serves as a kind of parable, illustrating principles important to drug history.

The subject and my approach to it require selectivity. I have concentrated on identifying and illustrating the most significant trends of the past 500 years, and have made no attempt to provide comprehensive histories of all psychoactive drugs. That task, rendered impossible by the weight of numbers, has been beyond the capability of any one person since Louis Lewin, the pioneering German psychopharmacologist, died in 1929. I should add that I have cited only a fraction of the voluminous literature on drugs. The reader will discover, however, that my documentation is not ungenerous, and will find in it many leads to the outstanding specialized scholarship on the role and impact of drugs in the modern world.

PART I

THE CONFLUENCE OF PSYCHOACTIVE RESOURCES

1

The Big Three: Alcohol, Tobacco, and Caffeine

THE EXPANSION OF OCEANGOING commerce is the single most important fact about the early modern world. Plants, animals, and microorganisms long confined to one continent or hemisphere spread elsewhere, with spectacular demographic and ecological results. New World foods such as the potato and maize made possible rapid population growth in Europe and Asia. Old World diseases such as smallpox and measles wiped out millions of Amerindians, creating a demographic vacuum filled by Europeans and Africans.

The exchange of diseases, so much to the Old World's advantage, was usually accidental. The exchange of plants was sometimes accidental, as anyone who has ever weeded a garden of hitchhiker species well knows. But the exchange of psychoactive plants, products, and processing techniques was seldom accidental. The globalization of wine, spirits, tobacco, caffeine bearing plants, opiates, cannabis, coca, and other drugs—each to be considered in its turn—was a deliberate, profit-driven process. It would transform the everyday consciousness of billions of people and, eventually, the environment itself.

Wine

Viticulture, the selective cultivation of grape vines for making wine, exemplifies the global diffusion process. Viticulture probably originated in the mountainous region between the Black and Caspian seas, where Armenia is now located, sometime between 6000 and 4000 B.C. Commercial wine production was well established in the Levant and Aegean by 1500 B.C. and was thriving throughout the Mediterranean world by the time of Christ. The Bible mentions wine no fewer than 165 times.[1]

The rise of Islam, which condemned wine as an abomination devised by Satan, discouraged viticulture in North Africa and the Middle East, but wine making and drinking flourished in medieval Europe. Greek wine made its way to Russia, along with Orthodoxy; the Kievan *Chronicle* attributes Vladimir I's rejection of Islam to the Russian fondness for drinking. Wine was a symbol of Christ's sacrifice, the preferred beverage of the European aristocracy (commoners mostly drank locally brewed ale or beer), and a safe, germ-free alternative to polluted water, possibly the single greatest menace to human health since the advent of civilization. That the Good Samaritan poured wine rather than water into the traveler's wounds was no coincidence.[2]

Viticulture also spread to northern India and China, though wine drinking never became as popular there as in Christian Europe. As a result of a minute genetic variation, roughly half of all Asians produce an inactive form of an enzyme necessary for complete alcohol metabolism. They experience an "alcohol flush reaction" of bright red facial flushing, heart palpitations, dizziness, and nausea. Those with milder versions of the syndrome, called "slow flushers," sometimes take to drink, but "fast flushers" are vulnerable to acute alcohol poisoning and typically have a stronger aversion. Though alcohol researchers differ over the deterrent power of the flush reaction, some have suggested that it slowed the progress of viticulture and other forms of alcoholic beverage production in East Asia. The Chinese, moreover, had less need of wine or other alcoholic beverages as alternatives to contaminated water. They had tea, made with boiling water and thus potable.[3]

During the Renaissance *Vitis vinifera*, the European wine vine, was successfully transplanted to the eastern Atlantic islands. When Shakespeare's characters spoke of Canary, they meant the wine, not the islands. Though Columbus tried and failed to establish vineyards, Cortés and his followers succeeded in importing wine vines to Mexico. The local varieties of grapes would not do; like almost all native American grapes, they were small, tough, sour, and unpalatable. Cortés solved the problem by transplanting strains taken from the Estremadura by his own father, strains that were the product of seven thousand years of artificial selection for superior size, tenderness, sugar content, and flavor.

Between 1524 and 1556 viticulture spread south to Peru and Chile and across the Andes to Argentina, where a Jesuit priest introduced it. Missionaries were also responsible for bringing viticulture to Alta California in the 1770s. Within a century it became one of the great wine-producing regions of the world, exporting its produce to places as far distant as Australia, China, Hawaii, Peru, Denmark, and Britain.

The Dutch brought viticulture to the Cape Colony, established in 1652 on the southern tip of Africa as a victualing station for the Dutch East India Company. The idea was to provide crews with fresh wine, an antiscorbutic and palatable alternative to the three-month-old water in the ships' casks. It was, however, the British, anxious to develop alternatives to French imports, who rapidly expanded Cape wine production when they took over the colony in the nineteenth century. The British also introduced viticulture to Australia. The ships that arrived in 1788 to establish the penal colony also carried wine vines from Rio de Janeiro and the Cape Colony. The experiment was initially a disappointment, as transplanted convicts preferred the more familiar beer and spirits.[4]

What the British attempted to do in Australia and later in New Zealand, where they introduced wine vines in 1819, was part of a larger pattern, the deliberate mingling of the world's plants by European colonizers and traders. The exotic plants of Kew Gardens, just upriver from London, are living reminders of Britain's preeminent role in the imperial reshuffling of nature. His Majesty's ships served as the means of botanical discovery and exchange. In 1789, when Fletcher Christian decided that he had had enough of Captain William Bligh, the *Bounty* was transporting a thousand breadfruit trees from Tahiti to the West Indies, where they might provide a cheap new food source for slaves. The mutineers rid themselves of Bligh and his cargo, but the doughty captain survived and later successfully completed a second breadfruit voyage.[5]

Spirits

European ships carried new technologies as well as new plants. Among the most important of these was distilling. Known to the Greeks and Romans, preserved and advanced by the Arabs, distilling entered Europe via Salerno in the eleventh century. Printed books on distilling, which began appearing in the late fifteenth century, spread knowledge of the technique. Although stills extracted the "essences" of many plants, the manufacture of alcoholic spirits from wine and other fermented liquids assumed increasing economic importance. Larger, improved copper stills and cheaper base materials, nota-

A still in a botanical garden, anon., 1560. The illustration is a modified detail from the title page of *Liber de Arte Distillandi de Simplicibus . . .* (1500), commonly called the *Small Book of Distillation*. Written by the Strassburg surgeon Hieronymus Brunschwig, it was, like most seminal works on psychoactive drugs and techniques, widely imitated and translated.

bly sugar and Baltic grain, made the mass production of liquor possible. By the mid-seventeenth century stills were dripping their fiery waters from Ireland to Russia. The center of the emerging industry was Holland. The Dutch, already leaders in the wine trade, had efficient stills and were well situated to export their product. To this day their language is imprinted on strong drink. "Brandy" is an abbreviation of *brandewijn*, or burnt wine. "Gin" is short for *genever*, grain spirits flavored with juniper berries. The English first ascribed the eponymous "Dutch courage" to their hard-drinking rivals during the seventeenth century.[6]

Mass-produced spirits were a cheap source of intoxication and calories.

The ales, beers, and wines drunk by early modern Europeans were often of poor quality and spoiled quickly. Brandy and whiskey kept well and improved with age. Vintners also commonly added brandy to preserve wines, whose alcoholic content was thus strengthened or "fortified."

Distilling rendered perishable crops imperishable. The potato, for example, was the mainstay of the German distilling industry in the nineteenth and early twentieth centuries. Once harvested, potatoes kept only until the warm weather of the next growing season set in. Converted to alcohol in one of the Reich's 6,000 potato distilleries, they could last indefinitely—and be profitably exported to African colonies. Spirits of all sorts, which were cheaper and easier to ship than beer or wine, became important items in colonial trade. "She is the fountain of all good," the Maoris toasted Queen Victoria. "May she send us plenty of gun powder, plenty of rum and may both be strong."[7]

Europeans also brought or improvised stills. William McCoy, one of the *Bounty*'s mutineers who ended up on remote Pitcairn Island, managed to adapt a copper kettle salvaged from the ship, with tragic personal consequences: he leapt to his death from a cliff while drunk. Thirsty beachcombers on Ponape learned they could not count on rum or whiskey from passing ships. So they fermented coconut toddy ("a skill they very soon passed on to the islanders") and rigged stills to guarantee a supply of spirits.[8]

Native peoples caught on to distilling and were soon adjusting recipes to suit their tastes. Some Maoris fancied tobacco and human urine in their home brew. But a mixture of imported and locally produced liquor became the most common pattern, at least in agricultural societies. By the 1840s the Siamese were consuming imported spirits from China, Batavia, Singapore, and Europe as well as growing amounts of locally distilled rum and arrack. One government official complained that, despite flogging his slaves to the brink of death, he could not stop them from converting their rice ration into spirits, "so strong was their appetite for the poison."[9]

Similar complaints could be heard wherever distilled beverages took hold. The mass production of spirits and the fortification of wines exacerbated drunkenness and alcoholism in both European and non-European societies. Contemporaries and historians are unanimous on this point. The question is why. After all, fermentation is a natural process. Except for some Arctic dwellers and North American Indians, most people had access to at least one type of alcoholic beverage—palm wine, mead, corn and barley beers, fermented milk—before they tasted of the fruit of the tree of distilling.

One frequent explanation is that fermented beverages spoil quickly and are much weaker in alcoholic content, which is not more than 14 percent in wine and 7 percent in beer, and often less. (Early modern wines—less potent than today's beverages—were also commonly diluted with water before being drunk, lowering the percentage of alcohol further.) Spirits packed a far heftier ethanol punch. "This changed profoundly the economic and social role of alcoholic drinks," writes the historian David Christian, "for distilled drinks were to fermented drinks what guns were to bows and arrows: instruments of a potency unimaginable in most traditional societies."[10]

Some traditional societies fared worse than others. Hunter-gatherers were hit harder than sedentary agricultural peoples, who were more constrained by community controls. Festive northern and eastern European drinkers and their American descendants had more trouble with grain spirits than the Romanized wine drinkers of southern Europe, who preferred their alcohol in moderation and on a full stomach. *Les misérables* swilled more gin than *les bourgeois*. Everywhere the cultural norms and social circumstances of those who were exposed to liquor, as well as those who did the exposing, influenced the prevalence of problem drinking.[11]

Yet it is hard to escape the logic of David Christian's observation. When familiar drugs are processed in unfamiliar ways, increasing their potency to unprecedented levels, heightened abuse inevitably, if not always evenly, follows. This is an important and recurring theme in drug history. Wine is to brandy as opium is to morphine, coca is to cocaine, or shag tobacco is to the modern cigarette. The history of psychoactive substances resembles that of the arms race. Technological change continuously raises the human stakes.

Tobacco

Europeans learned of tobacco in 1492, when two members of Columbus's party observed Tainos Indians smoking leaves rolled into large cigars. Subsequent contacts revealed that Indians also chewed and sniffed the drug, methods of administration that one day would be emulated by millions of Europeans. But for most of the sixteenth century tobacco was a sideshow—a botanical curiosity, an exotic medicine, or a raffish toy introduced to English courtiers by Sir Walter Raleigh. Sailors spread the smoking habit in humbler circles, in the taverns and brothels of numberless ports of call. With more deliberation, the Spanish used one of their Manila galleons to transplant tobacco to the Philippines, where after 1575 it quickly became a cash crop.

Around 1600 Fukienese sailors and merchants brought the plant from the Philippines to China, soon to become a nation of enthusiastic smokers.

Tobacco cultivation began in West Africa sometime in the late sixteenth or early seventeenth century, recent scholarship inclining toward the latter period. It was brought by the Portuguese, who revolutionized African agriculture by introducing maize, beans, sweet potatoes, tobacco, and many other New World crops. Between about 1590 and 1610 the energetic Portuguese also introduced tobacco to India, Java, Japan, and Iran. Like ripples from a handful of gravel tossed into a pond, tobacco use and cultivation spread by secondary and tertiary diffusion: from India to Ceylon, from Iran to Central Asia, from Japan to Korea, from China to Tibet and Siberia, from Java to Malaysia to New Guinea. By 1620 tobacco was, by any definition, a global crop.[12]

But it was not yet an item of widespread consumption. It was still expensive in 1620 and would remain so until colonial tobacco production—an object of all European imperial powers, even minor ones like Sweden—expanded. Virginia and Maryland were the most productive colonies. They were too productive, in fact, for their own good. Farm prices, measured in shillings per pound in the early 1620s, fell to less than one pence per pound by the late 1670s. The average weight of tobacco exports to England rose from 65,000 pounds a year to more than 20 million pounds during the same period.

Much of this tobacco was reexported, particularly to Amsterdam. The Dutch and the English were the first European peoples to achieve genuine mass consumption. The Dutch averaged 1.5 pounds per capita in 1670, the English a little more than a pound. Amsterdam and London served as rival headquarters of the psychoactive revolution in the seventeenth century, with Amsterdam the more advanced and aggressive of the two. Amsterdam had its own lively reexport trade. Its enterprising merchants mixed Virginia and other colonial tobaccos with cheaper Dutch varieties, which flourished on the sandy, manured soils of the inner provinces. They shipped the mixture to Scandinavia, Russia, and other markets dominated, to the chagrin of the English, by Dutch tobacco imports.[13]

Spanish, English, and Dutch soldiers fighting in the Thirty Years' War (1618–1648) introduced tobacco into the German-speaking lands of central Europe. From there it spread to northern, eastern, and southern Europe. Soldiers, along with sailors, merchants, diplomats, students, immigrants, guest workers, refugees, and tourists, have long constituted the advance guard of the psychoactive revolution. Armies, whose ranks are filled with single, lower-class men plagued by alternating cycles of boredom, fatigue, and terror, were natural incubators of drug use. Highly mobile, they introduced novel drugs and drug-taking methods into the countries in which they fought, and returned home with drug knowledge acquired abroad. The troops who fought under Gustavus Adolphus during the Thirty Years' War brought smoking to the interior of Scandinavia. (English and Dutch sailors had already exposed the seaport populations.) Veterans of the Mexican War (1846–1848) boosted cigar smoking in the United States, and veterans of the Crimean War (1853–1856) did the same for cigarettes in Britain. Demobilized Greek soldiers, who learned to smoke hashish in Turkey, helped spread the practice in Greece in the 1920s. American deserters who had begun using heroin in Vietnam brought the drug to Amsterdam in 1972.[14]

Whether advanced by military or by other means, two things are remarkable about tobacco's conquest of Europe and Asia during the seventeenth century. The first is that use of the drug cut across all social categories. Lowborn and high, ortho- and heterodox partook of its pleasures, though whether by quid, pipe, or snuff varied with class, gender, and local custom. The second is that tobacco managed to overcome sharp and sometimes violent initial opposition by civil and clerical authorities. English smokers risked the disapproval of James I, who declaimed against the Stygian weed. Monarchs of more absolute sway meted out cruel punishments. Russian smokers suffered beatings and exile; snuff-takers had their noses torn off. Chinese smokers had their heads impaled on pikes. Turkish smokers under the reign of Ahmed I endured pipe stems thrust through their noses; Murad IV ordered them tortured to death. Priests who indulged in tobacco during Mass—one vomited up the Sacrament after dipping snuff—were threatened with excommunication.

Added to the fines, floggings, mutilations, and threats of death and damnation was the everyday obloquy of those who did not indulge. Tobacco, as its critics tirelessly pointed out, fouled the breath, stained the teeth, soiled the clothing, and brought forth umbered streams of snot and spittle. Smoking also entailed the risk of fire, a mortal danger in a world of combustible dwellings. Yet nothing checked tobacco's progress. The drug was so reinforcing—the historian V. G. Kiernan called it the most universal new pleasure human beings have acquired—that it triumphed over all legal obstacles and offended sensibilities.[15]

Official statistics suggest that tobacco consumption, measured in pounds per capita, leveled off in Europe during the eighteenth century. This trend is

A tobacco sign popular in the late seventeenth century. Note the aristocratic dress and demeanor of the Frenchman. Despite Louis XIV's objections, snuff taking had caught on among courtiers by the 1650s, later spreading downward to the wealthy Paris bourgeoisie and rural gentry. By the eighteenth century it had evolved into an exquisite art form at Versailles and other courts that followed French fashion.

misleading, however. The figures omit clandestine domestic production and unreported American imports, equivalent to perhaps a third of the total. The eighteenth-century rage for snuff also helps explain the apparent stagnation. Pound for pound, tobacco could be stretched further in the manufacture of snuff than in smoking products. Europeans were not consuming less nicotine in the eighteenth century, but rather were consuming it more efficiently — or, in the case of contraband, illegally.

Smoking again became fashionable in Europe during the nineteenth century. Romantics, bohemians, soldiers, and dandies led the way. By the 1850s pipes and cigars were rapidly gaining ground, though oral snuff remained popular in Sweden and Iceland. In the first half of the twentieth century cigarettes triumphed over all competitors, becoming the smoking norm — or, more accurately, a kind of international language and freemasonry — in Europe, the United States, Turkey, China, and much of the rest of the world.[16]

Smoking in general and cigarettes in particular increased tobacco consumption. In France, a bellwether for continental drug practices, the use of tobacco products per person was only about three-quarters of a pound in 1819. Snuff then accounted for 58 percent of the market. In 1925, when the French were using well over three pounds per person, snuff held just 7 percent of the market, chewing tobacco only 2 percent. The French, remarked an American physician in 1909, after visiting the spotless modern tobacco factory at Issy les Moulineaux, did not indulge in the vile mastication so beloved of his fellow citizens.[17]

He need not have concerned himself. Within a generation spittoons were antiques and Americans were in thrall to the cigarette. The victory did not come easily: the cigarette had many enemies. One of the more implacable, Mrs. John Stuart White, objected to smoking during the sinking of the *Titanic*. "Before we cut loose from the ship two of the seamen with us . . . took out cigarettes and lighted them," she complained during a Senate inquiry into the disaster. "On an occasion like that!" More pragmatically, a coalition of evangelical and progressive reformers, who blamed "the little white slaver" for corrupting the young and poisoning the race, endeavored to throw up legislative barriers to its progress. But widespread military use during World War I, rapid urbanization, changing gender roles, and clever advertising ("Reach for a Lucky Instead of a Sweet") paved the way for the cigarette's triumph. In 1930 the authoritative *Tobacco Industry Annual Review* reported that U.S. leaf production was at an all-time high. It attributed the good news to heavy advertising and the "present great consumption of cigarettes by women," brought into the smoking fold by a "masterly" campaign. "Today, therefore, the cigarette industry cannot only look forward to annual accretions to its ranks from the generations of new male smokers but has added the opposite sex to this group, while continuing its efforts toward those women for whom smoking is still, if not among the taboos, at least a debatable question."[18]

By the late 1950s American men and women were purchasing upwards of 15,000 cigarettes a *second*. World production had climbed to over 8.4 billion pounds annually. N. *tabacum* was a cash crop on all continents save Antarctica, whose explorers smoked anyway. A third of global production came from North America, two-fifths from Asia, one-sixth from Europe, and the remaining tenth from South America and Africa—the latter then expanding its production rapidly. America led the world in tobacco production and export; its gold-standard cigarettes could be found on every continent. Bushmen begged for them in mime, puffing the tips of their fingers. Though consumption leveled off in the United States and other western nations during the 1960s and 1970s, it continued to expand in developing nations. By the mid-1990s the world's estimated 1.1 billion smokers—a third of the population over age 15—smoked 5.5 trillion cigarettes annually. That sum represented a pack a week for every man, woman, and child, smoker or non-smoker, on the planet.[19]

Caffeinated Beverages and Foods

As impressive as the cigarette's triumph was, its principal active ingredient, nicotine, is by no means the earth's most widely used drug. It is in third place. Alcohol ranks second, caffeine first. World per capita consumption is about 70 milligrams a day. In some countries, such as Sweden and Britain, the average is well over 400 milligrams a day, roughly equivalent to four cups of coffee. According to the anthropologist Eugene Anderson, the most widespread words on the planet, found in virtually every language, are the names of the four great caffeine plants: coffee, tea, cacao, and kola.[20]

Economically, coffee became the most important of the caffeine plants. By the late twentieth century it consistently trailed only oil as the world's most widely traded commodity. In its own way, coffee had become just as indispensable as a fuel of industrial civilization. Yet it began its career in the relative obscurity of the Ethiopian highlands, whose residents chewed rather than infused the beans for their stimulating effects. Coffee drinking made its earliest appearance outside Ethiopia in Yemen, in southern Arabia, sometime in the fifteenth century, likely before 1470. By the late fifteenth century it had spread to Mecca and Medina; by the early sixteenth to Cairo; by the mid-sixteenth to Istanbul. Iran, connected to the Ottoman Empire by warfare and commerce, soon followed. Exporters shipped the beans to southeastern Europe. They sold in Venice as an exotic drug as early as 1615, and came into more general use by the 1640s. Except for tea, coffee was the only important stimulant beverage whose use spread beyond its original zone of cultivation prior to and independently of European commercial expansion.[21]

But it was Europeans who made coffee into a worldwide drink and global crop. Coffee caught on in Europe in the second half of the seventeenth century. As in Islamic lands, the public center of consumption was the coffee house. Itinerant vendors also sold coffee, though fixed distribution was more practical because of the bulky equipment and fire required to brew and warm the drink. Coffee houses quickly emerged as centers of male conviviality, gossip, and business. Luminaries such as Voltaire—"the most illustrious of the coffee addicts," as one French physician styled him—gathered to discuss literature and politics. Coffee houses became incubators of liberal and revolutionary ideas: Camille Desmoulins delivered his "to arms, to arms" speech to a crowd gathered just outside the Café Foy, two days before the storming of the Bastille. Secular and religious authorities were, with good reason, suspicious of coffee houses, and sometimes ordered them closed. But they did so because they feared what went on inside them, rather than the stimulating effects of coffee itself.[22]

Many coffee houses doubled as local drug emporiums, offering everything from chocolate to strong drink. Patrons of Paris's famous Café Procope could, besides savoring fresh-brewed coffee, sample imported wines and exotic liquors like *rossoly*, a mixture of crushed fennel, anise, coriander, dill, caraway, and brandy steeped in the heat of the sun. Such delights were denied the patrons of Islamic coffee houses, who could not generally purchase alcoholic beverages. That trade was relegated to the taverns, disreputable institutions on the fringes of society. But patrons did indulge in smoking, as did their western counterparts. The air of many a coffee house hung thick with acrid haze. This was, in hindsight, good for business. Smokers metabolize caffeine at a rate 50 percent faster than nonsmokers and thus require more frequent cups of coffee to feel the same stimulating effects. It often happens that drugs are not merely substitutes for one another, but serve to increase demand for other psychoactive products. Drug commerce is more than a zero-sum game.[23]

European coffee consumption exploded in the eighteenth century, rising from an estimated 2 to 120 million pounds. Tea imports rose from 1 to 40 million pounds, cacao from 2 to 13 million. Allowing for smuggling, customs fraud, spoilage, adulteration, and other sources of measurement error, the growth of caffeinated beverage consumption clearly outstripped that of population, up 50 percent during the same period. Price and social-class usage moved in the same direction, downward, as cooks and chambermaids took to greeting the day with *café au lait*.

Coffee could not have become a beverage of the masses if the Europeans had not organized production in their own colonies. When coffee came into fashion in Europe, the Dutch East India Company purchased Yemenite coffee at the port of Mocha. They resold it in Amsterdam at a markup of 100 to 200 percent. Profits like that drew competition from the English and French, who bid up the price of Mocha coffee. So the company's directors shifted their efforts to western Java, where they had introduced coffee on an experimental basis in 1707. By 1726 they controlled 50 to 75 percent of the world bean trade, and coffee was on its way to becoming an international cash crop.[24]

This story was repeated time and again. Indigenous producers tried to maintain cultivation monopolies, but without success. Europeans and their colonial descendants expanded the production of, and eventually the markets for, plant drugs and spirits in regions under their political influence or control. The French turned Saint-Domingue (Haiti) into a sort of Java of the western hemisphere. They produced so much coffee that by 1774 they were exporting 2 million tons annually via Marseilles to their former suppliers in the Levant. The Portuguese managed a similar feat in Brazil, as did the Spanish in their South and Central American colonies. Today coffee covers 44 percent of the permanent arable cropland in northern Latin America. Although the Americas dominate world production, Subsaharan Africa, South and Southeast Asia, and Hawaii, home of Kona coffee, have joined the Ethiopian and Arabian hearth lands as significant sources of beans.[25]

A disproportionate share of those beans found their way to the United States, long near the top of the table of per capita coffee consumption. Coffee and America grew up together. Cowboys (and Indians) took theirs hot, black, and strong: "It don't take as much water as you think it do." Frontiersmen of a different sort, the Apollo 11 astronauts, were drinking coffee three hours after landing on the moon. Theirs was history's first extraplanetary drug use.[26]

The conventional explanation for the beverage's enduring American popularity is that in the 1770s tea became a symbol of British taxes and tyranny, and an object of colonial boycott and vandalism. Coffee became the patriotic drink. But protest politics have a short half-life, and any account that omits cost is incomplete. More significant over time were the country's proximity to Caribbean and Latin American coffee plantations and its low duties on coffee—a few pennies a pound for most of the nineteenth century, sometimes no duty at all. The cost per milligram of caffeine in coffee was thus lower than for any other caffeinated beverage. This was particularly true after the Brazilians, beginning in the 1820s, unleashed a flood of slave-produced coffee. American per capita consumption, three pounds per year in 1830, rose to eight pounds by 1859. Declining price had a similar effect on the habits of the Dutch, another heavy coffee-drinking people. There tea lost out to coffee after 1760, when import duties fell and Dutch per capita coffee consumption quadrupled.[27]

Coffee remained cheap throughout America for most of the twentieth century. It was a widely advertised loss leader in supermarkets and a come-on at lunch counters. One drugstore fountain in Canon City, Colorado, still sold it for three cents a cup in inflation-plagued 1969. (When the store had previously raised its price to four cents, half its coffee customers ungratefully departed.) Coffee was practically a free good—literally so in soup kitchens and at grand openings, fairs, and picnics. In the 1970s it took the average American just 30 seconds of work to pay for a cup of home-brewed coffee, less time than it took to drink it. Revolutionary America's "prenatal disinclination for tea" makes for a good story. However, the Occam's Razor of the modern American coffee experience, and the moral to be drawn from it, is that when psychoactive drugs are widely available, heavily promoted, and cheap they become extremely popular, particularly if they are habit-forming.[28]

As with coffee, the use of tea became progressively more widespread as the price came down. Tea is indigenous to the region where India and China meet. A Chinese text of 350 A.D. mentions it as a medicinal beverage. It came into general use—taxation was a sure sign—by the late eighth century. When the Japanese first learned to drink tea is uncertain, but firm evidence establishes its presence by 815. Buddhist priests brought seeds from China and planted them in temple gardens. Eventually the tea ritual, embodiment of the Zen conception of greatness in the smallest moments of life, became more central to Japanese culture than to Chinese.

The Dutch first imported tea to Europe in 1610, but it remained quite expensive until the British East India Company commenced direct trade with Canton in 1713. After that the trade, legal and illegal, steadily increased. In 1784 the British government removed most of the duties on tea. Low taxes undercut smugglers and further increased consumption, which reached over two pounds per capita—about 400 cups per year—in England and Wales at the end of the eighteenth century. By then consumers were paying only a quarter of what they had paid for tea in the 1720s.[29]

The steady expansion of the China trade by the British East India Company and its rivals was the first stage of the development of the world tea industry. The second was the appropriation, in the mid-nineteenth century, of tea cultivation by the European colonial powers. The Dutch introduced tea bushes to the *koffie moe* (coffee-tired) lands of Java. The British did the same in India and Ceylon, where a blight had so devastated the coffee industry that dead trees were stripped and shipped to England to make legs for tea tables. April 1887 marked the turning point. In that month the British, Europe's leading tea consumers, first imported more Indian and Ceylonese tea than Chinese. Cost was again decisive. The Chinese taxed their tea more heavily at the point of export and produced it less efficiently than on the large Indian plantations. Chinese attempts to maintain the price by putting less tea on the market proved futile, as they no longer held a monopoly on production; Indian and Ceylonese producers simply took up the slack. Aggressive retailers like Thomas Lipton made large, direct purchases of Indian and Ceylonese leaves. By using heavy turnover to compensate for low profit margins, Lipton could sell his tea for a little more than a shilling a pound, a sum within the reach of the poorest families.[30]

The third stage was the spread of tea cultivation from Asia to eastern, southern, and central Africa in the late nineteenth and early twentieth centuries. In 1952 more than 97,000 African acres were planted with tea bushes, yielding over 47 million pounds. By then commercial tea production had blossomed throughout the southern arc of Asia. Plantations stretched from Formosa in the east to Iran and Russian Transcaucasia in the west. Tea growing had also spread to Brazil, Argentina, and Peru. Though it does well in lands suited to coffee farming, tea never became a leading cash crop in South America. Perhaps it suffered from too much caffeinated competition, not only from coffee and cacao, but from guarana and yerba-maté. The latter yields a potent tea drunk by more than twenty million people in southern Brazil, Uruguay, Paraguay, Argentina, Chile, Bolivia, and portions of Peru.[31]

Cacao, another plant destined to become an important African crop, originated in the American tropics. The Olmecs domesticated it sometime after 1500 B.C. The Spanish learned of it from the Maya and the Aztecs, for whom chocolate, made from pulverized cacao beans and various spices, was the beverage of the social elites. They served it at the end of banquets, along with tobacco, rather like the port and cigars of later European aristocracy.

Chocolate bore similar aristocratic connotations in seventeenth- and eighteenth-century Europe, where it came to be drunk warm and sweet rather than cold and bitter in the Aztec manner. Particularly popular among the secular and clerical elites of Spain, Italy, and France, chocolate had about it an air of *ancien régime* decadence. The obese Marquis de Sade was obsessed with it in all its forms. From prison he badgered his wife for ground chocolate, *crème au chocolat*, chocolate pastilles, and even cacao butter supposito-

Caffeine confluence: Frontispiece from *Tractatus Novi de Potu Caphé, de Chinensium Thé, et de Chocolata* (1685), an influential and widely translated compilation of writings about the exotic new beverage drugs coming into fashion across Europe in the seventeenth century. A *molinillo*, or swizzle stick, can be seen in the foreground next to the chocolate pot. This device was used to beat the thick chocolate to a froth.

ries to soothe his piles. "I asked . . . for a cake with icing," he wrote in 1779, "but I want it to be chocolate and black inside from chocolate as the devil's ass is black from smoke."

Chocolate was democratized in the nineteenth century. Technological innovation, industrialized production, and expanded cultivation—Europeans were importing more than 100 million pounds by 1899—made it widely affordable as both beverage and solid food. In 1828 Coenraad Johannes Van Houten, a Dutch chemist, patented a process for pressing most of the cacao butter from chocolate. The resulting cake, powdered and treated with alkaline salts, could be mixed with water to make cocoa, a cheap beverage that required no gilt pots or beating of heavy liquids. Cocoa became a breakfast drink for children, chocolate candies tokens of middle-class affection.

While Van Houten and others were revolutionizing the manufacture of chocolate products, the Portuguese were successfully transplanting cacao across the Atlantic, beginning with Príncipe, a small island off the African coast, in 1822. (Spanish efforts to spread cacao had focused on the Philippines, where both cultivation and consumption caught on.) Cacao was growing on the African mainland by the 1870s. Although the imperial powers pushed cacao cultivation ever eastward, establishing plantations from Ceylon to Samoa, West Africa became the center of world production in the twentieth century, supplanting Latin America. By 1991 Africa was supplying 55 percent of the world's cacao, while Mexico, where domestication first occurred, supplied just 1.5 percent.[32]

West Africans also produced kola nuts, a crop that entered world commerce late and in an unusual fashion. Kola nuts are richer in caffeine than coffee beans and contain traces of theobromine, a milder stimulant also found in cacao. Kola nuts were traditionally broken into small pieces and chewed for their stimulating, mood-elevating, and aphrodisiac effects. Because they dried out easily and required special packaging, their long-distance trade was largely limited to western Savanna Muslims, who prized kola as an alternative to alcohol. Coffee, tea, and cacao were less perishable and hence better suited to international commerce. Coffee, for instance, could travel long distances without much detriment to quality, provided supercargoes took some elementary precautions, such as keeping the beans out of holds that had contained pepper.[33]

Kola did not enter world trade in any significant way until it became an ingredient in medicinal and "soft" drinks. The international success of Vin Mariani, a coca wine introduced in the 1860s, led to experimentation with other alcohol-stimulant combinations like Vino-Kolafra, a kola extract in Marsala wine. ("A liberal dose will sober a drunken negro in half an hour.") The most famous of these new products was Coca-Cola, a blend of "the two most massive stimulants known to pre-industrial cultures," their bitter aftertaste masked by a mix of flavors and citrus oils. It began life as Pemberton's French Wine Coca, but its inventor, Dr. John Pemberton, removed the wine to placate prohibitionists. He repositioned Coca-Cola as a temperance drink. In 1903 his successors also removed the coca, by then a controversial drug associated with black crime sprees. They replaced it with a decocainized extract to maintain the flavor and added crystalline caffeine powder, extracted from refuse tea sweepings and other sources, to maintain the kick.[34]

This raised the wrath of Dr. Harvey Wiley, the great American apostle of pure food and drugs. Wiley defined a drug habit as "the taking of any stimulating, exciting drug which has no food value, and which produces directly excitation of any of the organs of the body or nerves controlling them in such a way as to suggest or compel a repetition of the dose." By that standard caffeine was habit-forming, and toxic in the bargain. Wiley's conviction grew out of medical observation and personal experience. During the Civil War he traded his coffee ration for milk, and felt much better as a result. He took Coca-Cola to court in 1911, declaring caffeine to be a dangerous and unlabeled additive in a product marketed and sold to children. After lengthy litigation, the company reduced the caffeine content by half.[35]

In 1910, the year before the trial opened, Coca-Cola was available in every U.S. state and territory. But it remained a largely American product until World War II opened the window of global opportunity. Coca-Cola's Robert Woodruff made it a policy to supply U.S. soldiers anywhere in the world with nickel Cokes, whatever losses the company might absorb. ("We're playing the world long," he later remarked.) The government went along, exempting Coca-Cola's military sales from sugar rationing. The GIs in turn introduced millions of Europeans and Asians to the drink. Sixty-four bottling plants, some manned by German and Japanese POWs, sprouted in their triumphal wake.[36]

By 1955 this "sublimated essence of all America stands for, a decent thing honestly made, universally distributed, conscientiously improved through the years"—according to James Farley, New Deal politico turned chairman of the Coca-Cola Export Corporation—sold in 89 different lands. That figure rose to 155 in 1991. Pepsi-Cola, its chief rival, was by then available in 151 countries. One of the "conscientious improvements" of Coca-Cola and its competitors was the removal of the kola extract as cheaper sources of caffeine and taste became available. Modern cola drinks, observes the historian Paul Lovejoy, are just as "uncola" as 7-Up.[37]

Like most good puns, this one limns a deeper truth. The key psychoactive ingredient in soft drinks is caffeine, whether it comes from kola, guarana, or any other plant. The same is true of coffee and tea. Of course, these drinks are much more than stimulating drugs, as any anthropologist or advertising executive will attest. They are rich with cultural significance and political connotation. Citizens of Warsaw lined the streets and cheered the arrival of the first Coca-Cola trucks. But none of these drinks would have achieved the same degree of worldwide popularity had they not contained caffeine or an equivalent stimulant. Although he became a bit of a crank on the subject, Wiley had a point: no caffeine, no Coca-Cola phenomenon. Caffeine was an essential booster stage in the rocket of drugs that lifted Coca-Cola into planetary orbit, an orbit sustained by cleverly exploiting its status as American icon and embodiment of the western consumer life-style.[38]

Sugar in the Psychoactive Revolution

Coca-Cola contains a good deal more than caffeine. Would it have conquered the world without sugar as an ingredient? This is in fact a deeply useful question, important for understanding more than the fortunes of cola beverages. The production and consumption of sugar and the history of psychoactive drugs are linked in many ways, and neither can be fully understood without the other.

Sugarcane cultivation originated in New Guinea or Indonesia and spread to ancient China, where it was chewed as an aphrodisiac sweetmeat, and to India, where sugar and molasses were first refined from cut cane. Arab merchants, conquerors, and colonizers brought the crop to the eastern Mediterranean, North Africa, and the Iberian peninsula: "sugar followed the Koran." In the fifteenth century the Portuguese and Spanish introduced cane cultivation to Madeira, the Azores, São Tomé, and the Canaries. Columbus brought the plant to Hispaniola during his ambitious colonizing voyage of 1493–1494. He fared no better with sugarcane than with wine vines. But others persisted and, over the next half-century, showed the feasibility of producing at least small amounts of West Indian sugar. After 1550 the combination of abundant rainfall, fertile soil, and slave labor made possible the rapid expansion of sugar and molasses production throughout the New World's tropical zone. During the seventeenth century, when the world sugar trade grew at an estimated 5 percent per year, Brazil and then the eastern Caribbean islands became the leading centers of sugar and molasses production.

The demand for sugar was phenomenal. During the eighteenth century the annual growth rate rose to 7 percent, and during the nineteenth century, when beet sugar production also became a factor, to 10 percent. The British possessed Europe's sweetest tooth—and perhaps the continent's worst teeth. Their per capita consumption rose from 4 pounds in 1700 to 18 pounds in 1800 to about 90 pounds in the decade before 1900. As with caffeinated beverages, expanded colonial production made sugar affordable to all social classes. During the eighteenth century British tradesmen, and during the nineteenth the lowliest laborers, began dumping West Indian sugar into tea brewed from imported Chinese or Indian leaves. Whether such customs were a means of adding ready calories and stimulants to the working-class diet, or an effort to achieve respectability, or a new form of "addicted nervous dependence," bad for consumers and worse for enslaved producers, toiling unto death on despoiled tropical islands, is a matter of varying historical interpretation.[39]

Today sugar is not commonly considered a drug except by those who blame it for children's hyperactivity and a host of other human ills. But early modern Europeans considered it a potent medicine as well as an exotic spice. As overseas production expanded and price dropped, they increasingly used it as a sweetener for coffee, tea, and chocolate, all of which were bitter, psychoactive plant infusions. "Tea without Sugar makes but a very ordinary Tipple to most People," a physician observed in 1750. Residents of Lisbon were said to dump so much sugar into their Brazilian coffee that their spoons stood up in the cup. A taste for bitter liquids can be developed, of course, and millions prefer their coffee black. But, as the anthropologist Sidney Mintz points out, it requires "culturally grounded habituation." You have to learn to like it.

Not so the taste for sweetness, which is universal, observed in infants, and almost certainly a product of evolution. Mother's milk is sweet, and so is the ripe fruit favored by our primate ancestors. Adding sugar, often lots of sugar, to alcoholic or caffeinated beverages made these drinks more palatable to Europeans and increased their popularity. "If sack and sugar be a fault," boomed Falstaff, "God help the wicked!" Sweet liqueurs, sold by Italian distillers in Paris as early as 1332, caught on quickly. The distilling revolution increased the demand for sugar, as did the growing consumption of stimulating

THE OLD MAID

A consoling cup (or, rather, saucer) of tea with cream and sugar, English print, 1777. "Oh! Puss forbear to lick the cream," runs the unkind accompanying verse, "Your mistress longs to do the same."

beverages during and after the seventeenth century. In the last half-century the caffeine-sugar connection has assumed a carbonated dimension with the "coca-colanization" of emerging nations by aggressive soft-drink manufacturers, assisted by the worldwide spread of electrical refrigeration.[40]

In Asia sugar, or less commonly honey, has long been an ingredient in cannabis preparations. Opium-smoking mixtures sometimes featured sugar as an ingredient. Tobacco manufacturers everywhere employed it to preserve, flavor, and color their products. A typical nineteenth-century recipe for bright tobacco, marketed for chewing or smoking, required 13 pounds of sweetening for every 100 pounds of leaf. The bulk of the sweetening consisted of sugar, licorice, rum, and glycerine, all common ingredients in tobacco "sauces" or "casings."[41]

Molasses, a by-product of the manufacture of sugar, figured prominently in the psychoactive revolution. It coated and preserved the great ropes of spun tobacco leaves exported from Brazil and the French Caribbean colonies. It was a common additive to the tobacco quids that Americans so relentlessly chewed and spat. And it was the basic ingredient in rum. This potent (100 to 200 proof) beverage was first distilled in the West Indies sometime in the 1640s. In its eighteenth-century heyday it was the preferred beverage of millions of Europeans, Africans, and Amerindians who inhabited the Atlantic littoral. It was also a key commodity in the slave trade that provided the labor which produced the sugarcane in the first place. Between 60 and 70 percent of all transplanted African slaves ended up in the European sugar colonies. The percentage would have been lower if they had managed the same rate of natural increase as their American tobacco- and cotton-growing counterparts. But disease and unending, dispiriting toil in the canebrakes and boiling houses kept mortality high, fertility low, and the slave ships coming.[42]

What happened with sugar, rum, and slavery happened, in one form or another, with all major plant drug products. The psychoactive revolution entailed—required—the massive exploitation of labor. In the most naked version of exploitation, plantation owners and foremen drove bound laborers, both indentured servants and African slaves, to the point of death to produce sugar, tobacco, coffee, and other drug crops. But labor exploitation assumed many guises, as elites learned to use drugs to control, placate, and fleece their workers. As will become apparent, these practices were no less exploitative for being subtle.

2

THE LITTLE THREE: OPIUM, CANNABIS, AND COCA

ALCOHOL, TOBACCO, AND caffeinated products were the big three of the psychoactive revolution. The sheer scale of their production, distribution, and consumption and the degree to which they were integrated into cultures around the world made them relatively impervious to prohibition. Opium, cannabis, and coca were the "little three." They were less frequently consumed than alcohol, tobacco, or caffeine, and reformers eventually succeeded in making them objects of worldwide restrictions and prohibitions. Nevertheless, they remain highly profitable commodities. Tens of millions of people use them in crude form or in concentrated products such as heroin, hashish, and cocaine. These are what most people think of when they hear the word "drugs."[1]

Opium

Suggestions as to the geographical origins of the opium poppy have been all over the map, from southwestern Europe to western China. Mark David Merlin's careful review of the evidence indicates that the most likely route of dissemination was from central Europe down into the eastern Mediterranean from about 1600 B.C. Neolithic peoples in the Swiss Foreland and adjacent areas may have discovered opium as a weed species growing in dump heaps. They came to value it for its nutritious seeds and oil, as well as for its medicinal and psychoactive effects. In this regard opium resembled cannabis, another plant drug that paid high nutritional dividends to its cultivators. Opium may have spread to the southeast either accidentally, in contaminated grains, or deliberately, as an exotic trade good. In either case it became well known in Greece, Crete, Cyprus, Egypt, and throughout the eastern Mediterranean littoral.

Opium was uniquely suited to treat the ills of civilized peoples: anxiety, boredom, chronic fatigue and pain, insomnia, squalling babies in close quarters, and, not least, diarrheal diseases, ubiquitous and often deadly afflictions inherent to concentrated populations. Infections spread by fecal discharges did not much trouble wandering bands. Settled populations without sanitary facilities—practically nonexistent before the nineteenth century—were plagued by them. Greek and Roman physicians skillfully employed opium preparations to combat gastrointestinal and other ailments. Marcus Aurelius, the emperor of Rome from 161 to 180 A.D., habitually took opium to sleep, to cope with the ardors of military campaigns, and perhaps, as one historian has speculated, to wall himself off emotionally from the world he famously despised. Roman suicides swallowed the drug to end life *cum valetudo inpetilibus odium vitae fecessit,* when unbearable disease had rendered it hateful. Some scholars believe that the wine with "gall" offered to Jesus as he hung on the cross contained opium. His refusal to partake was analogous to a stoic soldier declining a blindfold or a cigarette before execution.[2]

Opium figured prominently in Arab medicine, and it was Arab traders who took the drug to Iran, India, and China during the eighth century. All three lands ultimately became important centers of production and consumption. A century ago Sir William Moore, a British physician with long experience in India, set out to explain why opium use was so widespread in the East. With a few qualifications, his analysis still commands respect.

Moore's first point was proximity to supply. Though opium poppies have been grown experimentally on every settled continent, sustained commercial production requires ample water, good soil, manuring, and, most critically, ready access to skilled peasant labor. Harvesters equipped with special tools score the unripe seed capsules and collect the exuded sap—"opium" *(opion)* means poppy juice in Greek. Because opium is collected in small amounts by hand, with daily yields per worker measured in ounces, the labor must be cheap as well as careful. Turkish harvesters in the early twentieth century earned 30 to 50 cents for a 14-hour day. The densely populated peasant societies of South and East Asia offered an abundance of this sort of labor. Though much of the opium they produced was exported, some of it leaked into the local market, even when authorities tried to prevent this.

Another reason for opium's popularity in the East was religious: Islam frowned upon alcohol. Opium was a more acceptable alternative. It was also medically imperative. Victims of diarrhea, so common in India that it was known as *morbus bengalensis*, resorted to opium. So did those wracked by malarial fevers, endemic to the warm and damp regions of India, western China, and Southeast Asia. The marshy English Fens, as Moore shrewdly noted, featured a similar pattern of heavy opium use to combat malaria.

Moore thought climate was significant in another way. The prevailing heat had made easterners more "indolent" than westerners and hence better suited to opium. The remark seems at first a classic piece of High Imperialist nonsense. Yet, if one digs deeper, the idea that people use opium in response to the debilitating effects of climate is neither wrong nor racist. It has a long history of more sympathetic exposition in both western and Arabic medicine. "People who live in the tropics or hot climates, especially those in Mecca," wrote Al-Bīrūnī (973–1048), "get into the habit of taking opium daily to eliminate distress, to relieve the body from the effects of scorching heat, to secure longer and deeper sleep, and to purge superfluities and excesses of humors. They start with smaller doses which are increased gradually up to lethal dosages."

Opium, finally, was a frugal drug. It enabled the poor to do with less food, tea being commonly taken for the same reason. And it cost less than alcoholic beverages or other recreational diversions. A pipe of opium was one of the few comforts affordable to common laborers in the East, who lived without access to the music halls, parks, libraries, and other recreational diversions taken for granted by their western counterparts.[3]

Of all the Asian lands in which opium use and cultivation became entrenched, the most significant was China. Chinese opium smoking began as an offshoot of tobacco smoking, introduced in the early seventeenth century. At some point the Chinese began experimenting with *madak*, a mixture of shredded tobacco and semi-refined opium. Later, about 1760, they discovered how to prepare opium so that they could smoke it without tobacco. Smoking pure opium was initially a pastime of the wealthy. By the 1830s, however, it had spread among palace eunuchs, imperial officials, soldiers, and merchants. By the 1870s it was common among chair-bearers, boatmen, and other laborers, and by the early 1900s, among the peasantry itself. In 1906, according to one recent estimate, 16.2 million Chinese (3.6 percent of the total population; 6.0 percent of the adult population) were dependent daily smokers of opium. Perhaps half of the adult population smoked opium at least occasionally, to celebrate festivals or ward off disease.[4]

For opium use to have become so widespread required a huge increase in supply. Here the stories of opium and tea intersect. Before they had their own tea plantations in India and Ceylon, the British depended on China for tea, Japan being closed to the West. They also imported silk, porcelain, and sundry *chinoiserie*, creating a serious balance-of-payments problem. British ascendancy in India after 1757 provided a solution. Though the British were by no means the first colonial power to export Indian opium, they perfected a monopoly system for its sale and manufacture. The system proved so lucrative that it eventually furnished one-seventh of the total revenue of British India. The lion's share of the crop, more than offsetting the cost of tea, went to China.

The private merchant houses that shipped—or, more precisely, smuggled—opium into China also prospered. James Matheson, a partner in Jardine Matheson & Co., made enough money from the trade to become the second-largest landowner in Britain. In 1844 he bought the Isle of Lewis off Scotland's northwestern coast and spent over 500,000 pounds building Lews Castle, a crenelated, mock-Tudor folly. As the local terrain did not meet his horticultural needs, he shipped thousands of tons of soil from the mainland to plant his trees and shrubbery.

Though British merchants dominated the traffic, Americans also participated, especially during the three decades following the War of 1812. In some years Perkins & Company, a Boston concern, bought up half or more of the Turkish opium crop for shipment to China. Warren Delano II—founder of the family fortune and grandfather of Franklin Delano Roosevelt—prospered as the head of Russell & Company, another leading American firm. "I do not pretend to justify the prosecution of the opium trade in a moral and philanthropic point of view," Delano wrote home from Canton, "but as a merchant I insist that it has been a fair, honorable and legitimate trade; and to say the worst of it, liable to no further or weightier objections than is the importation of wines, Brandies & spirits into the U. States, England, &c."

In Chinese eyes—and in the eyes of many historians—men like Matheson and Delano were criminals. Delano's rationalization omitted the inconvenient fact that imports of opium into China (unlike those of wine or spirits into the United States) were patently illegal. The opium trade had been explicitly forbidden by imperial edict since 1729. When conscientious Ch'ing officials finally attempted to suppress the traffic, the British resorted to force, defeating the Chinese in the First Opium War (1839–1842). Cannon reduced Chinese fortresses to ruins; marines gathered up the bodies and dumped them into mass graves, leaving behind mocking, hand-lettered signs: "This is the Rode to Gloury [sic]." A second Anglo-Chinese conflict in 1856–1858 resulted in the complete legalization of the Indian opium trade. The volume of trade, already more than 6 million pounds of opium in 1839, peaked at over 15 million pounds in 1879.[5]

By then China itself was annually producing an estimated 32 million pounds of opium to feed the growing demand. The bulk of it came from the southwestern provinces of Kweichow, Yunnan, and especially Szechwan. Opium was an ideal and easily transported winter crop, yielding peasant cultivators two to four times what they could earn from wheat. As with tobacco in the colonial Chesapeake, opium served in Szechwan as a medium of exchange, source of tax revenue, and preferred local drug. "Nowhere in China," summed up one observer, "are the people so well off and nowhere do they smoke so much opium." When the imperial government tried in 1906 to gradually eliminate domestic cultivation, the move was popular in eastern China but not in the opium-rich southwest. Szechwan officials tried to implement the policy by prohibitive taxation; agricultural land values plummeted. Rioters destroyed four tax offices, and officials called out police to suppress them. When the revolution came in 1911, the people of Szechwan rejoiced. They thought the Republic meant license to plant opium.

The disintegration of imperial China, one of history's great political dramas, played out against a background of accelerating population growth. Westerners had brought more than tobacco to East Asia in the seventeenth century; they had also introduced sweet potatoes, peanuts, and other nutritious crops that made possible sustained population increase. As in Europe, population pressure drove migration. Between 1848 and 1888 two million Chinese, mostly young men, left for the Malay peninsula, Indochina, Sumatra, Java, the Philippines, Hawaii, California, and Australia. Soon the diaspora became global, with Chinese districts springing up in the great entrepôts of New York, London, Rotterdam, and Amsterdam.

Opium smoking took root in every one of these places. Expatriate Chinese "coolies" and sailors were mostly bachelors, de facto or otherwise. Lonely, oppressed, indebted, and far from restraining family influences, they sought release in a constellation of bachelor vices, including gambling, prostitution, and opium smoking. The tax farmers and syndicates that controlled these vices prospered. William Skinner's observation about Thailand, that the country depended on Chinese virtues for the expansion of commerce and industry, while the government relied on Chinese vices for the expansion of public revenue, holds true for many diaspora lands.[6]

It is tempting to view the worldwide diffusion of opium smoking as Chinese revenge for the primal narcotic sin of the Indian opium trade. The actual impact, however, varied from country to country. The opium dens of London's East End acquired an infamy out of all proportion to their number, thanks to the imaginative talents of Charles Dickens, Arthur Conan Doyle, Oscar Wilde, Sax Rohmer, and lesser literary lights. However, opium smoking did spread widely in the United States in the 1870s and 1880s, becoming an important ritual in the white underworld and laying the groundwork for a criminal drug subculture.

Opiate use and addiction were also increasing rapidly in the upper and middle classes. Per capita imports of medicinal opiates doubled in the United States between 1870 and 1890. "If it were possible to stop the sale of opiates today," complained one journalist, "in a week's time there would be raving maniacs, and people dropping dead on every corner of towns and cities." The causes of the increase were the Civil War (a minor factor, whose actual influence has often been exaggerated), the flourishing patent medicine industry, and, most important, the vogue for the hypodermic injection of morphine.[7]

Saint Morphine

Morphine is the principal psychoactive alkaloid of opium. The German pharmacist Friedrich Sertürner worked on its isolation in 1803–1805, publishing his results in a short note in 1805. The significance of his findings was not generally understood until he published a longer piece in *Annalen der Physik* in 1817. Commercial production began when Heinrich Emanuel Merck, founder of the pharmaceutical dynasty, undertook it in 1827. By then Sertürner had moved on to other projects, among them the improvement of military firearms. A multi-talented but erratic man who may have become addicted to his own discovery, Sertürner faded into obscurity after his death in 1841, only to have his reputation revived during World War I. His contributions to alkaloidal chemistry were widely recognized, as was morphine's indispensability in treating the maimed and wounded.[8]

Morphine had other therapeutic virtues, as well as one great liability. The alkaloidal content of opium varied with soil and climatic conditions. Human greed added to natural variation. Opium was the most frequently adulterated—in early nineteenth-century parlance, "sophisticated"—of all drugs, mixed with everything from licorice to lead. One reason for the heroic therapeutics of that era is that practitioners knew or suspected they were dealing with adulterated drugs, weak in active principle. So they compensated with massive doses. Morphine eliminated the guesswork and the mess: no more wormy opium. Morphine was pure and therefore of predictable therapeutic action. It was soluble in water and injectable; hypodermic medication had been developed chiefly with morphine in mind. Injection was free of gastric side effects. It had a more rapid onset of action. And it was more potent and euphorigenic. Consequently, it had a much greater addiction liability.[9]

The consumption of morphine rose with the spread of hypodermic medication. In 1855, the year Alexander Wood introduced hypodermic injection as a therapeutic procedure, patients in Paris hospitals received a scant 272 grams of morphine from the central pharmacy. By 1875, when the technique was well established among physicians, the total was well over 10,000 grams. One of morphine's great attractions, and dangers, was that it could alleviate the symptoms of conditions whose root causes doctors could not treat.

In 1886 Jules Verne was shot by a deranged nephew, the bullet lodging just above his foot. Because Verne was diabetic, his doctors judged that they could not safely operate. A long recuperation was the only course. Meanwhile they eased his suffering with morphine. The grateful Verne wrote a sonnet—not his best medium—to the drug that killed his pain and stifled the tedium: "Oh, jab me with your fine needle a hundred times / And a hundred times I will bless you, Saint Morphine."[10]

Not all the morphine went to patients. Late nineteenth- and early twentieth-century European studies consistently showed physicians and pharmacists to be heavily overrepresented among "morphinists," a nice illustration of Moore's first principle of proximity to supply. No occupational or social group was entirely exempt, however. Prostitutes used morphine; so did politicians, one of whom, Georges Boulanger, was discovered injecting himself on the grounds of the Elysée.[11]

The case of Otto von Bismarck is particularly fascinating, and demonstrative of the ways drugs can interact in and ultimately dominate an individual's life. The 272-pound chancellor was a heavy smoker, drinker, and all-around glutton. He paid the price, suffering from gout, indigestion, insomnia, migraines, and a host of other ills compounded by hypochondria and paranoia. In 1883 he came under the care of a no-nonsense Bavarian physician, Ernst Schweninger, who promptly put him on a spartan diet and tried to restrict his intake of drugs. Bismarck cooperated at first, but soon relapsed to buttermilk and cognac. Told that he had aggravated his facial neuralgia by smoking, Bismarck agreed to limit himself to four pipes of after-dinner tobacco. He then purchased the largest pipe he could find, three feet long with a huge porcelain bowl, and snuck a fifth bowlful if no one was watching. He also took morphine, mostly to cope with his tormenting insomnia. Though Schweninger denied that the chancellor was addicted, others in Berlin political circles were not so sure. "There are two factors to be considered in all the Chancellor does or neglects to do from now on," Friedrich von Holstein wrote in his diary in February 1888, "morphia and Prince Wilhelm."[12]

The morphine that Bismarck and hundreds of thousands of other Europeans and North Americans injected in the late nineteenth century came from opium grown in the eastern hemisphere. Scattered experiments and wartime emergencies aside, no one cultivated opium on any significant scale in the western hemisphere prior to the twentieth century. That would change when laws and treaties enacted in the 1910s and 1920s gave rise to a black market for narcotics. Proximity to the United States, the largest and most lucrative market in the Americas, simplified smuggling. By 1926 numerous poppy fields grew in Sonora, in northwestern Mexico. Their opium went both to resident Chinese and across the border to the United States. The illegal export traffic expanded steadily, prompting charges of corruption and straining U.S.-Mexican relations. In 1947 Harry Anslinger, head of the Bureau of Narcotics, estimated that Mexican poppies covered 4,000 to 5,000 hectares, or roughly 10,000 to 12,500 acres. They yielded between 32 and 40 metric tons of opium, at least half of which became morphine or heroin. Mexican and American officials used airplanes to observe and photograph the fields; their opponents used them to fly the drugs into the United States.

War-surplus aircraft and the postwar expansion of commercial aviation proved a great boon to traffickers everywhere. In the 1960s Colombia emerged as a major center for air and sea shipments of marijuana, followed by cocaine in the 1970s and 1980s and heroin in the 1990s. By 1995 Colombia, already providing an estimated 70 to 80 percent of the world's refined cocaine, was also one of the world's major opium producers, with 20,000 hectares reportedly under cultivation. With the help of hired Chinese chemists, most of the crop was refined into an unusually pure heroin destined for the United States.

Though Mexico and Colombia have become important hemispheric producers, most of the world's opium is still grown in Asia. Two countries, Afghanistan and Myanmar (Burma), expanded production especially rapidly in the 1980s and early 1990s. Afghanistan became the major source of supply for the European heroin market, Myanmar for the renascent Chinese market—though some Burmese heroin was also transshipped to the United States.

The net result of all these changes was the emergence, in the late twentieth century, of an illicit international heroin industry whose size, smuggling capacity, and marketing sophistication surpassed anything that had preceded it. To explain the simultaneous spread of mass heroin addiction, observes the historian Alfred McCoy, commentators have stressed the reasons why addicts have turned to its use: unemployment, alienation, the youth drug culture. Granting that these are all factors, an exclusive emphasis on addicts' motivations "ignores the fundamental fact that heroin is a mass-market commodity with salesmen and distributors just like cigarettes, alcohol, or aspirin. The rising numbers of younger users can sample drugs like heroin because they are sold at standard prices and are available at hundreds of distribution points in major cities across the globe. . . . Without global production and distribution systems, there can be no mass addiction to cocaine or heroin."[13]

The Ganja Complex

Cannabis originated in central Asia and was first extensively cultivated in China 6,000 or more years ago. It was a valuable, multipurpose crop, yielding a potent drug as well as cooking oil, edible seeds, animal fodder, and hempen fibers. Hemp was the source of rope, fishing nets, and textiles for the Chinese masses, silk being reserved for the clothing of the rich.

The many uses and remarkable hardiness of cannabis—it flourishes in a variety of climates and at altitudes from sea level to more than 10,000 feet—assured its widespread diffusion. Of the many societies in which the plant's psychoactive properties came to be prized, the most important was India. The earliest written reference to *bhang* appears in the *Atharva Veda*, dating to ca. 2000–1400 B.C. Bhang consists of dried cannabis leaves, seeds, and stems from male and female plants, wild or cultivated. Often mixed with sugar, black pepper, and water or milk, it is the mildest of the three traditional Indian cannabis preparations. *Ganja*, made from the dried flowering tops of cultivated female plants rich in delta-9-tetrahydrocannabinol (THC), is two to three times stronger in effect. Ganja is smoked as well as ingested; when ganja smoking first emerged in India is uncertain. *Charas* is the pure resin processed from the female plant. Translated into western terms, bhang is equivalent to inferior grades of marijuana ("stems and seeds"), ganja to higher-quality marijuana, and charas to hashish.

India has been called the world's first cannabis-oriented culture. Ayurvedic (Hindu) and Tibbi (Islamic) practitioners gave it orally to treat endemic diseases like malaria and painful afflictions like rheumatism. Ordinary Hindus and Muslims used it as a folk cure and to ward off boredom and fatigue, particularly during the harvest. Warriors drank bhang to steel their nerves; mendicants to concentrate their prayers; newlyweds to stoke their ardor. Cannabis was a cheap and popular aphrodisiac, given even to mares before they were mated.

Indian cannabis use apparently peaked during the Mogul era (1526–1857), when cultivation and preparation of various cannabis drugs flourished in all parts of the subcontinent. The British discouraged its use as an intoxicant, as did their westernized Indian successors in the twentieth century. Both popular and elite opinion generally tolerated the mild bhang, whose use cut across all social categories. However, the smoking of ganja and charas, associated with the lower and criminal classes, became increasingly suspect.

It is not known when cannabis first appeared in Europe, though it seems probable that nomads from the steppe introduced its use and cultivation. A famous passage in Herodotus' *Histories*, composed in the third quarter of the fifth century B.C., describes Scythians "howling with pleasure" in a vapor-bath of burning hemp seeds. ("This is their substitute for an ordinary bath in water, which they never use.") Arabs knew of cannabis from Greek medical and botanical authorities and, more directly, from trade with India via Iran. An Indian pilgrim, according to folk tradition, introduced Iranians to the use of hemp as a drug in the mid-sixth century. However, some scholars believe that hemp appeared much earlier in the ancient Near East, possible references to the plant appearing in both the Hebrew text of the Old Testament and in the Aramaic translation.

Cannabis was controversial in the Islamic world, owing in part to its association with the Sufis, who used it for mystical purposes that orthodox authorities regarded with suspicion. Sporadic attempts to suppress cultivation failed, and by the fourteenth century hashish production was well established, particularly in the Nile Delta. By then Arab traders had succeeded in spreading cannabis down the east coast of Africa, whence it spread to the central and southern regions of the continent. The smoking of cannabis, in contrast to that of tobacco, flourished among the Khoikhoi, San, and other peoples of southern Africa well before European contact. Cannabis, in short, had spread through most of the Old World by the time Columbus and his three ships, webbed with hempen rope, dipped below the Palos horizon on the morning of August 3, 1492.[14]

The Spanish cultivated cannabis in their colonies from the sixteenth until the early nineteenth centuries, when hemp farming enjoyed a brief efflorescence in California. The French and the British did likewise, with plantings at Port Royal in 1606, Virginia in 1611, and Plymouth in 1632. Their concern was for fiber, particularly for the manufacture of naval rigging. In no instance were European colonizers primarily motivated by the plant's medicinal and psychoactive properties.

Their imported laborers thought otherwise. Angolan slaves (paid for, in part, with rum and low-grade tobacco) brought cannabis with them to the sugar plantations of northeastern Brazil, where cultivation was established sometime after 1549. One story has it that the slaves carried the seeds in cloth dolls tied to their ragtag clothing. The planters permitted slaves to grow their *maconha*—the word, like other Brazilian terms for cannabis, is of Angolan extraction—between the rows of cane, and to smoke and dream during the periods of inactivity between harvests. The planters stuck to their perfumed cigars.

Some Indians and rural mestizos adopted cannabis for their own medicinal and social purposes, as did eventually urban laborers. The anthropologist Vera Rubin called this pattern the "ganja complex." It included the use of cannabis for cordage and clothing, comestible and spice, energizer and invigorant, medicine and euphoriant, the last mostly in convivial male groups. "Except for ritual purposes involving members of the priestly class," Rubin wrote, "regular multipurpose use in the folk stream has been generally confined to the lower social classes: peasants, fishermen, rural and urban artisans and manual laborers."

The Old World ganja complex replicated itself in Brazil, where cannabis came to be regarded as the opium of the poor. Yet no such pattern emerged in colonial North America, although hemp was more widely and successfully cultivated there than in South America. The most likely explanation is that the slaves shipped to the British colonies came from farther up the West African coast, where cannabis had not yet taken root—that, and the fact that European settlers were culturally primed to seek release in alcohol and, beginning in the seventeenth century, tobacco.

Cannabis's hemispheric center of gravity shifted from northeastern Brazil to the Caribbean in the late nineteenth and early twentieth centuries. As with the globalization of opium smoking, migration and long-distance transportation were key factors. The demise of slavery in the region, beginning with the British West Indies in 1838, created a demand for low-wage labor on the sugar plantations. Planters imported indentured workers from India, nearly half a million of whom eventually came to the Caribbean. The ganja complex came with them, much to the regret of the white establishment. "We have seen a coolie gardener—by nature a quiet, retiring man—behaving like a raving maniac while under the influence of the weed," the Jamaica *Daily Gleaner* editorialized in 1913. The writer noted with alarm its spread to the island's African descendants, who had taken to growing cannabis, and predicted an outcome not unlike the opium situation in China.

Which, more or less, is what happened. By the 1970s, 60 percent of Jamaica's adult rural males smoked ganja, half of these heavily. The folk medicinal use of cannabis teas and cordials was also widespread, but even devout Christians did not regard it as vicious or déclassé. This may seem paradoxical. Whether inhaled from a "spliff" or poured from a spout, THC is THC. But distinctions based on intention of use, mode of administration, and social background are among the most enduring themes of drug history, and may be encountered in many guises.[15]

By the 1920s the ganja complex was well established in circum-Caribbean nations. Regional labor migration was again a decisive factor. In the years between 1900 and 1924 tens of thousands of Jamaicans sought work on the banana plantations in Costa Rica and the sugar plantations in Cuba, rapidly expanding with U.S. capital. Panama attracted waves of West Indian immigrants: 5,000 for the railroad (1850–1855), 50,000 for the abortive French canal (1880–1889), 150,000 for the successful American project (1904–1914). Many stayed after the work was complete. The first reports of cannabis smoking by American troops stationed at the canal date to 1916; a full-blown Army inquiry in 1932 concluded that Panamanian farmers were growing cannabis for their own use and selling the surplus to American soldiers. The officers who investigated the matter somehow managed to write a small gem of ethnography, a perfect evocation of the ganja complex. "The plant is used to make tea," they noted. "There is among the colored people great faith in the efficacy of this drink as a mild stimulant which gives a feeling of well being, and also as a preventive of malaria. The smoking of dried leaves and flower heads in the form of cigarettes seems also to be not uncommon."[16]

The Marijuana Complex

Cannabis smoking came to the United States proper via Mexican laborers, more than a million of whom entered the Southwest in the three decades after 1900. Tens of thousands of these newcomers fanned out through the Midwest, taking railroad, construction, and mill jobs as far away as Chicago. At the same time cannabis was spreading north and east from New Orleans, where Caribbean and South American sailors had introduced it around 1910. By the mid-1930s dealers could be found peddling the drug throughout Louisiana, even at remote Civilian Conservation Corps camps. The ongoing cigarette revolution, which taught Americans to absorb drugs through their lungs, facilitated the spread of marijuana smoking, as did the abundant domestic supply. Raised commercially for fiber and seed, cannabis also grew luxuriantly around derelict rope factories and abandoned hemp farms—hence "weed." ("I'd rather have weed; it do me better than whiskey do.") In Tennessee convict laborers simply dried and smoked the flowering tops of the wild cannabis they found along the roads. San Quentin inmates grew their own, right on the prison grounds. In 1936 New York City police destroyed 40,000 pounds they found growing within city limits.

Widespread availability kept the price low, from 5 to 50 cents for a reefer. That was well within the means of young urban blacks who identified with the emerging hip subculture. The heroes of this subculture, jazz musicians, spread marijuana smoking by example or, in one famous case, by design. Milton "Mezz" Mezzrow, the original white Negro, a Chicago-born Jewish clarinetist convinced he was a black man, became the apostle of pot, peddling fat, high-quality reefers on Harlem street corners, three for 50 cents. "Light up," he told his customers, "and be somebody."[17]

During World War II Army psychiatrists, concerned with morale and discipline problems, took a close look at marijuana smoking by enlisted black men. One 26-year-old soldier's experience survives in their case notes. The patient spoke in a whisper. A dreamy, rhapsodic expression came over his face. "You get hot all over, and you get cold all over. You like to look at freaky things. You like to go to one of those freaky 'pads' where you can look at nude bodies sprawled out. That's the height of the 'junky.' He likes to see those things. He likes them to kiss his body all over. He's freakish for those things. When you go to a 'pad' you want to listen to the frantic tom-tom of the Duke. You want to see some nude frantic women." Diagnosis: drug addict. Discharge: section VIII—the category for men of unsuitable and unadaptable habits or traits of character.[18]

Escapist and hedonic use of cannabis by working-class men was nothing new. But cannabis in America was not just a syncopated version of the ganja complex. It was more narrowly geared toward pleasure: no medicinal teas or folk remedies, just smoking to get high. This American pattern, which Vera Rubin dubbed the "marijuana complex," is distinguishable from the older and more variegated ganja complex.

In the 1960s the marijuana complex edged into the mainstream. From the 1840s heyday of the *Club des Hachichins* in Paris, educated men had experimented with cannabis, seeking novel sensations and the "intensification of individuality," as Baudelaire memorably put it. Their numbers were always minuscule, their disciples few. That changed when millions of bell-bottomed students lit up. "Marijuana was transformed from a lower-class drug to a middle- and upper-class drug through the mediating role of the hippy movement," was the psychologist William McGlothlin's crisp summary of the matter. The hippies emerged from the small but intellectually fashionable Beat movement of the 1950s. Favorable (or at worst transmogrifying) media exposure aroused interest among the young, as did disenchantment with segregation, suburban materialism, and the Vietnam War. Marijuana was a convenient multivalent symbol of rebellion, popular among high school students and undergraduates. Analysts at the University of Michigan reported increasing use from freshman to senior year, with a falloff in graduate school. Graduate students preferred tranquilizers.[19]

Though the emergent marijuana complex attracted the most notice in the United States—an estimated 55 million Americans had tried some form of cannabis by 1979, including two-thirds of those aged 18 through 25—it quickly became a worldwide phenomenon. From Australia, Canada, Colombia, Hong Kong, India, the Philippines, Scotland, Venezuela, West Germany, and other countries came reports of sharply increased cannabis smoking in the 1960s and 1970s. The modal user was a nonreligious male student in his teens or early twenties. Big cities and their suburbs were the primary markets. Danish hashish smokers were most likely to be found in Copenhagen, Swedish in Stockholm, and so on. In all countries youthful cannabis users were far more likely than nonusers to experiment with other drugs, including LSD, amphetamines, cocaine, and, of particular concern to European authorities, heroin.[20]

Some blame the spread of the marijuana complex and other countercultural drug practices on a handful of determined "vice entrepreneurs." Allen Ginsberg and Timothy Leary head the list of usual suspects. The media, slavering after the latest trend, magnified their bad examples, foisting another American folly on an unsuspecting world. Perhaps. But, as Eric Hoffer once observed, aspiring leaders cannot create mass movements unless conditions are historically ripe. In this case the critical precondition was demographic. Birth rates in industrialized nations dipped sharply during the Depression years, then rose again in the late 1940s and early 1950s. Birth rates in developing nations also rose after the war. The result was that 969 million of the world's 3 billion people—nearly one person in three—were between their fifth and twentieth birthdays in 1960. That is, they either were already in their teens or would enter their teens or early twenties sometime during the 1960s.[21]

This made for a record number of "susceptibles." Young people, who were better able to tolerate the aversive effects of drugs, were also more likely than older ones to seek new experiences, discount future consequences, and emulate peers. These psychological traits were conducive to drug experimentation, particularly in affluent western or westernizing cultures in which expressive individualism, hedonism, and sexual liberation were in the ascendant.

The marijuana complex and related forms of countercultural drug use also got a boost from the mass media. No fewer than 72 films released in the United States and Europe from 1955 through 1972 contained drug-related episodes and themes. Television news and entertainment programs informed viewers about novel forms of drug use like pot smoking, while at the same time broadcasting commercials that reinforced an ethic of unlimited personal gratification. The radical thrust of the old Schlitz ad, as Christopher Lasch once pointed out, had nothing to do with beer. It was the solipsism in the jingle: "You only go around once in life, so you have to grab all the gusto you can." The more young people thought of themselves as once-around consumers, the more they lived in a disenchanted world of self-gratification, the likelier they were to view cannabis as another choice in the vast ensemble of commercial pleasures.[22]

Middle-class youths who used cannabis and other drugs in the 1960s and 1970s also traveled a great deal, thanks to parental affluence, study-abroad programs, cheap fares, and easy hitchhiking. They were thus potential vectors of drug use. Ravinder Singh, born in India, the land of ganja, was a poster boy for the marijuana complex. The son of an army officer, he enjoyed an elite education. He learned to smoke hashish in boarding school. Cut loose from home, he drifted from Kathmandu to Goa. What stands out in his memoirs, published posthumously by his father, is how his life in those places constantly intersected with peripatetic "freaks" from Europe, North America, and Australia. Drawn by the prospect of cheap hashish, the freaks were heavily into, or at least willing to experiment with, LSD and heroin. It was with one of their company, a blue-eyed, jeans-clad, sandals-wearing French-Canadian girl, that Singh first injected heroin, the drug that claimed his life at 21.[23]

Cannabis came to Micronesia, Fiji, Samoa, Tonga, and other Pacific islands courtesy of Peace Corps volunteers. Official policy strictly forbade such practices, but youthful enthusiasm trumped distant bureaucracy. Volunteers in Truk planted seeds on several islands. The natives were at first uncertain what to do with the hardy new crop, but Trukese college students returning from study abroad clued them in, as did movies and videotapes from the United States. Travel and transportation are crucial variables in drug history, just as they are in the history of infectious diseases.[24]

Coca and Cocaine

It was in fact a shortcoming in transportation technology that delayed the globalization of coca and its principal psychoactive alkaloid, cocaine. Archaeological evidence of coca chewing dates back as far as 3000 B.C. The first human use probably occurred thousands of years earlier, when hunter-gatherers in the eastern Andes sampled the plant's tender new leaves as famine food, discovering their stimulating and medicinal properties. In any event, coca was one of the first plants domesticated in the western hemisphere. Coca leaves, mixed with alkalis such as vegetable ash or lime, which ease cocaine absorption, were used by natives for both sacred and secular purposes; they chewed the leaves to cope with the effects of altitude, hunger, and fatigue. Alcohol makes you feel good, explained one old coca chewer, but coca puts strength in your limbs.[25]

In the sixteenth century the Spanish debated the merits of toleration and suppression. Toleration prevailed on practical grounds: coca sustained labor in the silver mines. Though a lively coca trade developed in New Spain, transatlantic commerce failed to take root. Ineffectively packaged for long sea voyages, the few leaves shipped to Europe lost potency. Weak and uncertain effects contributed to scientific confusion and therapeutic skepticism about the drug. It was not until 1860 that Albert Niemann, a graduate student

Salut, mes enfants: Vin Mariani ad featuring school children from a working-class district of Paris. The manufacturer probably furnished the coca wine; it ordinarily supplied a free case to those from whom it sought an endorsement. Garden-variety physicians were allowed, in the words of the company's promotional literature, "a liberal discount."

at Göttingen, described the isolation of cocaine in his dissertation. He worked with specimens from a specially packaged 30-pound shipment, the largest amount of properly prepared coca leaves ever to reach a European laboratory.

Though Niemann died just a year after publishing his findings, things began to fall into place after his discovery. In 1862 Merck, the Darmstadt firm that had pioneered morphine production, began producing small amounts of cocaine, mostly for sale to researchers. The following year a Corsican pharmacist, Angelo Mariani, patented a preparation of coca extract and Bordeaux wine. Promoted by a campaign keyed to youth, health, and celebrity endorsement, Vin Mariani enjoyed international success as a tonic beverage. By 1884 the company had diversified into other coca products, including liqueurs, lozenges, and Thé Mariani, a coca infusion that helped Ulysses S. Grant complete his memoirs before succumbing to cancer. The success of

Mariani's products inspired imitations, Coca-Cola among them, and encouraged investigation of the plant's therapeutic potential.[26]

Sigmund Freud's well-known 1884 paper, "Über Coca," was a boosterish review of the existing literature on the drug. Noting coca's persistent use as an adjunct to Indian labor and the promising findings from his own and others' self-experiments, he professed optimism about its potential to counteract nervous debility, indigestion, cachexia (wasting), morphine addiction, alcoholism, high-altitude asthma, and impotence. (Andean *coqueros* reportedly sustained a high degree of potency into old age.) Freud also hinted at cocaine's use as a local anesthetic. To his regret, he did not follow up on the suggestion. Carl Koller won international fame when, a little later in 1884, he demonstrated cocaine's ability to numb the cornea. In an age when cataract removal was likened to a red-hot needle in the eye, the discovery was a godsend. Other demonstrations of cocaine's anesthetic properties, including spinal block, soon followed.

Therapeutic interest in cocaine initially outstripped the drug's supply. It was very expensive, "an obstacle to all further experiments," as Freud complained in early 1885. The situation triggered a kind of coca gold rush. Parke, Davis, the leading American manufacturer, dispatched Henry Rusby to the jungles of Bolivia to find coca leaves and to investigate other potentially profitable plant drugs. Brilliant, energetic, stubborn, self-promoting, and racist to the bone, Rusby was the Theodore Roosevelt of bio-imperialism. On this, the first of his seven expeditions to South and Central America, he rounded up 20,000 pounds of coca leaves, only to have his shipment delayed by a revolution. The shipment spoiled while waiting to cross the Colombian isthmus. Assembling a crew of soldiers of fortune, he nevertheless kept on, somehow making his way across the Amazon and gathering 35,000 to 45,000 botanical specimens—the number increased in the retelling—before reaching Pará half dead.[27]

American manufacturers were close enough to make the shipment of leaves feasible. What Rusby and others came to understand was that extracting the crude alkaloid in the Andes made more sense, especially for shipment to distant markets. This was how Merck and other German manufacturers initially solved the transportation problem. By 1900–1905, when the legal Peruvian export industry was at its peak, shippers dispatched more than 22,000 pounds of crude cocaine annually, together with more than 2 million pounds of leaves. Most of the crude cocaine (varying from 85 to 95 percent purity) went to European manufacturers for further processing; most of the

Henry H. Rusby

A latter-day caricature of Henry Hurd Rusby, one of a long line of great white drug hunters. Rusby, who identified nearly a thousand new plant species, embarked upon his last Amazon expedition in 1921, at the age of 66. One of his objectives was to study native use of a hallucinogenic drink made from the vine *Banisteriopsis caapi*. Though the journey proved too strenuous for Rusby, who turned back after seven months, the photographer Gordon MacCreagh managed to capture a *caapi* ceremony on film. He then skewered Rusby in a delicious, irreverent memoir, *White Waters and Black* (1926).

leaves, bundled and sealed with turpentine to prevent moisture damage, went to the United States. The seemingly odd behavior of American manufacturers—why import the bulky, perishable leaves?—was due to tariff policy. Leaves entered duty-free, while crude cocaine paid a 25 percent ad valorem duty.

The Peruvian boom was undercut, predictably, by expanded global cultivation, something that had already happened with every other important plant drug for which there was significant European and North American demand. Although coca would be grown commercially in many places, from Nigeria to Ceylon to remote Iwo Jima, Javan coca emerged as the most important rival to the Andean product in the early twentieth century. Initially reluctant to introduce yet another plant drug to the East Indies—there was concern that coca chewing would take root among the native inhabitants— the Dutch began small-scale commercial production in the 1880s. They succeeded in producing a variety of coca rich in cocaine, up to twice as much as the Peruvian leaf. The catch was that its efficient extraction required a special process under patent to a single German firm, effectively the only customer of Dutch leaves. But the establishment of the *Nederlansche Cocainefabriek* (NCF, or Dutch cocaine factory) in Amsterdam in 1900, which was under no treaty obligation to honor the patent, increased demand. So did the expiration of the patent in 1903, which brought in several additional German manufacturers. Javan coca exports rose from 26 metric tons in 1904 to 800 metric tons in 1912, a 30-fold increase in just eight years.

By the early 1910s the world cocaine situation was extremely dynamic and potentially explosive. NCF claimed to be the largest cocaine manufacturer in the world. Exporters supplied both NCF and its German rivals with potent East Indian leaves, carefully packaged to preserve quality. (The Dutch also planned to extract cocaine in Java itself, but were prevented from doing so by the outbreak of World War I.) The surge in world supply and expansion of manufacturing transformed cocaine from a rare and expensive drug to a common and inexpensive one. Its price plummeted from 280 dollars an ounce in early 1885 to around 3 dollars in 1914.[28]

Cheap cocaine fed a global epidemic that lasted from the 1890s to the mid-1920s, with peaks in different nations at different times. It began in the United States and India. The first American cases of cocaine poisoning and addiction were medical in character, involving patients and, not infrequently, doctors who had used too much of the drug or used it too often. By the mid-1890s cocaine sniffing and injecting had also spread to the underworld, where drinking and opium smoking were already well established. In India many users of cocaine were already heavy consumers of opium, ganja, or alcohol. Cocaine was essentially another drug in their repertoire, although Indian users generally swallowed the powder or chewed it with betel leaves and lime.

Reports of sharply increased cocaine abuse, typically followed by adverse publicity and efforts at restriction, poured forth from Canada and Europe in the two decades after 1905. The problem was essentially one of big-city low life and night life: Montreal pickpockets, Montmartre prostitutes, West End actresses, and even, wrote a horrified Louis Lewin, a few university men who descended to the Berlin cocaine dens. ("They give all that they possess, even indispensable articles of clothing, in order to indulge their mad craving.") Export figures and fragmentary police and treatment statistics strongly suggest that the continental situation was worse after 1918 than during the war, when the flow of East Indian coca was disrupted.[29]

Then, in the late 1920s, the epidemic subsided and world exports began a sustained decline. Japan had become a cocaine producer and was soon diverting an unknown percentage of its production to India and China. But this was strictly a sideline to its opiate trade. Cocaine was little in evidence in Europe by World War II (though the Danish resistance ingeniously used cocaine mixed with dried rabbit's blood to foil Gestapo bloodhounds trying to sniff out escaping Jews). The drug was also scarce in the United States. "We rarely hear of cocaine being used," one Bureau of Narcotics supervisor reported in 1940—this from New York City, easily the largest illicit drug market in the country. Mexican papers seldom mentioned cocaine trafficking; seizures throughout the country remained quite modest until the 1970s.[30]

David Musto, the historian who pioneered the study of the first cocaine epidemic, thinks the mid-century decline illustrates a generational learning pattern. A new drug generates enthusiasm. Use rises. Then problems—overdose, compulsion, paranoia—begin to appear among a significant minority of users. Would-be recruits think twice. Use declines. It is as if harsh experience immunizes a generation. The catch is that, when this generation passes, its immunity passes with it. When cocaine again became fashionable during the 1970s, baby boomers had no living memory of its downside. Having sampled and survived the forbidden fruit of cannabis, they were openly skeptical of official warnings about cocaine and other drugs.

Pot to coke was an easy transition, particularly in the Americas. Coca supplies had dried up in the eastern hemisphere, but were expanding in the western. A combination of international limitations on manufacture, declining demand, and Japanese competition had ruined the Dutch East Indian coca trade after 1925; then defeat in World War II put the Japanese traffickers out of business. But Andean coca production expanded rapidly in the last third of the twentieth century, particularly from 1982 to 1992, when leaf output rose some 300 percent. Some of this production, manufactured into illicit cocaine, made its way to western Europe. A trickle reached East Asia. The bulk stayed in the Americas, where it fueled the second great cocaine epidemic. Because of the economics of smuggling, the epidemic remained hemispheric. Larger, shorter-range shipments in specially outfitted trucks, boats, and aircraft were much more efficient than smaller, longer-distance, transoceanic shipments using couriers and false-bottomed luggage. The Colombians who came to dominate the traffic at first used planes to smuggle marijuana. Then, in the late 1970s, Carlos Lehder and others realized that they could make more money flying cocaine, which offered greater value for weight. (Locally manufactured heroin would later be added to the export mix.) The Colombians integrated backward and forward, developing an elaborate network for acquiring, processing, and transporting cocaine to the United States. Prices dropped as illicit production expanded. By 1988 wholesale prices were a quarter of what they had been in 1980. Cocaine was within the reach of the poor; crack had ignited the inner cities.[31]

Meanwhile, the smoking of semi-refined cocaine paste spread from the primary processing regions in the Andean nations throughout South America. *Basuco* was popular with those who could not afford refined cocaine and became a staple among the *abandonados* of Rio de Janeiro and other cities. The drug diet of these street children is a poignant symbol of the psychoactive revolution: cobbler's glue, gasoline fumes, cannabis, alcohol, and coca paste, straight or in cigarettes. When the smoking begins to wear, they swallow Valium and Rohypnol to take the edge off the *basuco* and blot out the miseries of their crime- and prostitution-filled lives.[32]

For all this psychoactive variety, there are many drugs these children have never heard of, let alone abused. It would be odd to think of them (or anyone in the Americas) chewing betel or qat, or seeking oblivion in a bowl of kava. These substances never became established in the western hemisphere, just as many American drugs never became popular in the eastern. Why they failed to do so is an interesting historical puzzle.

3

The Puzzle of Distribution

The key psychoactive substances discussed thus far—wine, spirits, tobacco, coffee, tea, chocolate, opium, morphine, cannabis, coca, and cocaine—all became global products. They were traded around the world and grown, or made from cash crops grown, in both hemispheres in the centuries following the Columbian exchanges. Coca is a somewhat special case: it went from Andean cultivation to bihemispheric cultivation, then back to expanded cultivation in the Andes. Its alkaloid, cocaine, is nevertheless a significant black-market drug in Europe and West Africa and is widely used throughout the Americas. Cocaine remains a global commodity, or at least a transatlantic one.

Yet dozens of substances with attractive psychoactive characteristics and long, culturally sanctioned usage never achieved worldwide cultivation and use in the way that, say, tea did in the eighteenth and nineteenth centuries. Why some drugs became global products while others did not is an important and complex question, as is the net impact of environmental changes wrought by successful globalization.

The European Distribution Engine

"A sense of such ease, such relaxation, had come on me that I felt I could not stand, I had to sink in a chair," the neurologist Oliver Sacks wrote of his first trial of kava. The beverage, in wide use throughout Oceania, is made from the root of *Piper methysticum*, a member of the pepper family. Sacks allowed that he was "stoned, but sweetly, mildly, so that one felt, so to speak, more nearly oneself." He slept deeply and awoke clear and refreshed—virtues not characteristic of caffeinated or alcoholic drinks. Taken in the right amount in the right circumstances, kava produces a wonderful, clean high. Why then is it not the world's most popular drug? Why has kava drinking remained largely confined to the Pacific islands?[1]

Betel is another interesting case. The chewing of betel quid, the areca palm seed mixed with slaked lime and wrapped in a betel leaf, dates to perhaps 7000 B.C. Something like a tenth of the world's population now indulges in the practice. It is a pleasant stimulant, similar in effect to tobacco. When asked what betel chewing was like, the British biologist J. B. S. Haldane, a man of considerable wit, rolled his eyes toward heaven and continued chewing. Yet almost all betel chewers live in east Africa, southern or southeastern Asia, or the western Pacific. Why has betel chewing failed to spread elsewhere?[2]

The most basic historical answer is that, for kava or betel or any other psychoactive plant to have achieved global distribution and cultivation in both hemispheres, it first had to catch on among western Europeans as a medicine, recreational drug, or trade good. Merchants, colonizers, and seamen from Portugal, Spain, Holland, England, and France were primarily responsible for distributing drugs in the four centuries after Columbus. They had the power and technology to ensure that what they valued and used spread around the world—often quite rapidly, as in the cases of tobacco and coffee. Their ships, terrariums, plantations, and bookkeeping were the essential means of the global psychoactive revolution. Still, why did they favor some psychoactive plants and not others?

One possibility is strength of initial aversion. All drugs produce unfavorable reactions in at least some of their users. Their taste ranges from the mildly bitter to the truly awful. The first taste of betel is acrid and disagreeable. Kava has been likened to chalk swimming in body sweat. Mescal buttons and other hallucinogens induce nausea. Yet the drugs that caught on with Europeans, tobacco especially, often had significant unpleasant consequences for neophytes. So initial aversion, while a possible factor, cannot be the whole story.

Another possibility is undesirable cosmetic effect, vanity being a greatly underrated factor in human history. Chronic kava drinkers often develop hard, scaly skin. Coca and betel chewing distend the face. In 1499 Amerigo Vespucci recorded his observation of coca chewers, the first European to do so. Their cheeks bulged with the mysterious herb, chewed in cud-like fashion. He declared them the ugliest and most bestial people he had ever seen. Betel also stains the teeth black and produces streams of red saliva. The lime in the quid eventually removes the calcium from teeth. It leaves only dentin stumps, which fall out because of chronic inflammation and hyperplasia of the gums. Old betel chewers did not present a pleasing sight to European eyes. But then, neither did tobacco "sots" nor bloated, red-nosed drunks. As with initial aversion, cosmetic effect is not by itself sufficient to explain why Europeans spurned some drugs and adopted others.[3]

Logistical drawbacks are more plausible. Coca's reception in Europe was clouded and delayed by the perishability problem. The requirement of growing and shipping more than one plant ingredient may have retarded the spread of betel-quid chewing. But the most clear-cut case of a drug whose progress was checked by logistical difficulties is that of qat (pronounced "cot," also spelled khat). As with coca, users chew or infuse qat leaves. One of its alkaloids, cathinone, closely resembles amphetamine. Although Europeans first encountered and described the plant in 1603, its commercial cultivation and use remained confined to East Africa and the Arabian peninsula. Qat leaves lost potency, and therefore value, faster than those of almost any other psychoactive plant. Not until after World War II did Ethiopian and other producers partially overcome this problem by the costly expedient of trucking fresh, night-harvested leaves to airfields for early-bird shipment in cargo planes.

Regular qat chewing also entails unpleasant sequelae, including fecal vomiting and severe constipation. Immediately after a 1957 ban on imports in Aden, sales of laxatives fell by 90 percent. Arab and western observers have often complained that the goat-like chewing of qat is a "time-wasting scourge," particularly among the Yemenis, known to spend as much as half of their scarce earnings on the drug. Although medical anthropologists have challenged the fairness of these perceptions, they discouraged consumption among Arab and western consumers who did not want for stimulants that left their bowels open, teeth white, and pocketbooks intact. Immigrants and refugees accustomed to qat's charms still seek the drug, but import seizures and raids against would-be qat farmers have kept supplies short. Drugs can, of course, become global commodities despite the efforts of police and customs, but they generally do so in such concentrated forms as heroin, cocaine, or hashish. Qat, by contrast, is bulky and difficult to conceal.[4]

New World Hallucinogens—and Old

Adequate shelf life, feasibility of shipment, and affordable cost were necessary historical conditions for drugs to become global commodities. They were not, however, the only conditions. Nonmaterial considerations also influenced Europeans' judgments about which drugs should become cash crops and international products. As Christians, they were suspicious of chemical shortcuts to altered consciousness. They were particularly suspicious of hallucinogenic drugs associated with Amerindian rituals.

The widespread native use of hallucinogens was probably not coincidental. One theory is that the Asians who migrated to the Americas across the Siberian land bridge were already familiar with fly-agaric mushrooms. Their shamans relied on these and perhaps other hallucinogenic plants to enter the spirit world, where they divined the source of troubles and interceded on behalf of ailing bodies and sick souls. They were culturally programmed to seek out substances that would help them slip into ecstatic trances. The people whose descendants would be called "Indians" brought this transformative quest for spirit plants into the western hemisphere along with their bows, spear-throwers, and dogs. And they were spectacularly successful, collectively discovering and using some 100 hallucinogenic plants. Peyote, mescal beans, morning-glory seeds, psilocybic mushrooms, and *Banisteriopsis caapi* are just a few of the better-known examples. Civilized Eurasians knew nothing of these plants and possessed only a puny folk armamentarium of hallucinogens, despite their greater land area and advantage of ancient habitation.

One might suppose that Europeans would have made up for lost time when they stumbled upon this psychedelic Eden. The reason they did not, argues the ethnobotanist Peter Furst, is that they saw hallucinogenic plants as instruments of the devil and obstacles to conversion. They clearly had supernatural effects, yet Christ was missing from Indian rituals. Ergo, the effects could only come from Satan. They were to be suppressed, not exported and certainly not commercialized.[5]

Tobacco is the obvious exception to Furst's generalization. Indians employed tobacco, especially the hardy *Nicotiana rustica*, in a variety of rituals. Modern strains of *rustica* yield tobacco products containing up to 16 percent nicotine. Shamans smoked, sniffed, infused, ate, or otherwise absorbed so much of this potent plant that they hallucinated to, and sometimes beyond, the brink of fatal overdose. Early English critics of tobacco, most notably

James I, mentioned the drug's idolatrous role. Why not, the king asked sarcastically, imitate the Indians' nakedness and devil-worship too? Yet moral arguments did not prevail. The black robes and their allies, who succeeded for centuries in suppressing, confining, and driving underground much native hallucinogen use, failed utterly to stamp out tobacco. Some missionaries became tobacco addicts themselves.

The explanation for tobacco's exceptionalism lies partly in its hemispheric ubiquity and variety of uses. Tribes that practiced no other agriculture cultivated tobacco. No colonists, wherever they staked out their plantations, missions, and trading posts, could escape exposure to Indian smoking. "The fondness they have for this herb is beyond all belief," wrote the Jesuit Paul le Jeune, superior of the Quebec mission, in 1634. "They go to sleep with their reed pipes in their mouths, they sometimes get up in the night to smoke; they often stop in their journeys for the same purpose, and it is the first thing they do when they reënter their cabins."

Colonists saw Indians use tobacco ritually, but also as a fumigant, panacea, and in other non-shamanistic ways that seemed more conventionally medical. Europeans had long imported drugs from the East. As a matter of cultural habit, they understood that valuable medicines came from faraway lands. They were on the lookout for new and cheaper plant drugs, a search specifically encouraged, in the Spanish case, by royal edict. Tobacco was an obvious candidate for the *materia medica*. It was a "drying" agent that fit neatly into the ancient scheme of humoral pathology, suggesting many possible therapeutic applications.

Europeans came to understand that tobacco use did not necessarily entail hallucinations. Drugs like peyote always produced hallucinations when used as intended, but not tobacco. The (Christian, civilized, rationalizing) Europeans were, to put it mildly, uninterested in shaky blastoffs to the spirit world. They did, however, value plant drugs of regular, predictable medicinal and psychoactive effects. Tobacco, particularly the less potent tropical strain of *Nicotiana tabacum*, filled the bill.[6]

This view, that early modern Europeans were deeply intolerant of shamans and spurned their hallucinogenic drugs, except for the milder variety of tobacco, represents the conventional wisdom of anthropologists and historians. The aversion is still in evidence in other lands where Christian missionaries remain active. Pacific Congregationalists take a dim view of kava, although the Catholics, perhaps as a result of their long experience of the Americas, are noticeably more tolerant.[7]

At least one influential scholar, however, dissents from the view that Europeans were necessarily hostile to or ignorant of strong hallucinogenic experiences—though he allows that their experiences were not of a religious character. In *Bread of Dreams* (1980; translated in 1989), an *histoire des mentalités* written in a stream-of-consciousness style, Piero Camporesi describes the early modern world as a hellish one of perpetual hunger and disease. The masses, suffering from protein and vitamin deficiencies, lived with

> the deliria of fevers, the festering of wounds, ulcers which ate away at the tissues, unrelenting gangrene and disgusting scrofula, the crazed patterns of 'St. Vitus's dance' and other choreographic epidemics, and the constant nightmare of worms and choleric diarrhoea. [They] also suffered the harmful effects of 'ignoble' breads . . . [It was] a hallucinating scenario, in which the feeble-minded and the demented, the insane and the frenzied, 'dazed' and 'drugged,' the chronic and temporary drunkards, tipsy on wine or—most incredibly—on bread, wandered about alongside cripples, the blind, scrofula sufferers, fistulates, those with sores or ringworm, the maimed, the emaciated, those with goitre, abdominal pains and dropsy.

Camporesi's thesis is that bread, the staff of life itself, had been poisoned. The desperate addition of cheap adulterants like darnel or hemp seeds, or the eating of rotten, ergot-infected crusts, produced hallucinations, individual and mass. Paradoxically, the absence of bread could also induce hallucinations, as starvation interfered with the production of enzymes necessary for normal brain functioning. Thus, whether starved of bread or fed with the contaminated stuff, "a huge stratum of the poorest part of the population . . . lived in a . . . universe of completely unreal extrasensory perceptions."[8]

It is hard to get a numerical handle on this extraordinary claim. I have found no hard evidence that a "huge stratum" of the vermiculous lower classes staggered about in a hallucinogenic daze, although accidental poisonings doubtless occurred. The ergot fungus, capable of producing hallucinations as well as death and debility, was one likely source of unintended intoxication. However, ergotism became less common over time. The fungus flourished on rye crops, particularly those harvested after unusually cold winters and wet springs. As Europeans began substituting wheat, potatoes, and maize for the more susceptible rye, and as a pattern of warmer, drier weather set in after 1660, exposure to ergotism diminished. The spread of distillation, which detoxified ergoty grain, may also have helped curtail fungal poisoning, or at least substituted for it a more predictable and conscious pattern of ethanol intoxication.[9]

The real value of Camporesi's work is that it underlines the dire utility of psychoactive substances in helping peasants and workers cope with lives lived on the verge of the unlivable. It is probably no coincidence that the rapid growth of European distilling, and the explosive growth of tobacco imports, took place during what historians call "the general crisis of the seventeenth century." Those born in 1590 who managed to survive until 1660 (as most Europeans assuredly did not) lived through a period of inflation, unemployment, pestilence, frigid weather, crop failures, riots, massacres, and warfare without parallel since the grimmest days of the fourteenth century. Plainly, these were people who could use a smoke and a drink.[10]

Coping drugs that did *not* entail hallucinations would have been of greater value to the gentry who controlled peasant labor. Quite apart from religious concerns, the floridly hallucinating commoners described by Camporesi would have been virtually useless for any sustained economic activity. The same could not be said of the pipe smoker or the tea drinker. Here is one last clue as to why "soft" drugs—chocolate, the milder strains of tobacco from the Americas, coffee and tea from the East—triumphed over what Jordan Goodman nicely calls Europe's ramshackle home-grown drug culture: they were more compatible with the emergent capitalist order. And they were capitalist goods in their own right. They produced profits for merchants and revenues for princes far greater than what they could extract from the old regime of stale beer and hemp-seed bread.[11]

The Future of Regional Plant Drugs

Explaining why (or when) a given substance became a global commodity while another did not is an absorbing task, carried out here with only the broadest of explanatory strokes. For particular cases there are countless reasons of timing, luck, finance, politics, organization, cultural predilection, elite preference, and even marital alliances, as between the chocolate-mad Spanish Habsburgs and the quickly infected Bourbon Court.

Any explanation of regional limits, however detailed or plausible, is in one sense premature. If a particular psychoactive plant has yet to become a global crop or commodity, this does not mean that it will never do so. One day betel and kava and other regional or hemispheric plant drugs may be as universal as cigarettes and beer. They could supplant them, given the health risks of tobacco and alcohol. The very corporations that now promote tobacco and alcohol may even market them. In 1969 a new-products task force assembled by the J. Walter Thompson Company suggested that Liggett and Meyers consider manufacturing "betel morsels," on the reasonable theory that millions of people must be on to something. When that particular idea was run up the flagpole, no one saluted. It shows, however, that sophisticated and well-financed capitalist institutions—J. Walter Thompson was then the world's largest advertising agency—were alert to the possibility of the further commercial exploitation of plant drugs.[12]

Also suggestive is the fact that, in recent decades, regional drugs have won new converts in or near established commercial zones, thanks to the growth of urban markets, cash economies, and innovations like "kava bars." Road-building in Papua New Guinea has helped to commercialize betel use by simplifying shipments to cities like Port Moresby. Such vigorous regional expansion may be a prelude to global usage, with long-distance immigration the bridge. The chewing of betel quid has become common in the rapidly growing Bangladeshi community in London. Kava drinking has appeared among Salt Lake City's Polynesians, and Utah has successfully prosecuted its first kava DUI case. The Mormons brought the Polynesians over, explained highway patrolman Paul Hiatt, and they brought their culture with them.

The herbal-supplement industry is another point of entry. Psychoactive substances such as St. John's Wort and ephedra have become popular in North American and European markets. Drawing on German clinical research, marketers have pitched kava and other "natural" remedies as safe and effective alternatives to drugs like Valium. Kava extracts are available through mail-order companies, Web providers, health food and grocery stores, and discount pharmacies. "We are very bullish on kava," comments one marketing vice president. "It's poised to be the next hottest garlic, ginkgo, or ginseng." Take your kava powder with lemonade, advises another promoter, and you will taste nothing at all. Add sugar and lemon-lime soda for a "party recipe," a suggestion that evokes uses beyond the purely medicinal and calls to mind the historical role of sucrose in popularizing the unpalatable.[13]

Environmental Consequences

Should kava or betel be commercialized further, and should they be extensively cultivated in the western hemisphere, they would have a significant and almost certainly harmful impact on the natural environment. Global drug crops, including that portion of sugar, grain, fruit, and tuber harvests converted to alcohol, have profoundly affected the ecosystem. We usually reckon the costs of drugs in terms of personal disasters like lung cancer or car crashes. It may be, however, that the most serious and long-lasting consequences are environmental. The psychoactive revolution has accelerated the degradation of regional environments and the fortunes of human communities dependent on them, through deforestation, soil exhaustion and erosion, chemical runoff, and weed and pest infestation.

The recent expansion of coca production, "the Attila of tropical agriculture," has destroyed millions of acres of primitive forest, much as the Brazilian coffee boom did in the nineteenth century. A dense haze of smoke covers Peru's Upper Huallaga Valley in August and September as growers slash and burn forests for coca. Many of these forests rise from "wet deserts," land with a thin soil base that quickly wears out after the initial infusion of ash. Producers move on to newly cleared lands. The depleted soil, minus its forest cover, erodes in the heavy rain. Flooding increases; mud slides bury villages; rivers silt up in a cascade of environmental disasters. Slash-and-burn cultivation of opium in Southeast Asia and Guatemala and that of cannabis in Colombia and Mexico have brought similar problems. The regeneration of mature forest in these places may take centuries. Meanwhile, carbon dioxide accumulates and the atmosphere warms.

The processing of illicit drugs, which often takes place near the point of production, is another important source of environmental damage. In the Andes the conversion of one hectare (2.47 acres) of coca into paste generates as much as two metric tons of waste. This includes the gasoline, kerosene, sulfuric acid, ammonia, sodium carbonate, potassium carbonate, and lime used in macerating and washing the leaves. Processors simply dump these chemicals onto the ground or into streams, where they poison aquatic life. Waste from morphine extraction produces much the same result. Adding ecological insult to environmental injury, cocaine smugglers also traffic in endangered jungle species, exporting them, alive or dead, as pets, skins, aphrodisiacs, and folk cures. The Cali cartel used regional fishing fleets to smuggle both drugs and exotic animals through the Caribbean to the United States.[14]

A critic of drug prohibition would argue that the problem lies not in the extraction of certain alkaloids, but in its illicit status. If this process were legal, licensed manufacturers would carry it out in factories with appropriate safeguards and supervision. No more *narcotrafficantes* operating in tarp-draped jungle labs, dumping solvents and eyeing the toucans while they oversee production of *pasta*. This is a fair point, but one that, taken out of context, is misleading. For in the larger historical scheme of things, perfectly licit drug crops have also had damaging environmental consequences.

Tobacco quickly depletes soil of potash, calcium, and nitrogen. Planters exhausted the richest Chesapeake lands after three years; no more tobacco could be grown for two decades. Field rotation on capacious plantations with at least fifty acres per laborer sufficed for a time, but eventually Chesapeake planters sought the rich, black mold of fresh woodlands, which fell before their servants and slaves. Long after the virgin forests of eastern North America have disappeared, tobacco remains an important source of deforestation in nations like Tanzania, where wood smoke cures the leaves. As much as an acre of forest is burned for every acre of tobacco cured, though the exact amount varies with the efficiency of local tobacco barns. Large applications of chemical fertilizers and pesticides pollute water supplies and breed pesticide-resistant mosquitoes and flies, a significant problem in the tropics.[15]

Changes in cultivation techniques have also disrupted the environment. South and Central American coffee bushes have traditionally been grown in the shade of fruit or other trees which protected the plants from direct sunlight and produced cash crops, such as avocados, of their own. The shade trees sheltered a variety of avian life second only to rain forests. However, since the 1960s planters have introduced a new species, *Café caturra*, in Colombia and other coffee-producing countries. *Caturra* grows rapidly without shade. It produces high yields, but at the price of heavy applications of fertilizers, as well as pesticides and herbicides to eliminate competing weed species. *Caturra* now flourishes on level or rolling land previously used for food crops and on older coffee plantations stripped of their fruit groves and forests. Ornithologists have found the high-tech fields of sun-coffee farms almost devoid of birds, and have begun promoting shade-grown beans as a green alternative.[16]

The cultivation of drugs necessitated clearing land for fields and for roads to get the crops to market. Both processes facilitated the accidental transfer of weed species. Planters and road crews moving into an area brought with them seed lots, tools, domestic animals, packing materials, ship ballast, and any number of alien objects to which "hitchhikers" adhered. "In Ceylon," reminisced the British botanist Henry Ridley, "I have had to walk many miles before I could get out of the area of South American weeds." Hitchhikers of a

Tobacco, wrote the Dutch physician Giles Everard, one of the plant's many early promoters, "loves a fat and pleasant soyl." But fat and pleasant soils did not love tobacco, which has a voracious appetite for nutrients. Unless carefully manured, a field like this one in the southern United States would be exhausted in three years. Slaves, shown here in an 1855 woodcut, are hoeing weeds that have sprung up among the small, man-made hills on which the tobacco plants are growing.

different sort attached themselves to exports. The Argentine ant, an aggressive agricultural and household pest in California and other parts of the United States, arrived in a shipment of coffee beans to New Orleans around 1891.[17]

Another danger, from the standpoint of human ecology, was that intensive cultivation of drug crops would supplant the food production necessary to sustain the population. The Chinese were particularly sensitive to this issue.

Critics accused British-American Tobacco of foisting Bright tobacco cultivation on the hungry peasantry. Company officials themselves professed concern about the abandonment of soybeans, grain, and other food crops. Even countries and regions which can easily import food, but which intensively cultivate psychoactive plants as cash crops, risk catastrophic failure due to pests and blights. The plant louse *Phylloxera vastarix* nearly destroyed European vineyards in the late nineteenth century. Only the grafting of vinifera vines onto resistant American roots saved the industry.[18]

All these problems—deforestation, pollution, blights—would have occurred in some degree anyway. They are inherent to commercial agriculture, not just plant drug cultivation. Still, the psychoactive revolution appears to have made a bad situation worse. Botanists have long noted that plants which provide human pleasure are often dispersed more quickly and freely than staple foods. Yet they drain the soil while providing (cacao, opium, and cannabis excepted) little or no nutritional benefit. A. H. Grimshaw, a physician and nineteenth-century opponent of tobacco, pointed out that thousands of acres of valuable land had been "run out," ruining farm families in the process: "Breadstuffs, wool, hemp, flax, or some *useful* article might be raised on lands now occupied in the cultivation of tobacco." If tobacco were not cultivated, Americans could get by with fewer imports; they would also have to clear less new land to produce essential foods and fibers. Setting aside the opportunity costs to tobacco farmers, it is hard to dispute the social and environmental logic of Grimshaw's argument.[19]

Except for one morbid detail. A demographer might argue that the psychoactive revolution actually *eased* pressures on the environment by killing people off. This is not as farfetched as it might sound. Relentless population expansion—Edward O. Wilson's "raging monster upon the land"—is the ultimate cause of agricultural expansion and habitat loss. Suppose tobacco and alcohol use had not spread rapidly over the past twenty generations. Because of the cumulative effects of lower mortality, a half-billion more people might now inhabit the planet. Their presence would surely have significant environmental consequences. But how do we know it would be a half-billion? And how much additional burden would they impose? Policies about drugs—whether and how they are taxed, regulated, or prohibited—are often justified in terms of their social impacts or costs. Yet working out the true net costs of drug cultivation, processing, and use is, in practice, maddeningly complex and highly imprecise.[20]

The Geographic Continuum of Drug Use

The global confluence of plant-derived drugs and alcoholic beverages can be thought of as ongoing movement along a continuum ranging from local to regional to hemispheric to worldwide use. The wider the use, the more extensive the environmental consequences. Tobacco's seventeenth-century boom is perhaps the most dramatic case of historically and ecologically significant movement along the continuum. However, the expanded production of wine, spirits, coffee, tea, cacao, sugar, opium, cannabis, and coca all fit the general pattern, with differences of detail in timing, direction and rapidity of spread, and degree of initial opposition.

The notion of a continuum implies that a drug can move — or be pushed — down the geographic scale. This has sometimes happened, though not often. The infrequency of movement back toward isolated local use is a clue to the transcultural biological foundations of drug reinforcement. It is also an indication of how entrenched psychoactive commerce has become, despite international efforts to control or prohibit it. The history of drugs is essentially a history of expansion, with technological change and capitalist enterprise providing most of the driving power. Drug control, to borrow a Cold War analogy, is more about containing use than rolling it back.

The notion of a continuum further implies that the confluence of psychoactive plant resources is not necessarily complete. Drugs that seem limited to local, regional, or hemispheric consumption may turn out to be incipient global products. A world of betel juice and kava bars may seem unlikely, but ruling out the possibility would be peremptory and ethnocentric.

Still, if betel and its ilk are to make further geographic progress, it will be against keen competition, not only from existing natural products but from synthetics. Mescaline must compete with MDMA (Ecstasy), nutmeg with MDA (methylenedioxyamphetamine), qat with the amphetamines. Plant drugs now compete with chemicals that produce similar effects but are superior from the standpoint of compactness, potency, cost, and taste, or lack thereof. Here is one last reason why some plant drugs have remained regional. They missed, so to speak, the historical window of opportunity, open from the late fifteenth through nineteenth centuries, but since closing rapidly. If a psychoactive plant did not, for whatever reason, achieve global cultivation and use by the end of the twentieth century, the odds of its doing so during the twenty-first will become increasingly long. The primary source of psychoactive novelty over the last hundred years has been and will continue to be the introduction of synthetic drugs by multinational pharmaceutical companies. Psychiatry's biological turn and the rise of "cosmetic psychopharmacology," the prescription of profitable new drugs to fine-tune mood and improve performance, assure the continued introduction of "clean" synthetic alternatives to natural drugs. Inevitably, some of these products will find their way into the drug underworld.

PART II

DRUGS AND COMMERCE

4

The Sorcerer's Apprentices

ONLY DRUGS THAT WERE widely used in western societies became global commodities. In no case, however, did novel psychoactive substances immediately become objects of popular consumption in Europe or North America. They began their careers as exotic medicines, about which physicians made heated claims and counterclaims. These intramural disputes seldom attracted official notice. Not until drugs began to be widely used in nonmedical contexts did they generate public controversy and state intervention. The story of the reception of new plant drugs, as well as the creation of wholly synthetic ones, is that of the sorcerer's apprentice. Again and again, promising new drug therapies slipped the bonds of medical discourse and control. They escaped into a larger realm of popular pleasure and mischief, prompting responses by national and international authorities.

An Hearbe of Great Estimation

It is an axiom of scientific medicine that particular diseases should be treated by particular medicines whose use has been justified by statistical studies. However, the principle of therapeutic specificity did not emerge (and then only gradually) until the nineteenth century. For most of medical history, doctors regarded drugs simply as tools to achieve broad physiological effects. Through such actions as quickening the pulse or regulating the bowels, they supposedly helped the body regain its natural balance. Seldom did physicians restrict a particular drug to a single illness. Quinine, for example, was an all-purpose tonic, not just a specific treatment for malaria. New drugs with pronounced effects were almost automatic candidates for medical curiosity and enthusiasm.[1]

This was especially true if physicians could administer them in a variety of ways. The Seville physician Nicolas Monardes, a student of New World drugs who published a seminal and widely translated work on tobacco in 1571, wrote that, applied topically, tobacco could heal all manner of wounds, sores, and aches. Taken internally, it acted as a vermifuge. Chewed, it allayed hunger and thirst; smoked, it overcame fatigue. Monardes noted that Indians also smoked as a "pastyme," reveling in tobacco drunkenness and diabolical visions. He was emphatic in his disapproval of these practices. From the start, moral lines were being drawn.[2]

Tobacco soon acquired a reputation as a "great Antidote against all venome and pestilential diseases," able to cleanse the air and disperse the poisonous "vapors" responsible for plague. "This day," the diarist Samuel Pepys wrote on June 7, 1665, "much against my Will, I did in Drury-lane see two or three houses marked with a red cross upon the doors, and 'Lord have mercy upon us' writ there—which was a sad sight to me, being the first of that kind that to my remembrance I ever saw. It put me into an ill conception of myself and my smell, so that I was forced to buy some roll-tobacco to smell to [sic] and chaw—which took away the apprehension." No London tobacconist, legend has it, ever succumbed to the Great Plague.[3]

Medical interest in and enthusiasm for Monardes's "hearbe of great estimation" peaked around 1600. While doctors were debating the means of administration and refining the indications for tobacco, sailors, soldiers, and men-about-town were smoking for their own pleasure, and urging their tavern-mates to do the same. As the supply expanded in the seventeenth century, and the practice became more general, many physicians grew alarmed by what they saw as the abuse of tobacco. One of the most interesting polemics came from the pen of the Danish court physician and academician Simon Paulli, who published his *Commentarius de Abusu Tabaci . . . et Herbae Theé* in 1665. Tobacco was valuable for its heating and drying properties, Paulli conceded, and had many uses as an infusion, syrup, or ointment. But when sniffed or especially smoked, it was "intolerable, and highly noxious." Tobacco smoke poisoned the brain and drained the purse. Foolish men smoked inordinate quantities, "whilst, perhaps, their Families are starving at

Home. . . Such is the Madness of some *Europeans*, that they will, for a Trifle, dispose of their Goods, in order to gratify themselves with *Tobacco*."

Paulli was a cosmopolitan with a wide knowledge of botany and many continental correspondents. He knew that tobacco was only one of many new drugs entering European medicine and commerce. Crediting as sincere reports that drinking chocolate, coffee, and above all tea produced healthful benefits, he pointed out that only those who lived in the plants' native regions were likely to enjoy these benefits. "The natural Produce of any Country is best suited to the Constitution of its Inhabitants," he argued, invoking an ancient medical maxim. Tea was best for the Chinese, coffee for Persians, chocolate for American Indians, and ale and wine for Europeans. Violating the natural order by mixing drugs and peoples had debilitating consequences, sterility among them. The importation of these products was wasteful as well as dangerous, as Europeans already had plants that yielded the desired effects. Spending immense sums for stale and adulterated foreign equivalents was "raging epidemical Madness"—especially in a country like Denmark, which had no drug-producing colonies of its own. Besides, why should Europeans ape base and cunning Asiatics, not to say the very Indian cannibals who had infected them with syphilis, and were doing so again with smoking? It was a shame, Paulli exhorted, "that we *Europeans* should thus brutally follow the Custom of the *Barbarians*, without listening to Reason, in which we so far excel them."[4]

Within the pages of Paulli's little book lie every one of the principal reasons why governments would one day assert control over or prohibit the use of certain drugs. They brought harm to those who abused them, misery to their families, and danger to their communities. They drained the resources of individuals and states. They were vices which originated with demonic others. Even the notion that drugs did not travel well, and could disrupt societies unfamiliar with them, survived as a commonplace of social science, though for reasons more anthropological than Hippocratic.

What also persisted was Paulli's distinction between tobacco as an occasional medicine, beneficent when the right people used it in the right circumstances, and tobacco as a habitual form of self-indulgence. Article titles and organization names concisely demonstrate the persistence of this distinction well into the nineteenth century: The effects of tobacco *when used as a luxury.* Is tobacco a good thing, *otherwise than as a medicine?* L'Association Française Contre *l'Abus* du Tabac. Deadly poison that it could be, critics conceded that tobacco had its uses, such as treating spasmodic asthma. Salvador Ruiz Blasco, a Spanish physician, once revived a stillborn child by blowing cigar smoke upon it. The motionless infant stirred, made a face, and began to cry. He was christened Pablo Picasso.[5]

Even today, long after tobacco has acquired a lethal reputation, nicotine retains some important therapeutic applications. Observing that the smoking rate in schizophrenics is as high as 80 percent, researchers have established that nicotine calms the agitating symptoms of the disease. It also mitigates the side effects of antipsychotic drugs prescribed to treat schizophrenia. Edward Levin has raised the possibility of switching schizophrenic smokers to nicotine patches, a suggestion that Paulli would have approved. Research, some of it sponsored by tobacco companies, is under way to investigate the use of nicotine and related compounds as a treatment for Alzheimer's and Parkinson's diseases, depression, attention deficit hyperactivity disorder, Tourette's Syndrome, and ulcerative colitis.[6]

A Most Excellent Thing

Wine was among the most ancient of medicines, employed therapeutically in all societies possessing viticulture. Greek and Roman physicians recommended it as wound dressing, fever fighter, diuretic, and restorative beverage. The Talmud says that "wine taken in moderation induces appetite and is beneficial to health. . . . Wine is the greatest of medicines." Wine and beer were commonly used as vehicles for other plant drugs, a practice that dates to the Ebers papyrus of about 1550 B.C. Medicated drinks were almost universal in medieval and early modern Europe. "To Procure easie Labour," ran a typical English recipe, "Take 3 spoonfulls of Oyle of Sweet Almonds in halfe a Pinte of white Wine every morning for 6 weeks together before the time of Delivery it is a most excellent thing." Cotton Mather, the Massachusetts clergyman-physician, recommended pulverized Green Turtle's penis in beer, ale, or white wine as a speedy cure for kidney stones.[7]

Before the seventeenth century, distilled alcohol was expensive, typically sold in apothecaries' shops, and reverently regarded as a life-giving "miracle," capable of dispelling everything from plague to melancholy. *Aqua vitae*, as brandy was called, means "water of life." (Likewise whiskey, which derives from the Gaelic *uisge beatha*.) Those who took a half spoonful of brandy every morning, declared one physician, would never be ill. Though couched in less enthusiastic terms, modern epidemiological studies have shown that the antiseptic properties of spirits confer protection against food-borne diseases like hepatitis.[8]

As with tobacco, physicians debated alcohol's therapeutic uses, a debate that turned heated in the late eighteenth and early nineteenth centuries. Few doubted, however, that it could be a lifesaving stimulant. "Alcohol, in full doses, seems to act as an absolute specific in snake poison, by overcoming the paralysed state of the heart and forcing it quickly to resume its natural action," wrote the Australian physician Julius Berncastle. His prescription: a wine glass full of brandy every quarter-hour until cured. Thomas Hicks, who essentially outlasted his competitors to win the 1904 Olympic marathon, took strychnine and brandy during the race to combat his exhaustion. The dubiousness of this (then-legal) tactic may be inferred from Hicks's time. It was 3 hours and 28 minutes, roughly an 8-minute-per-mile pace.[9]

Drinking spirits as a form of dissipation was an entirely different matter, and recognized as such long before Hicks staggered across the finish line. The historian Ann Tlusty, who has studied Augsburg's sixteenth- and seventeenth-century statutes on spirits, has shown how stubbornly authorities tried to enforce the distinction. "Brandy is not a drink to be taken immoderately," a 1614 regulation declared, "but only for strength or medicinal purposes." Brandysellers' customers had to take their medicine standing up and on the premises, rather like methadone patients three and a half centuries later. They could not drink brandy in taverns or other recreational settings. The strictures on gin, suspect as a waste of grain as well as a potent source of intoxication, were tighter still. Only four licensed apothecaries could sell grain alcohol for medicinal purposes. Popular demand, however, gradually undermined the regime. Soldiers demanded their brandy; widows and poor craftsmen distilled gin on the sly. Faced with persistent resistance and evasion, the city council finally acquiesced to taxed, nonmedical consumption, first of brandy, then of gin. Both were fully legal by 1683.[10]

One of gin's attractions was its cheapness. Its low price relative to beer and ale triggered a gin-drinking epidemic in early eighteenth-century England, immortalized in William Hogarth's *Gin Lane* and *Beer Street*. Writers such as Tobias Smollett and Henry Fielding—the former a physician, the latter a magistrate—denounced it as a new and unprecedentedly dangerous kind of drunkenness. Gin, complained Smollett, "was sold so cheap that the lowest class of the people could afford to indulge themselves in one continued state of intoxication, to the destruction of all morals, industry, and order. Such a

Duffy's Pure Malt Whiskey

FOR MEDICINAL USE.

No Fusil Oil.

ABSOLUTELY PURE AND UNADULTERATED.

In use in Hospitals, Curative Institutions, Infirmaries, and prescribed by physicians
everywhere. Cures CONSUMPTION, HEMORRHAGES, and all wasting
diseases; DYSPEPSIA, INDIGESTION, MALARIA. The only

PURE STIMULANT

For the Sick, Invalids, Convalescing Patients, Aged People, Weak and Debilitated Women.

For Sale by Druggists, Grocers and Dealers. - Price, $1 per Bottle

The Duffy Malt Whiskey Co, Rochester, N. Y.

For Sale by NOYES BROS. & CUTLER, Wholesale Druggists, St. Paul.

243

This 1894 whiskey advertisement cleverly evokes alcohol's venerable medical heritage. Even strict temperance families kept a bottle handy for medical emergencies such as fainting spells. Some radical prohibitionists, however, came to regard sales of medicinal spirits as a cynical dodge. In 1903 Blanche Boise, a disciple of Carrie Nation, made a point of smashing the windows of Topeka drugstores selling liquor, as well as those of saloons. The year before she had horsewhipped the mayor for winking at the liquor traffic.

shameful degree of profligacy prevailed that the retailers of this poisonous compound set up painted boards in public, inviting people to be drunk for the small expense of one penny; assuring them they might be dead drunk for two-pence, and have straw for nothing."

That this famous story was apocryphal and discredited soon after it appeared is beside the political point. Gin binges inspired anxiety among the respectable. They were, wrote Fielding, a direct cause of crime. They rendered men unable to work while destroying their sense of fear and shame. The results were theft and robbery—witness the parade of felons brought before him. And what, he wondered, would become of children conceived in gin? "Are these wretched Infants (if such can be supposed capable of arriving at the Age of Maturity) to become our future Sailors, and our future Grenadiers?" Like Paulli, who feared tobacco and caffeinated beverages as racial poisons, Fielding saw cheap gin as a threat to the future of the nation. So did Parliament, which in 1751 substantially increased licensing fees and requirements and imposed higher duties on spirits.[11]

Alarms over national fitness and security played a similar role in the fall of absinthe. Made by dissolving wormwood in alcohol with anise and other flavoring agents, this pale emerald-green drink contained the hallucinogen thujone. Although best remembered as a favorite tipple of poets and painters—Henri de Toulouse-Lautrec carried his supply with him in a custom-built cane—absinthe enjoyed growing popularity during the nineteenth century, particularly in France, where consumption reached 36 million liters a year by 1910. Advertising and mass production were the keys. The Pernod factory at Pontarlier was so efficient that only 170 employees, half of them women, could turn out 125,000 liters a day—bottled, corked, labeled, and packed in crates destined for ports as far-flung as Valparaiso, San Francisco, and Saigon. But temperance agitation and fears that absinthe drinking contributed to tuberculosis, epilepsy, heritable insanity, and crime led to bans in Switzerland, the United States, and other countries. The French government, concerned with military readiness and morale, issued an emergency decree against sales in August 1914. The following year the Chamber of Deputies formally outlawed all production, distribution, and sale.

Yet the prehistory of absinthe—the ancient use of wormwood, often with alcohol, as a medicine—presents a completely different picture. The plant was used in the treatment of intestinal worms (hence the name), fevers, epilepsy, and gout. Some believe that wormwood rather than opium was the drug offered to Jesus on the cross. Mixed with white wine and spices, it

ANOTHER IMPORTED FASHION.

Death pours another round while dangling an absinthe drinker by a string. This 1883 U.S. cartoon neatly combines three classic anti-drug themes: loss of control, loss of mind, and loss of life. Note also the reference to absinthe's foreign origins.

warded off contagion. Winemakers added sprigs to prevent spoilage. *Wermut*, whence our Vermouth, is the German word for wormwood. Wet nurses applied its bitter oil to their nipples to wean suckling babies. None of this was in the least controversial.[12]

Amphetamine Democracies

Four medical developments in the nineteenth century accelerated the psychoactive revolution and increased anxieties about its social consequences. These were the isolation and commercial production of psychoactive alkaloids such as morphine and cocaine; the development of hypodermic medication; the discovery and manufacture of synthetic drugs such as chloral hydrate; and the discovery and manufacture of semisynthetic derivatives such as heroin. Heroin is in the "semi" class because its basic ingredient is simply the morphine molecule, to which two small acetyl groups have been added, tripling its potency and speeding the onset of its action. Clinical trials of heroin and other experimental drugs demonstrated that small changes in molecular structure could produce large changes in effects. This principle revolutionized pharmacology and paved the way for the development of countless new medications, many with psychoactive properties.

Most synthetic and semisynthetic drugs originated in Germany, the center of pharmaceutical research and development during the late nineteenth and early twentieth centuries. One firm alone, Friedrich Bayer & Co. of Elberfeld, sold or licensed the manufacture of such sedatives and hypnotics as Luminal, Sulfonal, Trional, and Veronal, as well as its two best-known products, heroin and aspirin. (The company immodestly titled one of its publications *Materia Medica Bayer*.) Grateful doctors avidly purchased the sleep-inducing drugs; one Canadian practitioner bought them in 5,000-tablet lots. They soon learned, however, that barbiturates and other new drugs could mean trouble. One reason the word "drug" became associated with addiction in the early twentieth century was that physicians needed a term of convenience to link together the proliferating substance-abuse problems, much the way "cancer" described disparate forms of malignancy. "Drug habit" filled the bill.[13]

Cut off from German supplies and technology, the British and American pharmaceutical industries experienced hothouse growth during World War I. The American industry emerged as the world leader during and after World War II. More than 61 percent of new single-chemical drugs introduced from 1941 through 1963 originated in the United States, compared with 8 percent for Switzerland, 6 percent for Germany, 5 percent for Britain, and 3.5 percent for France. Whatever the country of origin, pharmaceutical companies marketed these products internationally, domestic sales being insufficient to recoup the large research and development costs. Those that had pleasurable or libidinal effects followed a trajectory similar to that of their organic predecessors. As they leaked from medical to popular experimentation and use, they engendered controversy and tightened control. This was true of heroin, barbiturates, anabolic steroids, tranquilizers, hallucinogens, synthetic narcotics like Demerol, and even, to cite a recent instance, Viagra, which prompted editorial head-wagging the moment it went from a treatment for erectile dysfunction to an experimental aphrodisiac. Similar controversies have erupted when nonmedical products have been used as intoxicants, for example, gasoline or glue sniffing. The sheer range of psychoactive chemicals available in the industrial environment is one of the main reasons why, in recent years, the terms "substance abuse" and "chemical dependency" have gained currency, being even more capacious than "drug abuse" or "addiction."[14]

The history of the amphetamines is particularly instructive. A group of related drugs whose molecular structures resemble adrenaline, the amphetamines stimulate both the sympathetic and central nervous systems, producing heightened alertness, wakefulness, and loss of appetite. Like cocaine, they increase the availability of dopamine, a neurotransmitter important in the brain's reward system. Methamphetamine is a potent and easily synthesized form of the drug popular with illicit manufacturers around the world. Users can swallow it or inject it like cocaine. They can also smoke high-purity methamphetamine crystals. Compared with crack cocaine, the effects of "ice" persist for hours rather than minutes. Chronic use leads to psychosis. It is a formidable drug.[15]

Amphetamine's first commercial use, however, was as a decongestant. Like heroin, which Bayer originally promoted as a cough suppressant, amphetamine was marketed by the Philadelphia firm of Smith, Kline, and French (SKF) for quick relief from cold symptoms. It was the base ingredient in their over-the-counter Benzedrine inhaler, introduced in 1932. When those who used the inhalers experienced stimulating, insomniac, and anorectic effects, it seemed that the drug might also prove effective against fatigue, narcolepsy, obesity, and other conditions. By 1946, according to one count, amphetamine had 39 indications, including such disparate conditions as low blood pressure, seasickness, chronic hiccups, and caffeine dependence.

College students found out for themselves that if they took amphetamine they did not need coffee. In 1936 University of Minnesota students, guinea pigs in experiments, quickly perceived the drug's utility for all-night parties and exam blitzes. (Human subjects in psilocybin and LSD trials in the 1950s and early 1960s would glimpse more cosmic possibilities.) Word of "brain" and "pep" pills spread to Wisconsin, Columbia, Chicago, and Purdue. Athletes, teamsters, and racehorse trainers got in on the act. So did the U.S. military, which issued upwards of 180 million tablets and pills to bomber crews and jungle fighters during World War II.[16]

The expiration of SKF's original amphetamine patents in 1949 brought new firms into the market. U.S. amphetamine production, 16,000 pounds in 1949, rose to 75,000 pounds in 1958, equal to 3.5 billion tablets. Nonmedical consumption accounted for half or more. In the 1950s, years not ordinarily associated with drug abuse in American history, an "amphetamine democracy" arose and spread rapidly. It included long-haul truck drivers, veterans, prisoners, students, teenage dabblers, and highflying celebrities. Max Jacobson, a notorious "Dr. Feelgood" whose patients included Yul Brynner, Alan Jay Lerner, and Johnny Mathis, injected John Kennedy with Dexedrine before his historic televised debates with Richard Nixon. By the mid-1960s, when production had reached 8 billion tablets a year, a flourishing amphetamine subculture was feeding off forged prescriptions, bogus wholesale orders, and other diversion tactics.[17]

Prescriptions were not even necessary. "I met a freak at the Hollywood Public Library," wrote James Ellroy, recalling his early life as a thief and drifter. "He told me about Benzedrex inhalers."

They were an over-the-counter decongestant product encased in little plastic tubes. The tubes held a wad of cotton soaked in a substance called propylhexedrine. You were supposed to stick the tube in your nose and take a few sniffs. You *weren't* supposed to swallow the wads and fly on righteous ten-hour speed highs.

Benzedrex inhalers were legal. They cost 69 cents. You could buy them or boost them all over L.A.

The freak said I should steal a few. I dug the idea. I could tap into a speed source without dope connections or a doctor's prescription. I stole three inhalers at a Sav-On drugstore and hunkered down to chase them with root beer.

The wads were two inches long and of cigarette circumference. They were soaked in an evil-smelling amber solution. I gagged one down and fought a reflex to heave it back up. It stayed down and went to work inside half an hour.

The high was *gooooood*. It was brain-popping and groin-grabbing. It was just as good as a pharmaceutical-upper high.

I went back to my spot in Robert Burns Park and jacked off all night. The high lasted eight solid hours and left me dingy and schizzy. T-bird took the edge off and eased me into a fresh euphoria.

I'd found something. It was something I could have at will. I went at it willfully.

This is an archetypal story of amphetamine abuse. A tip from a disreputable source. Diversion by theft. A bad initial reaction followed by a powerful high—Ellroy had swallowed the equivalent of 25 10-milligram tablets. He brought himself down with other drugs. T-bird is Thunderbird, a cheap wine. He kept using and built up a huge propylhexedrine tolerance, taking ten to twelve cotton wads at a time. Monsters jumped out of the toilet. Ellroy made a deal with God. "I told him I wouldn't drink or pop inhalers. I told him I wouldn't steal. All I wanted was my mind back for keeps." He quit alcohol and amphetamine, experimented with marijuana maintenance, then joined Alcoholics Anonymous. Westside AA swung hard in the late 1970s: "Hot Tub Fever" after meetings and nude pool parties. It worked anyway. Ellroy stayed clean and became a famous L.A. crime writer.[18]

This was not the sort of odyssey SKF had in mind for its consumers. The company tried various tricks to prevent abuse, such as adding denatured picric acid to discourage wick-eating. Determined users simply endured the bitter taste and nausea to get the high. Yet even if SKF and its imitators had succeeded in designing abuse-proof inhalers, the amphetamine democracy would still have taken root. They promoted the drug so aggressively for so many conditions that leakage was bound to occur.

Pharmaceutical detail men plied doctors with free samples and expensive brochures. "Fat people die first," proclaimed one, underscoring the point with anatomical renderings of fatty hearts and greasy livers. "Few therapeutic regimens have been adopted so widely, so quickly and with such generally satisfying results as the use of 'Dexedrine' sulfate in weight control." Dexamyl, an amphetamine-barbiturate combination, was just the thing for "the management of everyday mental and emotional distress," including patients experiencing money problems, family strife, anxiety over aging, bereavement, or spells of frustration. In other words, all of us. As late as 1953 SKF's official *Dexedrine Reference Manual* denied the possibility of addiction, conceding only and grudgingly that psychic "habituation" might occur in certain patients—but then "habituation may occur to pink water."[19]

When doctors treat a host of vague complaints by handing out powerful drugs flying the false colors of safety, they act as the sorcerer's apprentices. Some patients, invariably a minority, decide they can continue taking the medicine for other purposes. After all, it can't do any harm. They urge it on their friends. It helped my blues, my hangover, my fatigue, my weight problem, my sex life; it will help yours. Those who continue using get their supplies from physicians, concocting various stories to obtain prescriptions, or purchase directly from profiteering pharmacists and other illegal suppliers. Extramedical use evolves out of authorized medical use in a process of parallel chain reactions. The more pharmaceutical companies promote a drug and the more physicians prescribe it, the more parallel chains are set in motion and the sooner the drug is democratized.

Which eventually brings official intervention. In the case of the amphetamines, the hammer fell in 1971 when the federal government, alarmed by rising production (then 12 billion tablets annually) and the growing methamphetamine-based injection subculture, announced strict manufacturing quotas. Users could still purchase pharmaceutical amphetamine on the black market, though they ran an increasing risk of being cheated with "look-alike" products—counterfeit mixtures of caffeine, ephedrine, or other stimulant drugs. Clandestine methamphetamine laboratories, which filled the vacuum created by the federal crackdown on diversion, supplied the real thing.[20]

As it happened, 1971 was also the year in which the French banned Corydrane, an over-the-counter preparation marketed by Delagrange Laboratories. Each tube of twenty tablets contained 50 milligrams of aspirin and 144 milligrams of racemic amphetamine. The stated indications were for influenza, coryza, algia, and asthenia, the last two terms broadly referring to "pain" and "weakness." Corydrane was soon popular with customers other than those suffering from flu and runny noses. Men took it as an aphrodisiac; cyclists boosted their energy; students, artists, and intellectuals stoked their creative fires. Jean-Paul Sartre wrote his *Critique de la Raison Dialectique* (1960) on a diet of coffee, tea, cigarettes, pipe tobacco, alcohol, barbiturates, and Corydrane tablets, which he chewed like candy. The book was a prolix dud. Interestingly, when Sartre composed his more enduring literary works, he shunned all synthetic drugs, confining himself to a thermos of strong tea.[21]

The Japanese cracked down on pharmaceutical amphetamines much sooner than the French or the Americans; they consequently experienced an earlier shift to purely illicit supplies. During World War II Japanese soldiers and aviators used methamphetamine to sustain their *senryoku*, "war strength" or "war energy." Construction and munitions workers took the drug in a doomed attempt to keep up production in the face of incendiary raids and mounting labor shortages. In 1945 manufacturers began cleaning out stocks of war-surplus ampules, advertising them with such slogans as "elimination of drowsiness and repletion of the spirit." They were available at low cost, without prescription, and in an atmosphere of demoralization and weakened social controls.

Japanese physicians began seeing cases of amphetamine addiction in 1946. Most of the addicts were young men from slum districts, often of Korean or Chinese ancestry. No social group was entirely exempt, however, nor was dissipation necessarily the leading motive for nonmedical use. Stimulant drugs (not excepting caffeinated beverages) have intrinsic appeal in high-pressure, work-oriented societies like Japan's. "Japan is the type of society that needs methamphetamine," explained one longtime Tokyo resident. "The treadmill is very fast and people use it to stay on." Survey findings bear out the anecdote. In 1955 only 14 percent of current Japanese amphetamine users listed pleasure as the reason for beginning use of the drug. Night work and study accounted for 26 percent of users, curiosity 26 percent, peer endorsement 28 percent, and "despair" 5 percent.

As the amphetamine epidemic gained momentum, the Japanese government enacted progressively stricter measures governing advertising and availability and increased penalties for illicit manufacture and sale. In January 1955, when there were some two million users in the country, it launched a comprehensive national educational campaign. Slide shows, posters, and community meetings alerted the populace to the dangers of stimulants. The government mandated treatment and drastically increased the number of psychiatric beds available for addicts. This campaign—one of the first modern, multi-front drug wars—succeeded in ending the wave of postwar amphetamine abuse.[22]

Unfortunately, drug abuse in nations, like addiction in individuals, is a chronic relapsing disorder. "To say the Truth," wrote Fielding, "bad Habits in the Body Politic, especially if of any Duration, are seldom to be wholly eradicated." Amphetamine use persisted at a low, endemic level among Japanese *yakuza* (organized criminals), truck drivers, and laborers. Then came affluence, expanding night life, and baby boomers entering their twenties. The newcomers to the amphetamine scene lacked, as one Tokyo paper put it, knowledge of "the dreadfulness of the awakening drug whirlwind." Use took off again in the 1970s and 1980s, peaking in 1984. The supply was now wholly illicit in character. The *yakuza* derived 35 to 50 percent of their annual income from amphetamine trafficking, smuggling the drug from clandestine laboratories in Korea and, later, Taiwan and China.[23]

Amphetamines in Sweden initially came from licit pharmaceutical stocks. The drug was introduced in 1938 and restricted to prescription sale in 1939. But doctors were liberal: in 1942 they were prescribing amphetamines to 3 percent of the Swedish population. The vast majority, more than 200,000 patients, used amphetamines only occasionally, to cope with overtime or spells of depression. But 3,000 Swedes became near-daily or daily users, some building up tolerances as high as 100 tablets in 24 hours. A few of the early amphetamine addicts were also morphine users. They learned to dissolve and inject the tablets, a technique that spread in bohemian circles in the early 1950s. By then amphetamines were becoming popular with criminals, supposedly introduced by artists' models who had one foot in the atelier and the other in the street. Between 1949 and 1965, according to the psychiatrist Nils Bejerot, the number of persons addicted to amphetamine and related stimulants like phenmetrazine doubled every 30 months. From 1965 to 1967, during a brief experiment in medical maintenance—legal, state-financed amphetamines provided through doctors' prescriptions—the number doubled in just twelve months. The government reverted to a restrictive policy. By 1968 the prescription of stimulants required special permission, granted only 343 times that year for the entire country.

Bejerot, who looked broadly at the history of drug epidemics, likened them to infectious diseases. Their central feature, he decided, was proselytizing by young male enthusiasts not yet acquainted with the long-term destructive effects of drugs. Doctors might seed an epidemic or accelerate one in progress—Bejerot called the diversion-prone maintenance experiment of the mid-1960s the worst scandal in Swedish medical history. The real key, though, was youthful word of mouth. "If you go to a fine restaurant and you like it very much," explained one Stockholm addict, "then you tell your friends to go there. [This] is not recruiting. You tell them because you want them to enjoy. It is the same with us."[24]

Bejerot thought that only decisive government action, including the forced quarantine of addicts, could check the natural geometric progress of drug epidemics. He admired the campaigns of the Japanese government against stimulants and that of the Chinese Communists against opiates. History's lesson, he concluded, was that the mass abuse of drugs was not "a mysterious and inexplicable natural catastrophe, but a form of social disintegration which can be understood and even controlled."

But not one that could be entirely eliminated. Prescription restrictions and other legal countermeasures drove the Swedish traffic underground, where it survived by servicing the demands of its most reliable customers, the socially marginal and deviant users. Some illicit stimulants originated locally, but most were smuggled in from Germany, Spain, and other European countries. These included, after the end of the Cold War, former Soviet satellites and republics. The Soviet Union, lamented *Komsomolskaya Pravda*, had turned into "Narcostan," the land of drugs.[25]

In Sweden, as elsewhere, the injection subculture turned ugly. Emaciated injectors roamed aimlessly in condemned, needle-strewn flats, pausing only to get "freshly lit" or to "flame out" with sleeping pills and sweet wine. Desperate users forged checks and sold their bodies; paranoid ones pulled knives on police and passersby. Street sales became flash points of violence. Christer Pettersson, imprisoned for life for murdering Prime Minister Olof Palme in 1986, was an alcoholic and amphetamine addict. He confessed to a run of 600 robberies between 1970 and 1977. Most of his victims were amphetamine dealers.[26]

The epidemiologist John Ball calls the discovery, commercial exploitation, and popularization of synthetics like amphetamine the outstanding change in the world drug scene since World War II. "These new drugs," he wrote in 1975, "have had general acceptance by the medical profession, and their ethical use has been widespread, especially in Europe and the United States. Concomitant with their legitimate medical use, however, there has rapidly developed an illicit traffic and widespread abuse." Whether their medical use was invariably "legitimate" is debatable, though Ball's central point is not: pharmaceutical innovation greatly increased the number of potential drugs of abuse and potential abusers. Multiple patterns of recreational use proliferated among the young in western nations and soon spread elsewhere, as evidenced by the growing popularity of amphetamines and other synthetics in Guatemala, Nigeria, the Philippines, and other developing nations. Worldwide, the number of clandestine laboratories found to be manufacturing amphetamine and related stimulants increased six-fold between 1980 and 1994. The explosive growth of the Internet, which made more detailed information on more drugs available to more people than ever before, further simplified the illicit manufacturing process.[27]

The Medical Dilemma

The shift from medical to popular consumption has occurred for all types of psychoactive drugs: plant, alkaloid, semisynthetic, and synthetic. Over the years, physicians' concern about this process produced an impressive body of admonitory literature of the "damn fool" variety. The damn fool in these cautionary tales is, of course, the patient. He smokes or drinks more than his constitution can bear, dumps too much sugar in his tea, drinks too much coffee, takes too many pills, or otherwise abuses substances that are valuable when taken in moderation and in the right circumstances. Damn fools disinclined to heed published warnings got the message in person. Sir William Osler, remembered today as the apostle of scientific medicine, spent much of his time in private practice simply advising patients to mind their smoking, drinking, exercise, and diet. He once took matters into his own hands, scattering a box of forbidden candies over a patient's bed.[28]

Physicians frequently warned one another about drug potency, contraindications, side effects, and abuse potential. They offered tips on safety: Don't let the patient know what he is taking. Don't leave the syringe at her bedside. Such criticism and advice often appeared in journal articles and textbooks, but also in less formal settings—consultations, hospital rounds, lecture rooms, personal correspondence. "Incidentally, I have seen and treated two Milltown [sic] addicts in the past few months," cautioned one Dallas physician in a 1961 letter. "Too many people have been told that it is harmless or innocuous and they eat them like peanuts."[29]

The sheer volume and repetitiveness of such complaints are clues to a deeper conflict at the heart of medical practice. Historically, few physicians have abandoned psychoactive drugs when they first heard reports of poisonings, diversion, or addiction. As the physician Stephen Tabor wittily observed, if he and his colleagues set aside every medicine whose abuse had occasioned mischief, not one would be left. Eventually, doctors do become more circumspect about abusable drugs, though such therapeutic conservatism often takes years to develop. Sometimes, as in the Japanese and Swedish amphetamine episodes, the state forces their hands.[30]

One reason for medical foot-dragging is financial conflict of interest. From Hippocrates onward doctors have understood that, for most patients, they can do little other than prognosticate and let nature take its course. Yet patients and their families expect them to do something to cure the illness or at least to alleviate its symptoms. Doctors who succeed in meeting these expectations reap financial rewards; those who do not lose patronage. In these circumstances, drugs that provide pleasure, alleviate pain, dispel depression, restore energy, or bring sleep are attractive options. But how does one weigh their potential abuse against their humanitarian and financial advantages? Who should do the weighing, and on the basis of what information?

This last question is crucial. During the 1880s ethical drug manufacturers (those who advertised only to physicians and pharmacists, rather than to the public at large) began changing their marketing behavior. No longer content to react to shifts in medical fashion, they sought to shape physicians' demand for new products through aggressive sales tactics, such as the mass reprinting of favorable articles. One Parke, Davis production, *The Pharmacology of the Newer Materia Medica* (1892), included no fewer than 240 pages on coca and cocaine, then among the firm's leading products. Only 3 of the 240 pages dealt with cocaine's well-documented dangers, a ratio the historian Joseph Spillane dryly describes as "clear editorial bias against negative results." Reading medical trade ephemera, one quickly sees the general application of Spillane's observation: for more than a century physicians have been subjected to a well-aimed barrage of scientific-sounding advice that stresses drug benefits and minimizes risks. Any movement toward therapeutic conservatism has come against advertising's current. Recently the current has become stronger, as pharmaceutical companies have dropped the pretense of communicating only with medical professionals and have begun broadcasting claims for brand-name prescription drugs. Infomercials for Prozac air in the small hours and on weekends, when more depressed people are watching television. Physicians see patients who seek both relief and specific drugs — and who may go elsewhere if denied.

The conflict between loss of income and professional restraint is equally apparent in the history of pharmacy. A hundred years ago the big ethical question was whether pharmacists should sell drugs "indiscriminately" or to known addicts, lucrative customers who were nevertheless harming themselves and their families. One progressive New York pharmacist answered by suggesting that all reputable shops prominently display a sign: "A greedy criminal druggist will sell you morphine or cocaine; we are not of that kind." But things were not so simple in practice. Another prominent New York druggist wrote a journal article flatly condemning the sale of narcotics to addicts. One day his assistant observed the eminence dealing out a quantity of opium to a man who was plainly addicted. Confronted with the inconsistency, he protested that the man was the only one of his kind, that he had been supplying him for 25 years, "and that a refusal to sell it to him would only be the means of driving a good customer to another store."[31]

This was the control problem in microcosm. Profit-minded druggists or "dope doctors" or rogue manufacturers could frustrate attempts to confine drug usage to legitimate medical practice—the central goal of international drug policy as it evolved in the twentieth century. Though national drug laws differed over important details, such as addicts' eligibility for maintenance doses, the basic approach was everywhere the same: to control supply by regulating choke points in the producer-to-user drug flow through manufacturing quotas, licenses, prescription sales, triplicate record keeping, or other bureaucratic devices. The more dangerous the drug, the tighter were the regulations, a concept embodied in different "schedules," or lists of controlled substances, appended to statutes and international treaties. The object of this "bottleneck thinking" was to reduce both the aggregate supply of legally manufactured drugs and the likelihood of diversion, while maintaining a sufficient flow for ethical prescribing and research.[32]

The origins of this system are explored more fully in later chapters, as is the question of why some drugs like tobacco were exempted. One of the most obvious challenges to drug control, however, has been the ever-growing variety of potent synthetics. Before World War II the system regulated essentially three categories of drugs: those derived from opium, coca, and cannabis. Its creators did not envision the development of hundreds of new synthetics. They did not foresee that some of those synthetics, like etorphine, would be thousands of times more powerful than morphine. And they did not anticipate that millions of nonmedical users would surface after the new synthetics escaped clinical control.[33]

The parallel with nuclear weaponry struck several writers. Drug researchers, observed the psychologist Wayne Evans in 1971, faced moral dilemmas very similar to those encountered by physicists in the Manhattan Project. New psychoactive synthetics, like the release of nuclear energy, held an enormous potential for evil as well as for good. Help-the-patient, like defeat-the-fascists, was a powerful justification for their development. But what about those who might divert the technology to other ends? Nathan Kline, a brilliant and controversial American researcher—the Edward Teller of psychopharmacology—stated the issue concisely. The real question, he said, was not how to come up with new drugs to influence behavior and emotional states. That was comparatively easy. Much harder was "determining

Timothy Leary, apostle of LSD and veteran of 300 trips, outside his Millbrook, N.Y., headquarters in 1967. "I'm already an anachronism in the LSD movement," he modestly protested to an interviewer. "The Beatles have taken my place. That latest album—a complete celebration of LSD!"

who should make the decisions as to when they should be used, on whom and by whom."[34]

The refusal of some strategically placed individuals to submit to conventional authorities compounded the control problem. Timothy Leary abandoned a promising academic career ("LSD is more important than Harvard") and ultimately his freedom, spending several years in prison, to champion the psychedelic cause. Seeking political asylum in Switzerland, he encountered Albert Hofmann, the Sandoz researcher who had discovered the drug in 1943. One day in September 1971 the father of LSD and its apostle-in-chief met to discuss their differences over a meal of fish and white wine. Hofmann, who had entertained hopes that LSD might be used in the interests of psychiatric healing, was cordial but frank. Leary's efforts to seduce youth, for whom LSD was particularly dangerous, appalled him. Leary, he said, should have shunned publicity and stuck to quiet scientific investigation in an academic milieu.

Leary had three attributes indispensable to any true revolutionary: a contempt for caution, an indifference to casualties, and a knack for casuistry. He protested to Hofmann that the American teens whom he urged to turn on, tune in, and drop out had matured quite early. With so much information and life experience, they were comparable to adult Europeans! As for publicity, it was necessary to accomplish his historic mission. The overwhelmingly positive effects of getting out the good news about LSD would make any injuries and accidents, however regrettable, a small price to pay. Though Hofmann did not doubt Leary's idealism, he found it dangerously misguided. "Wrong and inappropriate use," he sighed in his memoirs, "has caused LSD to become my problem child."[35]

The use/abuse dichotomy, common in the world's medical literature, appears in its strongest form for narcotics and other highly addictive drugs, which Leary himself opposed. "The use of addicting preparations," declared Bejerot, "is medically defensible only in definite morbid conditions, and then, of course, under strict and competent medical control. All other use of these drugs is to be regarded as abuse." An anthropologist might question whether customary self-medication with opium to combat endemic diseases was "abuse" because it did not occur under the gaze of "strict" and "competent" authorities. Be that as it may, the distinction between medical use and recreational abuse has been present from the beginning of the psychoactive revolution; it has operated in Jewish, Christian, Islamic, Buddhist, and, to a lesser degree, Hindu cultures suspicious of intoxication; and it has hardened into the central moral assumption of the international control regime.[36] Natural or synthetic, drugs that have slipped from organized medicine's grasp have provoked cries of concern and appeals for control—eventually from the sorcerer's apprentices themselves.

5

A Trap Baited with Pleasure

THE IDEA THAT MOST DRUGS are dangerous substances best used in limited amounts under medical supervision has become the official attitude about their appropriate social role. But it is not the only attitude. Merchants, capitalists, and the political elites who tax them have long appreciated that drugs are seductive products and lucrative sources of revenue. The clash between opportunities for profit and concerns about health forms the central moral and political conflict running through the history of psychoactive commerce. Monetary motives and concerns are as historically significant as medical ones, and for some drugs doubtless more so. The first question to consider, however, is what is it about drugs that generates so much demand? And why do some people, as Simon Paulli observed more than three centuries ago, sacrifice everything they possess to acquire them?

The Evolutionary Paradox

Drugs are poisons. Psychoactive plant alkaloids evolved as a defense mechanism against herbivores. Insects and animals who eat them become dizzy and disoriented, or experience hallucinations. Yet some persist in eating intoxicating plants and fermented fruit, even though they disrupt their repertoire of survival skills. In evolutionary terms, *accidental* intoxication may be valuable: it warns an organism not to go near the plant again. *Seeking* intoxication, let alone profiting from it, is paradoxical. It seemingly defies the logic of natural selection.

One possible explanation is that the consumption of intoxicants satisfies a basic need. All people, argues Andrew Weil, possess an innate drive to alter their normal consciousness. Children at play will whirl themselves into a vertiginous stupor; holy men and women lose themselves in meditation. The desire to vacate ego-centered consciousness is deep-seated. However, some means of achieving this end are more dangerous than others. Drugs are powerful chemical shortcuts to altered states of mind. They do not alone determine the final state, which is a product of their interaction with the user's expectations ("set") and physical and social environment ("setting"). But they are key ingredients. Anyone who uses them to satisfy the drive is trading off toxic effects for potency and rapidity of action.[1]

Although Weil's postulated drive may be inborn, social circumstances have much to do with its strength. Bored, miserable creatures are more likely to seek altered consciousness than engaged, contented ones. Animals in captivity, for example, are much more likely to use intoxicants than those in the wild. And one could say that civilization itself represents a state of captivity. Humans evolved as hunter-gatherers in itinerant bands. After the Neolithic Revolution, most of them lived as peasants in crowded, oppressive, and disease-ridden societies. The misery and grinding poverty that were the lot of 90 percent of humanity in the early modern world go far toward explaining why tobacco and other novel drugs became objects of mass consumption. They were unexpected weapons against the human condition, newfound tools of escape from the mean prison of everyday existence. "There is no more profound way of understanding the course of history," Nathan Kline wrote, "than in terms of this effort to escape from one's own 'sweating self' and to experience even temporary states of euphoria or relief of discomfort regardless of the cost."[2]

Euphoria and relief are products of a molecular accident. Only a few toxic alkaloids have molecules that, if they succeed in entering the circulatory system and passing the blood-brain barrier, mimic or influence neurotransmitters in the brain's reward and pain-control centers. Nature is parsimonious with pleasure. Euphoria-inducing neurotransmitters are ordinarily meted out frugally and for some accomplishment that enhances survival or reproduction. Drugs fool the system, temporarily increasing the level of these pleasure-inducing neurotransmitters.

Though scientific knowledge has accumulated rapidly in the last three decades, researchers still do not know all of the ways the brain responds to different psychoactive drugs. Some, particularly alcohol, are "messy" in that they affect several neural systems. But they do appear to have at least one common denominator. They affect—directly or indirectly, strongly or weakly—the mesolimbic dopamine system, a primitive neural substrate that serves as a key pathway for pleasure and means of providing motivation for the choices we make. Drugs stimulate this system, and perhaps others not yet identified, signaling "good choice" by way of good feelings. Even a relatively nonintoxicating drug like coffee markedly elevates mood. A carefully controlled study of coffee drinking among nurses showed that those who drank two to three cups daily committed suicide only about a third as often as abstainers. It is a fascinating finding, entirely consistent with the notion of drugs as a coping tool.[3]

Before refilling your mug, however, bear in mind that the repeated use of caffeine and other drugs also alters the brain's natural chemistry in ways that are not healthful. Awash with external chemicals, the brain adjusts production of their internal equivalents or the number of receptors, becoming dependent on an outside supply. If that supply ceases, unpleasant consequences follow. Opiate withdrawal in particular triggers a cascade of symptoms: restlessness, sweating, extreme anxiety, depression, irritability, dysphoria, insomnia, fever, chills, retching and vomiting, explosive diarrhea, flu-like aches and pains. The cumulative misery has tempted many patients to suicide, as may be seen in the 1925 case history of Hermann Göring:

> Cause of illness: abuse of Morphine and Eukodal; severe withdrawal symptoms . . . The patient holds a prominent place in the "Hitler party" in Germany, took part in the Hitler putsch, during which he was injured and hospitalized; says he escaped from there to Austria, was given morphine by the doctors at the hospital, after which he became addicted to morphine. Admitted to Aspuddens [Nursing Home], the patient manifested violent withdrawal symptoms (in spite of the nurse allowing him more morphine), during which he became threatening and so violent that he could no longer be kept there. Threatened to take his own life, wanted to "die like a man," threatened to commit hara-kiri, and so on.

That Göring, winner of the *Pour le Mérite* (the "Blue Max"), should sink to such a state, or that he should continue to use opiates intermittently for the next twenty years, nodding off in *Luftwaffe* staff meetings, is a testament to the extraordinary hold this class of drugs can exert on the human system. "When the druggist sells me my daily box of Eukodol [sic] ampules he smirks like I had picked up the bait to a trap," William S. Burroughs wrote Allen Ginsberg from Tangier in 1954. "Allen, I never had a habit like this before. Shooting every *two hours*. Maybe it is the Eukodol, which is semisynthetic. Trust the Germans to concoct some really evil shit."[4]

Physical and psychological withdrawal symptoms can follow the regular use of any of the principal psychoactive commodities, including the less potent ones like caffeinated beverages. In 1989 doctors at London's Hammersmith Hospital discovered that the headaches commonly experienced by postoperative patients had nothing to do with anesthesia. They were a consequence of abstaining from caffeinated beverages before and during surgery. Depression, fatigue, and lethargy are other common symptoms. Though withdrawal is not synonymous with addiction, researchers have nevertheless found unequivocal evidence of a "caffeine dependence syndrome." This refers to patients who go to extremes to obtain caffeinated drinks, use them in dangerous or inappropriate situations, and continue drinking them despite adverse health consequences and warnings by their physicians. Honoré de Balzac, whose stubborn devotion to coffee hastened his death from heart disease, is the historical prototype.[5]

The notion of *reversal of effects* helps to explain the paradox of why people persist in manifestly unhealthful behavior. They have, as Burroughs put it, walked into a trap baited with pleasure. Having begun using the drug to feel good, they dare not stop for fear of feeling bad. If addiction is the hijacking of the body's natural reinforcement mechanisms, withdrawal is the gun held to the head. Even addicts who detoxify completely—a process that can extend over many months for a drug like cocaine—are not the same afterwards. The brain remembers the chemical shortcuts to pleasure. Environmental cues such as a familiar tavern sign can trigger powerful cravings. Addiction is a chronic, relapsing brain disease.

Why Exposure Matters

The last sentence takes us into fiercely contested terrain. Before exploring the economic implications of addiction and the related phenomenon of tolerance, it is necessary to take a closer look at compulsive use. Is it fundamentally a problem of repeatedly exposing brain cells to drugs? Or is it a problem of individuals who happen to have the wrong genetic, psychological, social, cultural, and/or moral characteristics? This issue has enormous implications for both understanding the history of drugs and implementing policies for their intelligent control.

At one extreme of the debate is a figure like Nils Bejerot who views drugs as germ-like pathogens that can artificially induce destructive drives in anyone: "No disturbed personality and no underlying social problems are required for an individual to develop a drug dependence." Exposure is the crucial variable. It explains why physicians in Germany, the United States, and other countries have historically had narcotic addiction rates up to 100 times that of the general population. "We almost never find a lawyer who plays around with the stuff," Harry Anslinger once remarked, "and nobody can tell me that lawyers are more moral or less inclined to get into trouble than doctors or nurses. You can't get away from it—if people lay their hands on the stuff, there are always a few who will try." Salvation lay in supply control.[6]

At the other extreme is a figure like Stanton Peele who views addiction as a people problem, not a drug problem. Addiction has nothing to do with a drug or its chemical properties. Indeed, people can become addicted to activities like gambling or drug treatment itself. In this view, addicts are essentially inadequate or misguided personalities who return again and again to drugs (or their behavioral equivalents) for a "reassuring absorption into a consuming sensation which takes away all consciousness of life's problems." Personal values determine whether people use, persist in using, become addicted to, and quit using drugs. Cultural values in turn shape personal ones. Cultures that tolerate drunkenness and invest alcohol with the power to control behavior suffer worse alcohol problems than those that frown on drunkenness and hold the individual accountable. Hence alcoholism is more widespread in Ireland than in Italy, despite high levels of per capita consumption in both countries. Supply matters less than the personal and cultural values that modulate demand and comportment.[7]

My own view of the matter (and that of most drug producers, distributors, and advertisers) is that both of these seemingly contradictory positions are true, though exposure is the critical precondition. Addiction following the use of any drug is the exception, not the rule. Only about a third of the young people who experiment with cigarettes, one of the most powerful addictive products known, become dependent users. Many individuals have inborn characteristics that confer immunity. The philosopher Karl Popper became so allergic to cigarette smoke that he turned into a virtual recluse. The real reason Bill Clinton didn't inhale marijuana is that he couldn't tolerate smoke in his lungs, despite repeated efforts by his friends to instruct him in this essential Oxonian art. Anyone with a persistent, violent reaction to a drug is essentially addiction-proof. Those with strong superegos and religious scruples are similarly less prone to experiment. Their opposite numbers, thrill-seeking sociopaths, are far more likely to light up. Peele has a point: individual values matter. So do collective ones. A strong taboo against consuming (as opposed to exporting) opium helped the Turks avoid a major addiction problem. LSD never became popular in Chinese cultures that equated hallucination with mental illness. The indulgent Japanese attitude toward alcohol abuse, by contrast, diminished the protective effect of the flushing genes carried by half its population.[8]

Yet history furnishes equally dramatic lessons about the importance of exposure. Iranian opium production expanded rapidly in the second half of the nineteenth century. The silk industry went into decline, and opium seemed an attractive export crop for which there was rising world demand. But with time the exports fell, and large numbers of Iranians took to obliterating their miseries with home-grown opium. An estimated 2.8 million of them were addicts when Reza Shah Pahlavi's government attempted to eliminate production in the mid-1950s. The predictable result was fewer addicts, somewhere between a quarter and a half million in 1968, but more users of smuggled heroin. Heroin smuggled from neighboring countries also proved to be the bane of the Shah's puritanical successors. Though they launched a crusade against narcotics, hanging dealers by the score, they could not stanch the flow of heroin from Afghanistan and Pakistan. Nor could they ease the severe unemployment that tempted Iranians to engage in drug use and trafficking.[9]

That Cubans once smoked 30 percent of all cigars made in Cuba, that Asian communities which grow and sell opium have consistently higher addiction rates than those which do not, that African transshipment points like Ghana or Nigeria have developed serious heroin and cocaine problems, that Kentuckians suffer exceptionally high rates of lung cancer—all of this strongly suggests that proximity, and hence familiarity and availability, matters. But how much? In 1973 Philip Baridon published the results of a unique global study in which he compiled officially reported addiction rates for 33 countries. He then compared these rates to twelve independent social, economic, and geographic variables (for example, urbanization, per capita income, proximity to opium- and coca-producing areas) in a multiple-regression analysis (a statistical technique for estimating relative causal weights). Proximity alone explained 45 percent of the variance, far more than any other variable. "The most fundamental fact about drug abuse is frequently overlooked in the welter of complicated psycho-social explanations," Baridon concluded. "If the drug is not available, there will be no abuse of it."[10]

This is why drug history is replete with giveaway promotions: bottles of Vin Mariani, cigarettes during rush week, smokeless tobacco at drag races, and surplus Brazilian coffee shipped gratis to Japan. The providers of the celebrated "free lunch" that accompanied the not-so-free beer in American workingmen's saloons a century ago played a clever variation on this theme. One Chicago salesman confided to a fellow worker that "he had had to swear off the free lunch when he realized he was beginning to go to saloons more for the beer than for the food." The idea behind all such schemes is to expose potential lifelong customers, particularly young ones whose consumption habits are still plastic. Young, single, undersocialized urban males who lack genetic or cultural protections and who are already using other drugs are on the A-list of susceptibility. They are most likely to experiment with and eventually become addicted to novel drugs, although, as Bejerot insisted, they are not the only types of people who become compulsive users. Given enough time and exposure, millions of others may join them. In 1915 American cigarette smokers were mostly confined to pool halls and street corners. In 1955 two-thirds of all American men between 25 and 64 smoked regularly, the vast majority of them cigarettes.[11]

Addiction, Tolerance, and Demand

Addiction—and it is addicted customers who consume a hugely disproportionate share of any drug—translates into relatively inflexible demand. Contrary to myth, addicts will not pay *any* price for drugs. Like other consumers, they are sensible of cost. If it rises high enough they will seek substitutes, make do with less, or quit altogether. Still, substances like opium or qat are qualitatively different from barley or oats. Dependent consumers will sacrifice more to continue using them than commodities that they do not crave. This is particularly true in the short run, above all while addicts are suffering through withdrawal.[12]

One summer evening, while strolling about on Hampstead Heath, the English essayists William Hone and Charles Lamb talked themselves into renouncing their habit of snuff taking. In a fit of resolution they hurled their snuff boxes from a hill into the brambles below and strode off in triumph. "I began to be very miserable," Hone later wrote. "I was wretched all night; and in the morning as I was walking on the same hill, I saw Charles Lamb below, searching among the bushes. He looked up laughing, and said, 'What, you are come to look for your snuff box, too?' 'Oh, no,' said I, taking a pinch out of a paper in my waistcoat pocket, 'I went for a half-penny worth to the first shop that was open.'"[13]

Experiences like Hone's—smokers hunting for an open tobacconist in the small hours; alcoholics shivering in the cold, waiting for the liquor store to open; bleary-eyed commuters digging for change to purchase their morning coffee—were to become commonplaces of urban-industrial life. The "must have" feelings of millions of consumers helped insulate drugs against the business cycle. The economic historian Alfred Rive studied British tobacco consumption over a 40-year period from 1860 to 1900. He found that when unemployment rose from 2 to 10 percent, tobacco consumption fell only about 1 percent, a sure sign of relatively inelastic demand. Internationally, the industry more than held its own during the Great Depression. British-American Tobacco, among other firms, enjoyed record sales and increased profits. In the United States, retail tobacco sales fell less than a dollar per capita, from $26.23 to $25.29, between prosperous 1928 and disastrous 1932. C. W. Barron, the owner of *The Wall Street Journal*, confided that he had purchased three stocks after the 1929 crash: General Motors, Paramount Pictures, and American Tobacco. Americans, he reasoned, drove cars even when they couldn't afford them, went to the movies more often than they should, and would sacrifice just about anything for their cigarettes. "If you want to make money pick out some good vice," he said. "In hard times they will give up a lot of necessities, but the last thing they will give up is their vices."[14]

Drugs are also fashion-proof—a counterintuitive claim that needs some elaboration. Particular brands and modes of administration come and go: 101-millimeter cigarettes, cocaine free-base kits. But, once established, a drug will typically persist in some form across many generations. Drugs have legs. They have outlasted beaver hats and hoop skirts and other once-fashionable items long since relegated to museums. Historically, fashion has moved from the upper to the lower classes in a "chase and flight" pattern. Social inferiors, anxious for marks of status, copy novel modes of upper-class dress, decoration, and behavior. The elites, vigilant in defense of social distinctions, then drop the vulgarized styles and practices. They move on to something else, which is copied in turn. Thus fashion constantly changes, or, as Georg Simmel wrote in a famous essay, "as it spreads it gradually goes to its doom."[15]

Coffee, tea, and chocolate were fashionable upper-class drinks in Europe before they passed into more general use. Why weren't the silver pots retired to the townhouse attics when commoners began imbibing? One answer is that these drinks (and perhaps the sugar so liberally spooned into them) possessed properties of physical reinforcement and habituation that the latest styles in dresses did not. British aristocrats might hold their gilt-rimmed cups in dainty fashion, signaling their status with refined manners, but they were not about to give up their beloved tea.

Dealers in tea had other advantages, among them lightness of weight and ease of adulteration. Although most people equate it with the black market, adulteration and its cousin in crime, brand counterfeiting, were common features of licit drug commerce everywhere before the twentieth century. Wine, spirits, tobacco, chocolate, coffee, tea, opium, and cannabis preparations were watered, sophisticated, doctored, or misbranded to stretch profits. Tea tampering was so notorious that London dealers placed Chinese attendants behind their counters to avert suspicion of sloe leaves.[16] Consumers' willingness to continue purchasing products of such doubtful content was, in a way, a measure of their dependency, another manifestation of inflexible demand. William Hone was unlikely to be too solicitous of the quality of the snuff he purchased after suffering a night of withdrawal.

Not all customers were as dependent as he. Yet, addicted or not, they soon developed a tolerance to their purchases. Tolerance occurs when repeated administrations of the same dose produce decreasing effects, or when users must take increasing doses to experience the original effect: the pub-goer who requires an extra pint to feel jolly. It is a built-in profit escalator, increasing demand without adding customers. Most people eventually reach a toxic plateau. The heaviest drinkers do not usually exceed 10 ounces of pure alcohol a day, or smokers two packs (40 cigarettes). But there are exceptions. FDR smoked as many as four packs a day, producer David O. Selznick five. John Wayne worked himself up to six. He wound up on the operating table with an egg-size tumor in his blackened left lung.[17]

By that time he had smoked well over a million cigarettes. The brief duration of psychoactive effects is another reason drugs are ideal products. Smoked drugs have a particularly quick and powerful effect, passing rapidly from lungs to heart to brain. Ingested drugs, such as alcohol or opium pills, enter the system gradually and are longer-acting. Nevertheless, apart from LSD, oral methadone, methamphetamine, and a few other drugs, they seldom have marked consciousness-altering effects beyond five or six hours.

Drugs are the opposite of durable goods. Although production surpluses can drive down prices, as has happened periodically with all the major drug crops, there is little danger that demand will suddenly dry up. It is in the nature of the product that individuals are continuously liquidating their personal inventories. This is particularly true of those who become addicted to the shortest-acting drugs. Sub-Wayne-class cigarette addicts who smoke two packs a day inhale tobacco smoke approximately 150,000 times a year, consume upwards of 15,000 cigarettes, and, at current U.S. prices, spend well over 1,500 dollars in the process. "I'll tell you why I like the cigarette business," the legendary investor Warren Buffett once remarked. "It costs a penny to make. Sell it for a dollar. It's addictive. And there's fantastic brand loyalty."[18]

Contemporary drug merchants who plead ignorance of these facts are liars. But did their early modern forerunners understand the economic logic of drugs, or were they simply buying and selling without knowing the true nature of the demand they serviced? They certainly weren't blind to the compulsive use of tobacco, widely remarked by Europeans at home and abroad. "Tobacco, in this age growne so common," Francis Bacon wrote in his *Historia Vitae et Mortis* (1623), gave men "such a secret delight and content, that being once taken, it can hardly be forsaken." Observers also recognized that longtime opium users could easily consume amounts that would be fatal to the uninitiated. "This is a great merchandise," the Portuguese apothecary Tomé Pires wrote from Cochin in 1516. "Men accustomed to eat it become drowsy and confused, their eyes go red, and they go out of their senses. They use it because it provokes them to lewdness . . . It is good merchandise, consumed in great quantity, and very valuable." And seventeenth-century Europeans knew that long custom of drink might "turne delight into necessitie" 150 years before Benjamin Rush and Thomas Trotter crystallized the disease concept of alcoholism. Although physicians did not articulate addiction as a related cluster of nervous diseases (morphinism, cocainism, *caféisme*, and so on) with their own distinctive symptoms until the late nineteenth century, those who lived through the formative stages of the psychoactive revolution had at least a rudimentary understanding of the possibility, and economic consequences, of compulsive drug use and toleration.[19]

Intercourse and Enterprise

Early modern buyers did not purchase drugs solely to assuage their private woes or satisfy their "secret pleasures," pressing though those needs were. They also prized drugs as aids to social, political, and sexual intercourse — another reason drugs passed so quickly from the joyless realm of medicine.

Coffeehouses in the Near East, for example, provided an ideal excuse for men to get out of the house, to consort with other men in societies conspicuously lacking in institutions of male conviviality. It was in fact suspicion of coffeehouses as centers of male sociability and vice that led some sixteenth-century clerics to oppose the beverage, rather than the *marqaha* or "coffee euphoria" itself.[20]

European coffeehouses played a similar liberating role. They provided the rising middle classes with a forum for relaxation, caffeine-energized conversation, and the serious business of politics and art. Coffeehouses connected men and ideas across class barriers. The barriers of gender proved more formidable: women seldom frequented coffeehouses in the seventeenth and eighteenth centuries. They were, however, able to create their own conversational institutions, the *Kaffeekränzchen*, in which they educated one another on the latest news and fashions, much to the resentment of traditionalists.[21]

Cannabis and opium may not have fueled the Enlightenment, but their smoking assuredly fell under the heading of male group recreation, as did the smoking of tobacco pipes and cigars. Cigarettes served everywhere as the small change of sociability. "Smoke?" became a standard greeting among Chinese men, displaying their packs in outstretched hands. Like treating others in a tavern or coffeehouse, the friendly offer of cigarettes increased exposure, consumption, and ultimately addiction. John Uri Lloyd, an Eclectic physician, pharmacologist, and wide-ranging student of drug history, argued that companionship was more often the cause of "dissipation" than drugs themselves.[22]

The appeal of drugs, in short, lies in their social utility as well as brain reward. Culture shapes drug use, but drugs also shape culture, inspiring all sorts of social practices, from ceremonial toasts to coffee breaks. After World War I, American women found the cigarette to be much more than a drug-delivery vehicle. It was a useful prop in their role as newly public persons, a protean symbol of independence, availability, friendship, or—stubbed out vigorously in an ashtray—of anger and defiance. So integral did cigarettes become to twentieth-century social life that some people took to describing them as surrogate persons. "I find that it's like a companion," said one woman, who smoked when her husband was away. "It's like being in company with somebody," said a man, describing his feeling of smoking alone in the woods while hunting.[23]

By the mid-twentieth century, when nicotinic breath had become a romantic given, smoking served as a frequent accompaniment to lovemaking. So

OSCVLA CVSVMIS QVID TV NISI TOXICA SVMIS. 14

The association between drinking and romance, illicit in this instance, is a frequent theme in art and literature. Alcohol, however, is most useful in the early stages of courtship, and then only in moderation. Knowing when to stop is tricky because of the lagged effects of drinking: the blood alcohol level keeps rising after the last drink, as alcohol already in the stomach continues to be absorbed. One more round before bed is generally not a good idea. From Theodor De Bry's *Emblemata Nobilitati . . .* (1592).

did alcohol, an ancient sexual facilitator whose amorous use remained widespread. "*No* is an extraordinarily complicated word when you're drunk," summed up the writer Caroline Knapp, who in her drinking days made it a point never to date an abstemious man. Alcohol, however, is more useful in the early stages of lovemaking than in its consummation. "It provokes the desire," as the porter says to Macduff, "but it takes away the performance."[24]

What many men have sought in aphrodisiac drugs is their ability to *delay* performance. Premature ejaculation is a commonly reported sexual complaint that has caused embarrassment and frustration in many cultures. In

1563 García d'Orta, a *cristão novo* physician in Goa (posthumously burned by the Inquisition as a secret Jew), published an account of drugs from India. It included descriptions of the hallucinatory and aphrodisiac uses of hashish, datura, and opium. Opium was "a merchandise in great demand everywhere," hoarded and eaten in small amounts to dispel daily cares. Yet opium eating often commenced for sexual purposes. (Recall Tomé Pires's allusion to "lewdness.") This was mysterious, Orta wrote, for all authorities testified that regular use led to impotence. Why were so many deceived? "This is not a very proper subject especially when we discuss it in Portuguese," he admitted, before launching into a circumlocutory description of simultaneous orgasm. "Taking Amfiam [opium] is here a help. It . . . assists to complete the venereal act more slowly."[25]

Morphine and cocaine have been put to similar dilatory uses. So have injections of amphetamine, known as sexual "pumps" in Swedish, a language full of colorful drug slang. Some antidepressants turned out to be surprise aphrodisiacs. "Incidentally," wrote a physician treating a patient with the antidepressant clomipramine, "his wife—a big film star type girl—wants him to stay on the drug as he can maintain an erection for considerably longer than ever before." The trap, as always, was baited with pleasure. Prolonged use of ejaculation-delaying drugs (and for that matter tobacco) commonly leads to impotence as well as addiction. In attempting to fine-tune one natural drive, men supplant it with another, artificial, and often more expensive one.[26]

Hallucinogenic drugs, which have less addiction potential, have frequently served as aphrodisiacs. "Compared with sex under LSD," Timothy Leary scolded the uninitiated, "the way you've been making love—no matter how ecstatic the pleasure you think you get from it is like making love to a department store window-dummy . . . In a carefully prepared, loving LSD session, a woman can have several hundred orgasms." The effects of cannabis, widely used as an aphrodisiac in ancient and modern cultures, are far milder, though no less appealing. It at once disinhibits, sensitizes, and distorts time, making orgasms seem longer—effects likely enhanced by users' expectations. In 1980–1981 George Gay, a physician at the Haight-Ashbury Free Medical Clinics, and his associates carried out a unique study of 102 drug and sex aficionados. They interviewed the subjects about their preferences, which, in pre-AIDS San Francisco, encompassed just about everything. Surprisingly, this expert panel picked marijuana as the champion of increased sexual pleasure, ranking it ahead of MDA, nitrites (popular with gay men), cocaine, and LSD.[27]

Cannabis also enhances the enjoyment of food and music. "When you're straight, sex is great. When you're high, *everything* is great," remarked a 21-year-old student. While not all drugs are as broadly pleasure-enhancing as cannabis, a variety of cultural linkages have developed: wine with meals, coffee with dessert, beer with darts. Drug merchants are selling more than a transient high or relief from withdrawal. They are selling products that enhance an array of pleasures, from sex to scones.

While modern advertising consciously reinforces these connections, at least for licit drugs, it does not usually create them, nor is it indispensable to the process. Word of mouth—the hushed advice in the tavern, the graffiti in the *pissoir*—is more ancient and fundamental. Drugs and their affiliated pleasures are self-advertising, especially within deviant hedonic subcultures. Heroin, for example, first got its reputation for prolonging intercourse among young men who frequented the vice districts of northeastern U.S. cities—one reason its use spread rapidly within this group.[28]

Word of mouth helps in another way. Some people fall in love with drugs the first time they take them. "You can never top that first rush," Jim Carroll wrote of heroin in *The Basketball Diaries*, "it's like ten orgasms." The more usual reaction, however, is distaste or outright sickness. Sometimes the sickness is mixed with pleasure, sometimes not. Bitterness, acrid smoke, and vomiting are visceral forms of sales resistance and the greatest drawbacks of drugs as products. Like Elizabeth I, who was said to have given up smoking after one trial, many dabblers never try again. They submit to the evolutionary logic of toxic alkaloids.

Yet others persist. Peer advice and pressure are crucial to their efforts. Don't worry, everybody gets sick the first time. It's no disgrace. You'll get the good out of it next time. And if you can't get the hang of it, well, too bad. Early twentieth-century Russian workers ridiculed the rare comrade who refused to drink as a *krasnaia devitsa* (red maiden), *mokraia kuritsa* (wet hen), or *baba* (peasant woman)—all feminine forms. Real men could handle liquor. And tobacco. "They can't believe I don't smoke," Frank McCourt wrote of his youthful Irish companions. "They want to know if there's something wrong with me, the bad eyes or consumption maybe. How can you go with a girl if you don't smoke?" "You couldn't get anywhere, in the high-school society of the late forties, without smoking," agreed his American contemporary, John Updike. Though he found his first drags disagreeable, Updike gamely stuck with it, and went on smoking for more than 30 years.[29]

Problem Profits

New drugs and drug products often take market share from existing ones. Hit by competition from gin in the seventeenth century and caffeinated beverages in the eighteenth, Dutch brewers went into a long decline. In Latin America alcohol had to compete with cannabis, a product that developed a reputation as an inexpensive high. After cheap gin made its appearance, Nigerians began substituting it for the expensive kola nuts traditionally offered to visitors. The cigarette triumphed at the expense of other tobacco products. In 1900 American smokers averaged two cigars for every cigarette; in 1949, 65 cigarettes for every cigar. The success of aspirin—introduced commercially in 1899, it was one of the world's most widely used analgesics by 1914—gave doctors and patients a safe alternative to opiates. Iatrogenic (physician-caused) addiction diminished. Meanwhile, novocaine and other synthetic anesthetics virtually wiped out the medical market for the more dangerous cocaine.[30]

The drug market is not, however, a zero-sum game. For there are just as many examples of new drugs enhancing, or being added to, existing ones. Cola drinks and tea were employed to color moonshine and quench the thirst of qat chewers. Tranquilizers and barbiturates boosted the effects of alcohol, nicotine those of cannabis and qat. Cocaine spiced up heroin injections—"cocktails" in Switzerland, "speedballs" in the United States. Alcohol, medicine's ancient drug omnibus, simply added new passengers in the synthetic era. It was a key ingredient in narcotic-laced patent medicines and ethical preparations like Terp-Heroin, a respiratory antispasmodic. Drug companies discovered that adding barbiturates to diet pills and other amphetamine products had a synergistic effect; patients felt more euphoric and relaxed than if they had taken either drug by itself.

Tobacco and cannabis were highly complementary. They have been smoked together in virtually every culture in which they have taken root—for example, *kif* in Morocco, spliffs in Jamaica, blunts in the United States. Tobacco was a gateway to cannabis experimentation. The marijuana complex could not have arisen as quickly or spread as far as it did without the antecedent cigarette revolution. Heavy drinkers were also more likely to light up, notwithstanding the countercultural cliché of marijuana as a benign alternative to alcohol. If anything, smoking and drinking have increased the demand for marijuana and other drugs, rather than diminishing it.[31]

Drugs have often served to counter the effects of other drugs. Barbiturates and coca wines eased opiate withdrawal. Tranquilizers, opiates, and alcohol modulated the effects of cocaine. Coffee beans and kola nuts helped drunks recover from sprees. So did morphine and heroin: hangover was a common source of opiate addiction well into the twentieth century. Soft-drink manufacturers pushed a more benign alternative. "Got a hangover? Drink Coca-Cola," advised ads in West German papers after World War II. Sankyo, the Japanese pharmaceutical giant, pitched "Regain," a popular caffeine-and-vitamin tonic, to those who had downed too much *sake*.

These are all instances of what economists call externalities: unanticipated effects whose costs and benefits are not borne by those who occasioned them. Drugs are notorious for their harmful externalities, such as accidents and fetal poisonings; this is one reason they were subjected to progressively stricter regulation in the nineteenth and twentieth centuries. But the psychoactive revolution also spawned many profitable externalities. Bobbing in its wake were manufacturers and distributors of clay and briar pipes, jeweled snuff boxes, porcelain cups, art nouveau absinthe spoons, spill-proof bongs, flavored rolling papers, and a hundred other types of imaginative paraphernalia. (In the mid-1970s the Drug Enforcement Administration began estimating domestic marijuana consumption simply by extrapolating from cigarette paper sales.) Something about drugs fires human ingenuity. The sellers of lichee nuts and charcoal balls prospered; their merchandise was handy for holding dollops of opium and keeping pipes lit. In 1876 London alone boasted 30 Meerschaum pipe makers and importers. Across the continent in Constantinople, society women wore jewelry concealing miniature syringes. A century later their American counterparts sported gold pendants and earrings in the shape of Quaalude tablets.

Externalities often took the form of "problem profits." That is, the problems associated with drug abuse translated into opportunities for providers of symptomatic relief and treatment. In the mid-1930s the marketers of Bromo-Seltzer, an over-the-counter preparation of acetanilid, bromide, caffeine, and citric salts, discovered that most of their customers were lower-income men looking for relief from hangovers. They promptly dumbed down their ads and ran them in the Sunday comics, "the day most Bromo-Seltzer is used." Not to be outdone, rival Alka-Seltzer devised cartoon ads aimed at men who smoked as well as drank too much. Matchbooks bore ads for cough drops: "Soothes your throat, cleans your breath."[32]

The biggest windfalls went to organized medicine, which treated the con-

The seventeenth- and eighteenth-century boom in caffeinated beverages led to many new products, rendered in high style for wealthy consumers. In this pastel after *The Beautiful Chocolate Girl* (1743), the *Mona Lisa* of chocolate painting, a servant bears on her tray a Meissen cup with *Höroldt* adornment. The original artist, Jean-Etienne Liotard, used as his model the chambermaid who brought him his morning chocolate.

sequences of drug abuse and provided assistance for those struggling to quit. Nowhere were the profits from the latter enterprise greater than in the United States. What began as a motley collection of mail-order cures and private asylums ("dip shops" in upper-class slang) in the late nineteenth century had matured into a vast chemical dependency complex by the late twentieth. In 1992 expenditures on alcohol and other drug abuse treatment were running more than seven billion dollars annually, with another three billion spent for prevention, training, research, and insurance administration. Twenty years ago I met an ex-addict researcher employed by the New York State Division of Substance Abuse Services. I told him about my plans to create a street-level history of American narcotic use by taping the life histories of elderly methadone patients. That's fine, he replied, but it was too bad that I was missing out on the real story—the rise of the drug-treatment industry.[33]

The insight was larger than he knew. Problem profits are not unique to drugs; they inhere in all enterprises that exploit evolved drives. Fat and sugar were scarce on the African savanna where the human design was fine-tuned. Those who had a tendency to consume large amounts of fat when given the rare opportunity to do so were more likely to survive famines. We, their descendants, retain the taste, though it has become a health disadvantage and a readily exploitable weakness in a world of fast food. In fact, the confluence and sensory enhancement of new foodstuffs after the Columbian exchange bears an uncanny resemblance to what happened with drugs. No New World, no chocolate bars, no pizza sauce, no popcorn, no french fries—currently the fate of one in every three American potatoes. By 1997 American food processors were shipping 386,000 metric tons of french fries overseas. McDonald's, which was feeding 7 percent of the U.S. population each day, had opened 10,000 stores in 105 countries, 2,000 in Japan alone. The company was serving Big Macs from Rovaniemi, Finland, just south of the Arctic Circle, to Invercargill, New Zealand, 13,200 miles away. Kentucky Fried Chicken was doing business in the shadow of the Sphinx. Ten years before, in 1987, the world's largest KFC outlet opened just across from Mao's final resting place in Tian'anmen Square, dispensing gravy and mashed "potato mud" to the willing masses.[34]

These popular sacrileges, like drug commerce, have a transcultural biological foundation. We all like sweet and fatty foods. Some obese individuals, like some susceptible drug users, add to the "natural" attractions of such foods by using them to cope with boredom, frustration, anger, depression, insecurity, and despair. "Capitalism and the medical establishment profit not just from our biological tendency to enjoy high-calorie foods and psychoactive drugs," comments the historian Susan Speaker, "but from the ubiquity and variety of human misery, physical, psychological, and spiritual." The human price of the profit varies. For those of us who have inherited "thrifty" fat-storage genes, or who live in exercise-poor automotive societies, overeating often results in catastrophic illnesses like diabetes. Yet, judging from weight-gain figures, we cannot stop ourselves. Our evolved tastes and desires, inflamed by corporate advertisements, defeat our intellect and willpower. "How ironic," remark Randolph Nesse and George Williams, authorities on Darwinian medicine, "that humanity worked for centuries to create environments that are almost literally flowing with milk and honey, only to see our success responsible for much modern disease and untimely death."[35]

Ironic, but also profitable for the providers of insulin, arterial stents, liposuction, diet pills, treadmills, and lite foods. The peculiar, vomitorious genius of modern capitalism is its ability to betray our senses with one class of products or services and then sell us another to cope with the damage so that we can go back to consuming more of what caused the problem in the first place. Dieting, as the critic Richard Klein wryly noted, is the most highly perfected form of consumption.[36]

Drug makers certainly cashed in on fat. Fashion models quickly discovered the slimming possibilities of amphetamines. The English model Jean Dawnay described her New York counterparts of the early 1950s as living on Benzedrine, Dexedrine, and black coffee: "Their incredible slimness staggered me." Millions of women who longed to emulate the wraith-like images of high fashion resorted to cigarettes, which suppress the desire for sweet foods, as their secret weapon in the war against weight. "If you look the word 'model' up in the dictionary, it means example," observed Andie MacDowell, who took diet pills and cocaine to stay thin while modeling. "Now kids'll try and be that size, they'll drink Diet Cokes and smoke cigarettes all damn day." Or worse. "There are certain, practical things that doing lots of heroin or cocaine takes care of," explained the actor Robert Downey, Jr., a man in a position to know. "Like weight problems, or attention deficit disorder."[37]

Diet books at supermarket checkouts, Viagra to restore erections lost to the cumulative effects of cigarettes first smoked to enhance manliness—it all seems impossibly contradictory, but only from a public-health perspective. From the standpoint of profit maximization and full employment it is quite logical, even inevitable. Problem profits are a defining feature of mature capitalism, which can no longer sustain growth simply by churning out innocu-

With regard to health and pleasure, a consumer society is like a dog frantically chasing its own tail. One product, pie à la mode, leads to demand for another—and profits for enterprising drug companies. Ads like this one for Methedrine (methamphetamine hydrochloride) ran in American medical journals in the 1950s. Their designers aimed to create a "response habit" among doctors so that they would, as a first resort, prescribe trade-name drugs for certain patient profiles.

ous commodities and durable goods. Soy beans and clothes driers generate only so much economic activity. Drugs, which radiate externalities, produce far more. They are a kind of perpetual motion machine, providing steady work for everyone from peasants to lawyers to drug historians.

"We live in a society," Thomas Merton complained in 1948, "whose whole policy is to excite every nerve in the human body and keep it at the highest pitch of artificial tension, to strain every human desire to the limit and create as many new desires and synthetic passions as possible, in order to cater to them with the products of our factories and printing presses and movie studios and all the rest."[38] That is exactly right. Drug dealers are to dopamine what pornographers are to testosterone or food engineers are to taste buds or plastic surgeons are to reproductive fitness. They are all profit-seekers who have managed, with the assistance of technology, to plug into internal reward or regulatory systems that evolved under circumstances radically different from those of the present. That such exploitation can be physically dangerous and morally subversive is apparent enough. What to do about it is a recurring political dilemma, one that grows more urgent with the wiring of the world.

6

Escape from Commodity Hell

IN 1997 GENERAL BARRY MCCAFFREY, the director of the Office of National Drug Control Policy, devoted a major speech to the drug problem in historical perspective. It was an unusual undertaking. U.S. drug czars are not, as a group, given to historical reflection on the subject. McCaffrey nevertheless captured the essence of the matter: "Illegal drugs are a byproduct of an industrial society that has led us to tamper—for better and for worse—with the body's inner environment."[1] *Legal* drugs, of course, are also by-products of the same process. The cigarette above all others is an industrial product, produced by mechanical means and consumed at a mechanical pace by smokers who have adjusted their habits to life in a mechanical age.

Cigarettes have several advantages as industrial products, among them addiction potential, tolerance, transient effect, social and sexual desirability, and weight control. They also have a significant disadvantage, one that they share with other mass-produced items. They are commodities, products interchangeable with those made by competitors. A cigarette is a cigarette, as blind product tests have repeatedly shown. In the early 1940s the Federal Trade Commission looked into an American Tobacco Company advertising campaign that suggested otherwise: "Sworn affidavits show that among the men who know tobacco best it's Luckies two to one." The investigators had little difficulty showing that the claim was pure bunk. Some 200 tobacco growers, warehousemen, auctioneers, buyers, and dealers unanimously testified that all standard brands were made from the same type of tobacco. Farmers grew it in the same type of soil with the same sort of fertilizers, gathered and cured it in the same fashion, and sold it at public auction to manufacturers who bought tobacco of similar quality.[2]

This reality cuts across all commercial drug categories. Casks of rum, bundles of kola nuts, bricks of opium, and kilos of cocaine are so many commodities. The big problem with being in the commodity business, or "commodity hell" as it is sometimes known, is that the only way to capture additional market share is to cut price. Competition exerts relentless downward pressure on profit margins, particularly in an industry like drug production, where start-up costs are comparatively modest and new competitors continuously arise.

Several means of escape from commodity hell present themselves. Producers can control output and stabilize prices through a cartel, trust, or other monopolistic device. Failing that, it pays to advertise. Creating attractive brand names allows producers to charge more because consumers are willing to pay for the brand and the product. Another approach, not exclusive of advertising, is to improve the product and cut manufacturing costs. Design a better tea bag and sell it for less. The drawback of innovations is that rival firms eventually copy them; patents provide at best a temporary competitive advantage. Finally, producers can increase market share without cutting profits if they succeed in opening new markets previously closed or indifferent to their products. Hence the logic of shipping free coffee halfway around the world.

The history of drug use offers any number of ingenious attempts to escape from commodity hell: cocaine manufacturing cartels, flavored coffees and liqueurs, nitrite ads in pornographic magazines. This chapter focuses on the manufacture and promotion of cigarettes. Cigarette makers created a large and uniquely profitable global industry, and the success they enjoyed in advertising, technological innovation, and exploiting new markets lifted the fortunes of other psychoactive products. Many boats rose on the cigarette tide. Cigarette smokers, for example, are four times likelier than nonsmokers (adjusting for age, gender, marital status, alcohol use, and other risk factors) to abuse amphetamines. They also consume more alcohol. Charles Towns, an early twentieth-century addiction specialist, went so far as to pronounce cigarettes the worst of all drug habits. Though less harmful in their immediate effects, they led to the use of alcohol and narcotics and created an ongoing scandal. The very openness and permissibility of the vice, he wrote, legitimated the process of "self-poisoning."[3]

Making People Disappear

"People underestimate energy," the novelist Jeffrey Archer once remarked. "One gift plus energy, you'll be a king; energy and no gift, you're a prince; a gift and no energy, you're a pauper." James Buchanan Duke—a figure who might have stepped from the pages of an Archer novel—combined a gift for business with boundless energy. "I loved business better than anything else," he recalled, "I worked from early morning to late at night." While still in his thirties, he became the undisputed king of tobacco production and prime mover of the cigarette revolution. It is not an exaggeration to call him the single most important figure in the history of psychoactive commerce.[4]

Buck Duke was the strapping son of a Confederate artilleryman whose North Carolina farm was looted by Union soldiers in 1865. He worked hard to restore the family fortunes after the war, eventually becoming a full partner in a Durham tobacco factory purchased by his father. The competition was merciless, particularly from the giant Bull Durham, which sold the makings for roll-your-own cigarettes. Ready-mades were not then a part of the Bull Durham product line, so the Dukes concentrated their efforts there.

It proved a wise choice. Cigarettes made with flue-cured Bright tobacco were, in several respects, superior to other tobacco products. Customers found them lighter and more palatable than pipes and cigars, and appreciated their "short smoke" qualities. Five to seven minutes with a ready-made cigarette fit the tempo of urban-industrial life much better than a leisurely half-hour with a cigar. "Short, snappy, easily attempted, easily completed or just as easily discarded before completion," wrote one editorialist, "the cigarette is the symbol of a machine age in which the ultimate cogs and wheels and levers are human nerves."[5]

The road to the nerves ran through the lungs. Smokers could inhale cigarette smoke deeply, delivering a powerful dose of nicotine into their bloodstream. The cigarette was to tobacco as the hypodermic syringe was to opiates: a revolutionary technology that permitted alkaloids to work more quickly and with stronger effect on the brain's reward systems. Though no one yet understood those systems in the late nineteenth century, the seductive, almost narcotic, power of cigarettes was clear enough. In America, where cigarettes were especially controversial, they earned the sobriquet "dope sticks" and the suspicion that their manufacturers spiked them with opium, cannabis, or cocaine.[6]

The suspicion was unfounded; nicotine alone sufficed to produce a powerful addiction. When the anarchist Emma Goldman, who smoked as many as 40 cigarettes a day, had to do without in Blackwell's Island Penitentiary, she experienced "torture almost beyond endurance." So did the prostitutes rounded up in vice sweeps. They shook their bars, cursed, and screamed for "dope *and* cigarettes."[7] In all strata of society cigarette smokers, like the users of injectable narcotics, were more likely to become dependent customers. They also consumed more tobacco per person than cigar or pipe smokers, or chewers and snuff dippers.

The one drawback of ready-made cigarettes when the Dukes got into the business in 1881 was their price. The federal tax, a vestige of the Civil War, was steep, and so were the costs of employing hand rollers. Ninety percent of the cost of manufacturing cigarettes went for labor. But the government slashed the cigarette tax in 1883, and in the following year Duke negotiated rights to the Bonsack cigarette machine, capable of spewing out 120,000 cigarettes in a 10-hour shift. The makers of this mechanical wonder, spurned by other manufacturers because of its doubtful reliability, agreed to charge Duke at least 25 percent less than any future competitors would pay. He in turn agreed to take as many machines as he could keep running.

Once mechanics had worked out the bugs, the Bonsack machines enabled Duke to cut prices and still earn handsome profits. But the size of the market for ready-mades—a rarefied dude product—remained limited. Duke, whose office spittoon brimmed with tobacco juice, personally shunned them, as did most men of his generation. He had to figure out what to do with the flood of cigarettes he was now capable of unleashing on an unsuspecting world.

Duke only seems to have invented tobacco advertising. Robert Louis Stevenson, who traveled across the Midwest by train in 1879, wrote that the only advertisements he saw plastered on the fences along the endless tracks fell into one of two categories, tobacco or remedies against the ague. But Duke poured unheard-of resources into promotions and ads, spending 800,000 dollars in 1889 alone. He and his salesmen tarted up their ads and cigarette cards with actresses and tights-clad models. Sex sold cigarettes, particularly to young, single men in cities. They were, as always, fertile ground for novel types of drugs.

Duke pushed hard to open new markets. His drummers fanned out across the country, distributing packages of Duke brands at baseball games and hir-

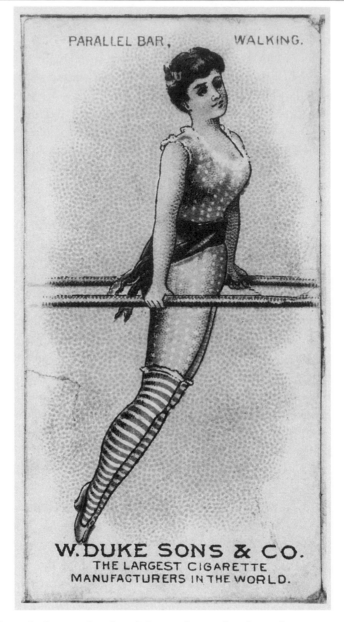

PARALLEL BAR, WALKING.

W. DUKE SONS & CO.
THE LARGEST CIGARETTE
MANUFACTURERS IN THE WORLD.

Collectible cards, first introduced in 1878, proved a popular ploy in the cigarette wars. They even gave rise to a new hobby, "cartophily," with albums, specialty dealers, and auctions. The images emphasized celebrity, exoticism, masculine adventure, physical vitality, and sex. This card is tame in comparison to the "Sporting Girls" series issued after Duke had taken charge of American Tobacco. In exchange for 75 premium certificates, smokers received a deck of "artistic pictures" featuring buxom models in harem attire puffing away at cigarettes and striking come-hither poses.

ing street urchins to give away samples outside tobacco stores. In 1884 Duke personally laid siege to New York City. He opened a small, Bonsack-equipped factory on Rivington Street, but soon had to move to larger quarters. He dispatched runners with bulging sacks to greet immigrants, many of whom were already familiar with cigarettes. Handing each arriving male a pack, they cast Duke's nicotinic bread upon the nation's waters. "These people will take our cigarettes all over the country," he reasoned. "It's whopping good advertising."[8]

Duke understood that large-scale machine production of cigarettes and other tobacco products would inevitably lead to concentration in the industry. So did his four leading rivals, who were steadily losing ground to his relentless cost cutting and lavish advertising. In 1889 they agreed to form American Tobacco, capitalized at 25 million dollars, with Duke as its president. His first move was to purchase exclusive rights to the Bonsack machines, assuring control of mechanized cigarette production. He also began acquiring other companies and factories, buying out 250 of them during his career. By 1900 his trust controlled 93 percent of U.S. cigarette output and the lion's share of snuff, chewing, and smoking tobacco hedges against the possibility that reformers might succeed in crippling the still-controversial cigarette industry. Duke was so entrenched that he could dictate retail profit margins and leaf prices for farmers, who received as little as three cents per pound.[9]

Still he kept driving to lower costs, installing machinery to make foil wrappers, fold coupons, and perform a hundred other tasks. "I stood by a machine into which the cut tobacco was poured through a chute," the Danish-American reformer Jacob Riis wrote of a June 1910 visit to a North Carolina tobacco factory,

> and [it] came out packed in the familiar little bags, all ready for the store counter. While it was on its way, at one point a pair of steel fingers reached down, plucked a revenue stamp from somewhere, pasted it on and then reached for another. It was the very perfection of mechanical skill. Where the bags came out sat a colored boy who caught them as they came and with a single twist tied two little cords that closed them up. He did it once every second, never anything else, day after day, year after year.[10]

Riis told this story to illustrate how assembly-line jobs could turn child laborers into mindless automatons. But it is equally, if backhandedly, a testament to the power of specialized machinery. With additional improvements, mechanical devices like this one took over almost all the manufacturing and packaging functions, further reducing the cost of tobacco products. What Duke really wanted to do was to make the colored boy disappear.

The Mustard Seed

Duke's Rockefellerian tactics inevitably provoked retaliation. Ruined rivals, reduced to working behind company store counters, stole from his tills. Night-riding farmers torched company warehouses. Editorialists fumed. The Justice Department filed an antitrust suit. After years of litigation, the Supreme Court ordered the dissolution of American Tobacco in 1911. By then, however, Duke had fashioned an even more ambitious enterprise, the British-American Tobacco Company, or BAT.

BAT was born of invasion. Duke bought up the Liverpool firm of Ogden Ltd. in 1901, intending to use it as a base from which to gain control of the British and ultimately the European cigarette trade. Rival firms united to form the giant Imperial Tobacco Company. Its sole purpose was to fend off Duke, whose very presence in the country inspired jingoistic panic. The war lasted until 1902, when the two sides struck a momentous deal. Imperial's directors purchased Ogden and retained control of the home market. American Tobacco would not independently distribute its products in England, nor Imperial its products in America. A third entity, British-American Tobacco (BAT), was to exploit all other foreign markets save those, like France or Spain, closed by government monopoly. Duke was to head the new company; American Tobacco owned two-thirds of its stock. BAT was, wrote Duke's biographer, the nearest approach to a world trust ever organized in any industry.

Duke used BAT to export technology, organization, and advertising techniques as well as cigarettes. His greatest success was in China, a country in which he already had sizable interests. When Duke first learned of the power of the Bonsack machine, he reportedly asked for an atlas. Turning the pages, he looked, not at the maps, but at the population figures. When he came to the legend "Pop.: 430,000,000," he said, "That is where we are going to sell cigarettes."[11]

In 1905 Duke chose fellow North Carolinian James Thomas to direct his China operations. A self-styled "missionary" for the cigarette, Thomas held the post until 1922, becoming the highest-paid foreign businessman in Asia. He combined energy and determination with an unusual degree of empathy and tact. Southern manners played well in China. Early on he recruited

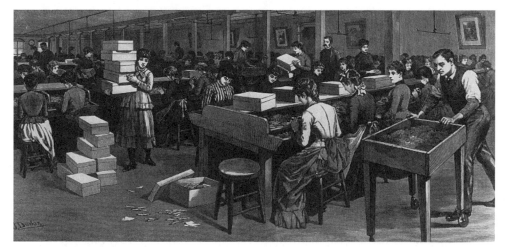

A Richmond, Virginia, cigarette factory in 1887. Duke's mechanization of the industry would soon drive such labor-intensive establishments out of business.

Wu T'ing-sheng, a 20-year-old Chinese college graduate who spoke excellent English. At first Wu told Thomas that the prospect of peddling cigarettes was disgraceful. Thomas did not argue. Instead, he told Wu the parable of the mustard seed. Grasping the point that great things might come from humble beginnings, Wu changed his mind and began hawking cigarettes. He rose to become BAT's leading comprador.

With the help of men like Wu, Duke and Thomas created an integrated system of mass production and distribution in China similar to that already operating in the United States. It stretched from the tobacco fields, whose cultivators were given free Bright tobacco seeds, to modern factories, to camel trains stretching across the Gobi Desert. Thomas thought of everything. Believing, as one recruit later put it, that only inexperienced and adventurous young men would be fools enough to risk what he and the directors proposed, Thomas recruited and trained bachelors as salesmen. He urged those who stuck it out to learn colloquial Chinese and become familiar with the dialects of their particular regions. Those who passed the BAT language tests earned a 500-dollar bonus. He hired native "teachers" of a different sort, men who simply walked about lighting and smoking cigarettes, demonstrating the technique to peasants who at first tried to bite their free samples.

BAT's success depended heavily on the collaboration of Chinese merchants, compradors, tobacco farmers, and factory workers, many of them female. Because foreign copy writers were apt to blunder into disastrous inadvertent puns, with which the Chinese language is strewn, native artists took charge of the advertising campaign. Their slogans and bright placards, so attractive that they were appropriated as home decorations, blossomed everywhere. BAT operatives imported the latest in printing presses and kept them humming. Eventually they built the single largest and most expensive advertising device in China, a tricolor clock sign in Shanghai, 130 feet tall, that touted Ruby Queen cigarettes in 10-foot-square neon characters. The company's own movie studios made films extolling the virtues of Ruby Queen, Pirate, and other BAT brands.

BAT's success also hinged on pricing. "We knew that our tobacco was good," Thomas recalled, "and we used every endeavor to distribute it economically, so that people with small purchasing power could enjoy it." A copper coin, worth about half a cent, purchased five cigarettes. "I often used to think"—Thomas again—"as I watched a native smoking his cigarette that nothing in the world he could have bought at the price would have given him the same amount of pleasure and comfort. The volume of our business testifies to this." So did BAT's annual dividend. It rose from 6 percent in 1902 to 26.5 percent in 1924.[12]

Duke apparently hoped that BAT cigarettes would supplant opium smoking, which was under increasing attack by missionaries, nationalists, and other reformers in the early twentieth century. When Duke died in 1925, one BAT official claimed that he had combined "business with humanity by weaning the Chinese . . . from opium by teaching them to smoke North Carolina cigarettes." Whether this was necessarily humane and whether or to what extent it actually happened are open questions. What is certain is that by 1916, a year when BAT's China cigarette sales were approaching—by some estimates they had already well exceeded—the 10 billion mark, this singularly addictive form of smoking had become popular with all classes and ages, including children. BAT's China operations, which continued to expand during the 1920s and 1930s, managed to survive sporadic nationalist boycotts, Chinese competition, and civil and world warfare. They did not cease until Mao, himself a heavy smoker, formally transferred them to the Chinese government in 1952.[13]

Duke did not succeed everywhere in Asia. To get around unfavorable tariffs, he bought a controlling interest in the Murai Brothers, a Japanese tobacco company, and sent a genteel ex-Confederate named Edward Parrish to oversee its expansion and operation. Parrish reached deep into the familiar

Shanghai
December 21st 1923

Cover of the program for a BAT staff dinner, held in honor of Sir Hugo and Lady Cunliffe-Owen's visit to China. He succeeded Duke, who stepped down as director of BAT in 1923. The program included a menu with four kinds of meat and a quiz for guessing the weights and heights of the well-fed dignitaries who constituted the company's China Board. ("Side bets permitted.") After Cunliffe-Owen returned to London, he announced another year of record profits.

bag of Duke tricks. Marching bands paraded through remote mountain villages; uniformed sales girls distributed Murai cigarettes beside the free smoking stand at the 1903 Osaka Exposition. As in Britain, the aggressive tactics provoked a nationalist reaction. Rival brands played upon patriotic sentiment in their ads: "Hard Fight of Tengu Cigarettes!!! Cruelty and Danger of the Foreign Trust!!!" The Japanese government, which had carefully studied the operation of European tobacco monopolies, had other plans. In 1904 it nationalized the cigarette industry. Working through Parrish, Duke negotiated the best compensation he could get and pulled out. He contented himself with the growing markets in China, India, Burma, and other lands where BAT gimmicks were winning over a new generation of smokers.[14]

A Stroll Down Madison Avenue

No one would ever again dominate the tobacco industry the way Duke did in the first decade of the twentieth century. Though companies occasionally conspired to fix prices and divide markets, as Philip Morris and BAT allegedly did in Latin America in the late 1980s, the industry long ago settled into a pattern of competitive multinational oligopoly—that is, a handful of large firms fighting one another for market share at home and abroad. The only true monopolies to survive were those run by governments, such as the China National Tobacco Corporation. Protected by heavy tariffs against imported brands, it reached the point in 1998 where it was producing a third of the world's 5-trillion-plus cigarettes and fully 12 percent of the Chinese government's revenue.[15]

The U.S. companies—American Tobacco, R. J. Reynolds, Liggett and Meyers, Lorillard, and others—that were spawned by the judicial breakup of Duke's empire had no such protective advantages. They had to struggle to stay out of commodity hell. They did, however, have help in the form of increasingly sophisticated advertising and public relations agencies. Their well-paid assistance enabled the tobacco companies to build brand recognition and loyalty, recruit millions of new smokers, improve their products, counter health concerns, and further expand the global cigarette market.

Unprecedented sums poured into advertising in the 1920s. Charles Lindbergh turned down 50,000 dollars to publicly endorse a cigarette after his epochal transoceanic flight in *The Spirit of St. Louis*. Tareyton had better luck with the *Question Mark*, an Army trimotor that stayed aloft for almost a week during a widely publicized endurance trial in January 1929. A thousand Tareytons passed from the refueling plane to the *Question Mark*'s grateful crew. Ad men pondered equipping all South American passenger planes with the brand: "One flight down there over the mountains is particularly hazardous and will make some excellent pictures and news copy." BAT sales teams in Chile used airplanes to parachute samples of Compadre cigarettes, while blaring their advertising pitch through megaphones. American Tobacco's promoters saw another possibility in aviation: they offered Major Jack Savage, the pioneering skywriter, a thousand dollars a day to inscribe "Lucky Strike" in chemical smoke in the sky above New York and other cities.[16]

In 1948 the Lucky Strike advertising account, swollen to 12 million dollars, moved to Batten, Barton, Durstine, and Osborn. Bruce Barton, a best-selling writer, former Republican congressman, and one of America's most successful advertising executives, immediately began brainstorming about new ways to sell the brand. His correspondence suggests the sheer ingenuity that went into promoting cigarettes and Madison Avenue's sophisticated understanding of their dual nature as psychoactive drugs and as social products.

Barton thought a lot about women smokers, who represented a critical growth area. Would Emily Post consider endorsing a series of advertisements on the etiquette of female smoking? ("Don't smoke while taking dictation in the office.") Would a health-based appeal to thinness work? Why not light a Lucky instead of taking those last few fattening mouthfuls? "Tension shortens life," mused Barton in another memo. "Tension makes one grow old faster. Best thing to do when you feel yourself getting tense is to light a Lucky . . . Amos and Andy coined 'unlax.' Could we coin 'un-tense'? It sounds silly, but probably L.S./M.F.T. sounded silly when it was first suggested."

L.S./M.F.T.—Lucky Strike means fine tobacco—had been the brand's telegraphic slogan since 1944. Barton thought the fine-tobacco angle lent itself to a new approach: "You live only once. Why not live like a millionaire?" The logic, he explained, was that "you can't have a Rolls Royce. You can't have a house on Fifth Avenue. You can't spend your summers in Newport. But in one thing, by God, you can be just as well off as the richest man in America. You can smoke the finest tobacco. Light a Lucky, and feel like a millionaire."

The every-man-a-king pitch would work even better if real kings smoked Luckies. Barton could try to arrange that. While dining in November 1949 at the Waldorf Towers with Mr. Hoover—Herbert or J. Edgar not specified, but in Barton's Olympian circles it was probably the former President—inspiration struck. Looking at the company around him, Barton concluded that the

Waldorf was becoming a haven for hard-up royalty. Why not hire the Duke of Windsor and his ilk to extol American cigarettes, saying: "They are so good and so much wanted that in many parts of the world they actually serve instead of money. I have tried all your brands since I have been here, and I like Lucky Strike the best." Negotiations for royal puffery would be delicate, Barton warned his staff. The publicity department would be out of its depth. "We ought to get Mrs. Astor, or some top-notch socialite who can use a little extra dough."[17] As it happened, the Duke never endorsed Lucky Strike, though Barton was right about his financial worries. He and the Duchess eventually left America and settled in less expensive France.

The means by which R. J. Reynolds's advertisers sought endorsements of Camel cigarettes were more cold-blooded still. For years they broadcast the reassuring claim that more doctors smoked Camels than any other cigarette. The claim had an empirical basis, of sorts. Interviewers stationed themselves outside a New York City hotel where physicians were attending a medical conference. They asked them a series of routine questions: Did you travel by car or plane? Did your family come with you? Buried inside the seemingly innocuous questionnaire was the following: "Doctor, do you smoke cigarettes?" If the physician said yes, the interviewer asked what kind he smoked and whether it was the kind he had on him now. As it turned out, a large percentage were carrying Camels. "Unbeknownst to the people who read the ads based on these claims," explained a confidential memo, "was the fact that the interviewers had placed in the doctors' hotel rooms on their arrival cartons of Camel cigarettes. The chances are that the doctors ran out of cigarettes on arrival, and conveniently put a pack of Camels into their own pockets."[18]

By the 1960s large, full-service advertising agencies were playing a role in the ongoing technological enhancement of the product. For years, manufacturers had been tinkering with cigarettes. They had experimented with different blends of tobacco; had learned to use reconstituted "sheet" made from tobacco stems, scraps, and dust; and had introduced filters and flavors and crush-proof boxes. Philip Morris began using ammoniated tobacco in 1965, freeing up more nicotine for absorption in the lungs—the hidden chemistry behind the Marlboro's success.[19] Those modifications that were not trade secrets were heavily promoted by the agencies, which pitched triple filters to health-conscious smokers and menthol brands to those who thought smoking hot and dirty. But the advertisers, who made it their business to understand consumer motivation in intimate detail, also suggested improvements to the manufacturers themselves.

In 1969 J. Walter Thompson put together an intra-agency task force to propose profitable new products for Liggett and Meyers. Its members reviewed market surveys, attitude and image studies, scientific reports, advertising analyses, and comments from focus groups. They concluded that most people smoked automatically, lighting up in certain situations without even thinking about it. The cigarette acted as an omniprop, giving people an excuse to pause, gather their thoughts, take a break from work. It provided tactile and oral pleasure. More sensuous, velvety paper might enhance cigarettes' appeal. So might a "soft, pliable filter that allows more sucking, chewing than present filter." A nipple-shaped filter "that fits more comfortably into [the] mouth and provides more contact points with lips" was another possibility. But nicotine remained the key to the cigarette's success. "Only plants with active pharmacological principles have been employed habitually by large populations over long periods," they noted, citing coffee, tea, betel, cannabis, qat, and opium as parallel cases. "Smoking becomes a habit because of the nicotine content." If nicotine was the essential ingredient, why not also put it in smokeless products like lozenges? Or concentrate it in lower-tar cigarettes aimed at health-conscious customers?[20]

Carry on Smoking

It was prescient advice. Between 1982 and 1991 the average nicotine content in U.S. cigarettes rose more than 10 percent, with the largest increases in low-tar brands.[21] The introduction of nicotine-rich, low-tar cigarettes was just one of many responses to consumers' health fears, undoubtedly the industry's central problem in the second half of the twentieth century. The problem first reached critical mass in the early 1950s after the publication of several reports linking cigarettes to lung and other cancers.

Tobacco executives hated the pioneer cancer researchers. They hated them for selfish reasons, because they threatened their profits, but also for sentimental ones, because they spoiled the "innocent" pleasure people took in cigarettes. America in 1950 was a smoker's paradise. The haze was so thick in New York's legendary Birdland nightclub that the canaries behind the bar died within weeks of its opening. Social custom and the millions invested in advertising over the years had fostered an ideal mind-set for smoking. Everybody's in on the fun, so relax and light up. Cancer destroyed this comforting illusion and, with it, the industry's pet rationalization. Tobacco executives liked to think of themselves as doing good while doing well. What James Thomas thought as he watched a native smoking a cigarette, that nothing in the world he could have bought at the price would have given him the same amount of pleasure and comfort, was in fact the moral foundation of the industry—that, plus jobs and government revenues. Alton Ochsner, Ernst Wynder, and other white-coated messengers of malignant doom were systematically undermining that foundation. By linking cigarettes to a specific lethal disease, they were transforming a product that alleviated anxiety to one that massively produced it. And they were turning the medical profession decisively against cigarettes. Doctors were quitting and advising their patients to do likewise.[22]

The industry initially responded with denial and buck-passing. "You hear stuff all the time about 'cigarettes are harmful to you' this that and the other thing," Arthur Godfrey reassured his television viewers in September 1952. Not to worry. Chesterfields wouldn't harm your nose, throat, or "accessory organs." A responsible consulting organization and a competent medical specialist had vouched for it. Industry leaders like American Tobacco's Paul Hahn realized, however, that every-brand-for-itself health malarkey was self-defeating. It only served to increase public awareness of the cancer issue. (It was a dull viewer indeed who didn't understand "accessory organs" as a euphemism for lungs.) What tobacco needed was a united front. In December 1953 Hahn met with his counterparts in New York's luxurious Plaza Hotel. They agreed to create the Tobacco Industry Research Committee.[23]

TIRC had money, talent, and clout. The tobacco executives endowed it by imposing upon themselves a tax of one-quarter cent per 1,000 cigarettes, plus additional appropriations as needed. They hired Hill and Knowlton, a leading public relations firm with headquarters in the Empire State Building, to direct TIRC's day-to-day operations. With Hill and Knowlton's assistance, it quickly became a smoothly running disinformation machine. TIRC ran full-page advertisements in (white) newspapers denying proof that cigarettes caused lung cancer. It distributed booklets quoting authoritative disavowals of the link between smoking and malignancy. It corrected "misstatements" about tobacco and health in the press and collected potentially damaging information about tobacco opponents, lay and scientific. It funded laboratory and epidemiological research to give the impression that the industry was anxious to get at the facts and not callous to considerations of health. Implicit in this effort was the assurance that, should this research turn up a cancer-causing agent, the companies would quickly eliminate it from cigarettes, restoring full consumer pleasure and comfort. In the short run, these tactics prevailed. Though the link between smoking and cancer remained a controversial and widely reported issue in 1955, the sense of crisis had eased and cigarette sales were again rising.[24]

TIRC researchers also monitored developments abroad. Lung cancer deaths were up sharply in Belgium, France, and other continental nations, but European smokers displayed more *sang-froid* than Americans. The only discernible trend among Parisian tobacconists, for example, was the increased sale of filter-tipped cigarettes. Reports from England were likewise encouraging. In 1956 the leading British firms established their own version of TIRC, blandly called the Tobacco Manufacturers' Standing Committee (TMSC). Because it had to operate under different institutional and cultural constraints, among them "the extremely prickly and reserved attitude of British doctors towards all forms of external patronage," TMSC necessarily behaved more circumspectly. Nevertheless, it adopted many of the same obfuscating and diversionary tactics pioneered by TIRC. It questioned the validity of purely statistical inquiries, called attention to the industry's generous funding of lung cancer research, and challenged the findings of particular scientists that ran contrary to tobacco interests.

TMSC did not limit its operations to disinformation. Anxious to discern the impact of government and Medical Research Council propaganda against smoking, it conducted surveys of public and medical attitudes toward tobacco and health. The news was mostly good. "The public," concluded the authors of one study, "appear to be quite content with the present state of affairs. They know that specialists are working in cancer research and no doubt in due time will provide the final answer; the tobacco manufacturers are aiding the research financially; in the meantime, carry on smoking!" Alan Campbell-Johnson, TMSC's public relations adviser, privately offered a blunter assessment: "The forces of inertia and addiction are still stronger than those of cost and risk." In Britain as in America, the tobacco industry, assisted by public relations consultants, won the first battle of the cancer wars.[25]

Yet the medical evidence continued to pile up: heart disease, emphysema, low birth weight. In the wake of the 1964 Surgeon General's report and televised public service announcements against smoking, cigarette consumption finally began declining in the United States. It fell steadily from about a half pack per adult per day in the mid-1960s to a third of a pack in the early 1990s. By then as many as half a million Americans per year were dying prematurely of smoking-related illnesses, a million were quitting, and another 15 million were trying to. The domestic consumer base was eroding.[26]

The tobacco companies had two ways out, both critically dependent on advertising. First, they could recruit teenage smokers to replace those who died or quit. Though the industry has, for legal reasons, steadfastly denied this intention, any fair reading of the confidential internal correspondence that has come to light suggests otherwise. "To ensure increased and longer-term growth for CAMEL FILTER," declared a 1975 R. J. Reynolds memo, "the brand must increase its share penetration among the 14–24 age group, which have a new set of more liberal values and which represent tomorrow's cigarette business." "To the best of your ability (considering some legal restraints)," advised a youth-conscious Brown and Williamson consultant that same year, "relate the cigarette to 'pot,' wine, beer, sex, etc. *Don't* communicate health or health related points." One J. Walter Thompson executive, reviewing a you-can-smoke-less pitch for Chesterfield's purportedly richer tobacco, turned his thumb down. "Not an appeal to youth—live dangerously," he scribbled in the margin.[27]

Ad men everywhere understood that recruiting new teenage smokers meant presenting cigarettes as a means of resolving their psychological quandaries and social anxieties. Young smokers weren't (yet) buying nicotine-delivery vehicles. They were buying accessories of identity. Cigarettes symbolized independence, sexual potency, and disdain for authority. (One Japanese brand was named "Dean," after the legendarily rebellious American actor.) Teenagers glimpsed, if at all, the future costs of such posturing through the darkened glass of adolescent temporal myopia. They made perfect targets for cool brands and gear. Industry salesmen zeroed in on fast-food restaurants, video arcades, and convenience stores—miniature bazaars of nicotine, alcohol, caffeine, sugar, fat, and salt that doubled as popular afternoon hangouts. They larded up the stores nearest to junior and senior high schools with extra premiums and promotions: discount prices, free cigarette lighters, colorful T-shirts. "We were targeting kids," confessed Terence Sullivan, a Florida sales representative for R. J. Reynolds. "I said at the time it was unethical and maybe illegal, but I was told that was just company policy."[28]

Company policy also stressed further expansion in foreign markets, the second means of maintaining or expanding the customer base. Cigarettes were already the most heavily advertised product in the American economy by the end of the 1970s, and manufacturers poured additional billions into promotions overseas, where they faced fewer regulatory obstacles. (Japanese warning label: "For your health don't smoke too much.") Winston T-shirts appeared in Saipan, Camel sweepstakes in Truk, L&M billboards in Senegal, the Marlboro Man everywhere. Norway, where a center-left parliamentary coalition enacted a total ban on tobacco advertising, was the exception that proved the rule. Following the law's implementation in 1975, smoking among 13- to 15-year-olds, which had been steadily rising, began to decline, as did adult consumption of tobacco products.[29]

By 1996, when the World Health Organization announced a public health emergency, the strategy of offsetting domestic losses with overseas gains was plainly succeeding. Global consumption of cigarettes per adult was holding steady, while the total world market, buoyed by population increases, was growing at about 1 percent a year. BAT, the leading British exporter, was expanding aggressively in developing nations and in former eastern-bloc countries. (The removal of the iron curtain, enthused BAT's Sir Patrick Sheehy, had created "the most exciting times I have seen in the tobacco industry in the last 40 years.") The big U.S. companies were doing more and more of their business overseas. Philip Morris, the most aggressive exporter, was selling two cigarettes abroad for every one in the United States. With the help of trade pressure from the Reagan administration, Philip Morris had even managed to crack the Japanese market, accomplishing what James Duke had not. In 1994 the company accounted for one in every eight cigarettes sold in Japan—a major coup, considering that two-thirds of Japanese men (and nearly half of Japanese doctors!) were smokers. By comparison, only about a quarter of all American adults were still smoking, and the best educated had practically quit altogether. Just 6 percent of the Harvard-Radcliffe class of 1970, a group not notable for pulmonary abstemiousness in the late 1960s, reported smoking in 1995. Relatively speaking, the United States, home of the world's most efficient tobacco companies, had become a nonsmoking island in a worldwide ocean of puffers.[30]

McWorld

Historians call accounts like this one "internalist." The story of the expansion of the cigarette industry is about insiders and innovators who, faced with recurrent problems such as how to increase market share without slashing profits or how to allay public fears, contrived a variety of organizational, technological, and media solutions. Competitors copied those solutions or they perished. The result of their collective efforts was that more people in more parts of the world smoked more tobacco in more efficient cigarettes, tricked out with the talismans of youth and health.

Similar internalist tales can be told of other drug industries. Two centuries of tinkering with yeast strains and fermenting tanks and stills turned the manufacture of alcoholic beverages into a highly efficient enterprise, capable of producing a steady flow of attractively bottled beverages of consistent quality. Faced with flat or falling per capita adult consumption in increasingly health-conscious developed nations, manufacturers mounted a two-front campaign. They pitched sweet, fruit-flavored alcoholic drinks and ices to the rising generation of young drinkers, while simultaneously expanding their trade through slick advertising in developing countries like Malaysia or Zimbabwe—Marlboro tactics in an Absolut world. Illicit drug distributors found their own creative ways to cope with commodity hell. Heroin dealers commonly employed brand names like "F-16" or "Hydrogen Bomb" to emphasize the potency of their always-suspect street bags.[31]

A complementary externalist account of the role of technology and advertising is also possible. Innovations *outside* an industry have often had as large an impact as the calculated ones that originate within it. Going back deep in time, it was a completely unrelated breakthrough, the domestication of fire, that made widespread drug use possible in the first place. If there had been no fire, there would have been no amphorae, pipes, tea, heated mash, refined opium, and so on. Controlled flame was the ur-technology of the psychoactive revolution. Moreover, as time passed, the flame became more controlled and portable. The invention of the friction match was a great boon for nineteenth-century smokers, who promptly liberated themselves, their cheroots, and their bad examples from the confining realms of hearth and tavern. Without friction matches and their successors, cheap safety matches, the cigarette revolution would not have occurred, at least not until someone invented the mechanical lighter.[32]

Railroads and highways cut transport costs for licit drugs and simplified life for the couriers of illicit ones. Most of the cocaine distributed in India in the 1920s and 1930s was smuggled into Calcutta and then shipped along the two main railway routes running northwest through the United Provinces into the Punjab and beyond. (Unsurprisingly, cities like Benares that fell along the routes suffered the highest rates of addiction.) Nineteenth-century American moonshiners hauled their kegs to market down mountain trails on mule-drawn sleds; their twentieth-century descendants drove souped-up cars on macadamized roads. Planes sped drugs and their promoters everywhere. The first commercial pilot in southeastern Alaska in 1923 was a salesman for Hills Brothers Coffee. "Civil aircraft," Lindbergh wrote in his autobiography, "laid every spot on earth open to the ravages of commerce."

Lindbergh, under no illusions about his own historic role in the transportation revolution, brooded about "the deadly standardization that fast communication brings." He dreaded the emergence of a homogeneous world dominated by North American consumer norms, intolerant of local customs, subversive of tribal ways, and destructive of the environment. The writer Benjamin Barber gave Lindbergh's nightmare a name: McWorld. Disturbing as McWorld may be for sensitive souls, not to say those of a fundamentalist turn, it has been a real boon to western drug manufacturers struggling to open new markets. It is perhaps the ultimate example of a technologically driven externality that turned out to be good for their business.[33]

A look at a failed international advertising campaign shows why. In 1963 Pepsi-Cola, trying to catch up with Coca-Cola, took its "Come Alive—You're the Pepsi Generation" campaign worldwide. It used a one-sight, one-sound approach, forcing the same images and themes on Pepsi bottlers everywhere. It didn't work. The generational pitch made little sense in cultures where teenagers did not think of themselves as a special non-adult group. In countries like Germany or Japan adults, not kids, controlled the discretionary income for soft-drink purchases. "Come alive" was meaningless or untranslatable in many languages. Pepsi, concluded Albert Stridsberg, an expert on international advertising, had ignored the prevailing wisdom of global marketing. People lived, and each sale was made, in local markets. International success meant adapting to many local markets, varying advertisements, sugar content, container size, and price as necessary. Promoters of new products had to traverse a cultural minefield. BAT, which recruited native talent to help sell its cigarettes, nimbly picked its way through. Pepsi blundered in and got blown up.

But the media-driven rise of McWorld and the concomitant spread of American English and juvenile mores made it progressively easier to navigate the minefield and simplified the international promotion of drug products. One of the first to spot the trend was Stridsberg himself. By the late 1960s he was describing the emergence of a viable international style of advertising, headquartered in New York, London, and Paris. Though national markets were not yet identical, Stridsberg cautioned, they were becoming more similar as affluence, travel, transistor radios, satellites, and commercial television facilitated the spread of western ways. These and other electronic advances (Stridsberg correctly predicted that "satellite relays, coaxial cables and memory banks" would coalesce into a global sound and image network) paved the way for dominance by western images and world products. International campaigns geared to youth themes worked much better in an MTV world. So, for that matter, did the much more informal promotion of illicit drugs. The stronger the western cultural orientation of Zimbabwean school children, for example, the more likely they were to experiment with cannabis and inhalants.[34]

Richard Rhodes, in his epic *The Making of the Atomic Bomb* (1986), meditates upon nation-states' appropriation of applied science and industrial technology to create weapons of mass destruction. To protect themselves and further their ambitions, they caused 100 million deaths in the wars of the twentieth century. Most of those 100 million died between 1914 and 1945; nuclear warfare was the climax of a mechanized annihilatory process that stretched from the Marne to Nagasaki. Rhodes thinks the decline in the casualties after 1945 was no coincidence. The capacity for military destruction became so great that it forced a political reassessment of total war, which the leaders of the great powers came to view as an exercise in mass suicide.[35]

Something similar, but also something different, has happened with drugs. The corporations and cartels that manufacture drugs have, with the connivance of tax- and export-conscious nation-states, utilized applied science and industrial technology to protect their profits and expand markets. Like the military, they have devised their own technologies and exploited those that evolved elsewhere. They have caused well over 100 million premature deaths during the twentieth century, 80 million from tobacco alone. The carnage has provoked a worldwide public health reaction to alcohol and especially tobacco products, which many reformers would like to see added to the schedules of restricted substances and banned from advertising.[36]

The reformers have not yet succeeded. The death toll from legal drugs has continued to rise. The reasons, reduced to their essentials, are money and power.

PART III

DRUGS AND POWER

7

OPIATES OF THE PEOPLE

AT THE OUTSET of my research for this book, I seriously underestimated three things: the extent of caffeine use and dependency; the ferocity of the early opposition to nonmedical tobacco use; and the variety of ways in which drugs have been employed to palliate, control, and exploit labor, animal as well as human. Marx's famous metaphor, religion as the opium of the people, would have worked just as well with alcohol or tobacco. Next to profits and taxes, the utility of drugs in acquiring, pacifying, and fleecing workers proved to be their greatest advantage to elites, at least until some of their number began to rethink the situation in the nineteenth and twentieth centuries.

The Labor Treadmill

Opium is the best known of the labor-palliating drugs, and the Chinese who ventured overseas during the nineteenth century are the best known of its devotees. The typical coolie found himself doing mind-numbing work in a barbarian land, bored and homesick and without parental supervision. He did what the junk crews and chair bearers back home did to soothe their troubles: he turned to the opium pipe. This did not disrupt his labors, at least not initially. "The opium smoking coolie," as one British official put it, "is probably as reliable a workman as any in the world." But he was often in debt, especially if he had journeyed far overseas. Until the debt was cleared he could not return to China. Regular expenditures on opium and other bachelor vices such as gambling and prostitution effectively kept him on a labor tread-mill, working for his creditors. More than a few sick and despairing Chinese finally stepped off the treadmill by the same means used to keep them on it: they took an overdose of opium.[1]

Opium farms raked in profits for the host nations. Their rulers or, more often, colonial administrators auctioned the right to sell opium to the highest bidders, usually syndicates of Chinese merchants backed by strong-arm societies. These societies kept rivals from infringing on the monopoly. The merchants kept the coolie supplied with monopoly-priced opium, often siphoning off half and in some cases as much as two-thirds of his wages in the process. And the government enjoyed a stream of revenue from the periodic auctions. Singapore, as the historian Carl Trocki points out, literally lived on the back of the opium-smoking Chinese coolie. The colony derived half of its nineteenth-century revenue from opium.[2]

Chinese laborers were not the only victims. A physician in the Egyptian provinces in the early 1930s reported that dependent *fellahin* spent most of their wages on drugs. A man earning five piasters a day allotted one for food, one for tobacco, and three for opiates. A landowner had to choose between sending his wife back to her parents and continuing to purchase drugs. He chose the drugs. A contractor for a Nile transport company decided to eliminate the element of choice altogether. He furnished his stevedores only rancid food and two packets of heroin a day. When the police seized his books, they discovered that he had been making an extra 30 percent profit on the in-kind wages.[3] Similar tactics are still used on large Thai fishing vessels, 20 percent or more of whose crews are reportedly addicted to heroin.

Jamaican teenagers who weed ganja fields are sometimes paid in kind, and are not infrequently high when they chop and pull. Cannabis is a popular adjunct to agricultural labor throughout the lands of the ganja complex. In the Punjab consumption increases by half during the harvest season. Colombian peasants boast that cannabis helps them to *quita el cansancio*, or reduce fatigue; increase their *fuerza* and *ánimo*, force and spirit; and become *incansable*, tireless. Critics of the marijuana complex have condemned the drug as leading to precisely the opposite state: lethargy, lack of motivation, and burnout. But how people behave under the influence of a particular drug is a matter of social and cultural circumstance as well as pharmacology. Learning to smoke cannabis to get through a hot day in a cane field is one thing; learning to smoke it to get through a long night at a rock concert is quite another. Different situations can lead to different sorts of intoxicated comportment.[4]

Before the arrival of mechanized agriculture, alcohol played a similar role to cannabis in Europe and North America. Workers drank to get through the harvest crisis, to celebrate after it, and to allay the fatigue and boredom of rural life. Alcohol, however, was more expensive than cannabis, and too frequent indulgence ensured poverty. Except for *shtetl* Jews and a handful of other religious minorities, eastern European peasants were notoriously prone to drinking away their money. Some landowners paid them in vodka for the potatoes and grain delivered to their stills. "When I was a child," the interpreter Juvenale Ivanovitch Tarasov recalled of his Russian village in the 1880s, "half the peasants would be drunk for days at a time."

> A bottle of vodka came to be used as a standard unit of value. When a peasant was asked what a job would cost, he would answer not in roubles [sic] but in bottles of vodka. If there was none to be had in the stores, the peasants would refuse to work; but when it came, there would be a rush to earn money to buy drink. Merchants from the larger towns came here with carts and wagons loaded down with vodka, and for this the half-crazed people parted with their grain, their cows, their very last belongings. . . . I remember seeing men in those days who went about wearing nothing but shirts. They had sold or pawned the rest of their clothes. And half-naked women, too, were by no means uncommon sights. Anything for alcohol.

Escapist drinking was also common in Europe's Coketown slums. Reformers blamed it on workers' monotonous lives and comfortless surroundings. "Work requires recreation," Émile Zola observed in 1868, "and when money is short, when the horizon is closed, one grasps at the pleasure at hand."[5]

An American story, cast with European immigrants, illustrates the point. In 1855 a group of Irish railroad workers, lumpenproles if ever there were any, happened across a German inn in a midwestern town. When a bystander made the nature of the establishment clear to them, they whooped and shouted, and began making popping sounds with their thumbs in their mouths to simulate the uncorking of bottles. "The German [innkeeper] immediately opened both his mouth and his door and began murdering the English language and tapping whiskey," wrote a disgusted Norwegian observer. "He is now well on his way to becoming a capitalist, because these fellows have tremendous capacities and swallow a quart of firewater without batting an eye."[6]

Bibulous workers—the beer-guzzling printers young Benjamin Franklin encountered in London, the drunken proletarians Friedrich Engels saw reeling through the streets of Manchester, cowboys at trail's end, *gauchos* in their *pulperias*, sailors of any nationality on liberty—had a way of going through their wages. Unless prematurely detoured into the local jail, they ended their binges with pounding headaches, empty pockets, and the necessity of returning to work. "And thus," Franklin wrote disapprovingly, "these poor Devils keep themselves always under." Alcohol kept them on a labor treadmill, just as opium did the Chinese.[7]

So, to a lesser degree, did tobacco. "Howsoever poor a man may be," runs a Sanskrit verse of unknown date, "he does not leave the use of tobacco." "Farmers, Plough-men, Porters, and almost all labouring men plead for it, saying, they find great refreshment by it," the English physician John Rowland wrote in 1659, "and very many would as soon part with their necessary food, as they would be totally deprived of the use of Tobacco." Well after expanded production brought down its price, critics still complained of parents who starved their children and bartered away their goods "for a Scantling of this inchanting Weed." The economist Sir William Petty estimated that two-sevenths of late seventeenth-century Irish peasants' expenditures on food went for tobacco. It is an odd and revealing statistic, inasmuch as Petty chose to conflate food and tobacco into a category of basic nutritional necessity. In any case tobacco remained a significant expense for low-income workers well into the twentieth century. Black tenant farmers in Georgia were spending 6 percent of their cash income on tobacco as the country moved into the Depression. In other low-income groups, reported the economist Jack Gottsegen, individuals spent practically all their pocket money on tobacco—more than they allotted for reading, personal care, and education.[8]

Drug use has thus historically operated as an impediment to upward mobility, whether this is defined as savings, land accumulation, education, or marriage and family formation. There is no grand conspiracy about this. In fact, the use of drugs to cope with fatigue and obliterate misery is in many ways a by-product of civilization itself. Humans evolved in itinerant band societies. Life in the sedentary peasant societies that succeeded them was less varied, fulfilling, egalitarian, and healthful. While hunter-gatherers prized certain drugs for shamanistic rituals, they rarely relied on them to cope with dawn-to-dusk manual labor. Taking drugs to get through the daily grind (or to treat the intestinal and parasitic diseases attendant to settled life) is peculiar to civilization. So is the stupefying of infants to free the labor of harried parents and caregivers. Quieting young children with opium or cannabis or alcohol was a common expedient of working people before the early twentieth century and persists in many developing regions. Such practices are further clues, if any are needed, that our social circumstances are out of sync with our evolved natures.[9]

Animals and Armies

The same is true of domesticated animals. Many species seek and consume intoxicants in the wild, but they do so more often and more compulsively under conditions of captivity. That, or humans provide drugs for them. Zoo animals, especially large or hoofed ones, are routinely sedated to control their transportation and tranquilized to help them adjust to new surroundings. Neurotic or stereotypic behavior brings out the prescription pad. It's Prozac for polar bears who pace too much.

Lab animals who "go down in their cages" or otherwise refuse to adapt to their surroundings are more likely to be euthanized than maintained on drugs, which would compromise their experimental value. Neurotic pets are another matter. Small-animal veterinarians have begun prescribing serotonin-specific reuptake inhibitors like Clomicalm to pacify them. Hong Kong, where owners leave their pets in cramped flats all day, is a particularly good market. Upwards of 20 percent of Hong Kong dogs suffer from separation anxiety, expressed by barking incessantly, soiling carpets, and chewing furniture.[10]

Humans have often drugged animals to facilitate their labor. Tibetans give large vessels of tea to their horses and mules to increase their ability to work at high altitudes. Commercial poultry farmers put amphetamines in chicken feed to increase egg production. Fighting cocks get cannabis mixed with onions to make them more combative. Elephants receive opium balls as part of their domestication. Trainers dispense them as rewards for logging tasks executed properly, much as a performing dolphin is rewarded with a fish. The driver simply offers the opium to the elephant who, recognizing the smell, eagerly scoops it like a peanut from his hand.

Elephant drivers have also employed opium to combat musth, a seasonal rutting condition of adult male elephants. Brimful of testosterone, these "mad" elephants are prone to destructive and sometimes fatal rampages. The malefactors have been shackled, shot by a firing squad, or hanged—civilized norms, so to speak, stubbornly visited upon the uncivilizable. But working elephants are valuable creatures, and their drivers have often tried to save them from the consequences of musth by increasing their opium allowance, which calms them down. The drivers have to be careful, though, not to dose them into a state of lethargy. Some Thai elephants too far gone on opium have lain down during tiger hunts, oblivious to the risk of mauling.[11]

Humans have plied horses with opium since at least the seventeenth century. Indian jockeys fed opium to horses before showing them to prospective buyers, that the animals might appear to be more tractable. Travelers in Turkey gave horses and other riding animals up to two grams before departing on a fatiguing journey. The Rajputs, the hereditary soldiers of northern India, made it a point of honor to share their opium with their horses and camels before embarking on desert patrols.[12]

The Rajputs took a fair amount of opium themselves. Of all of civilization's occupational categories, that of soldier may be the most conducive to regular drug use. Most people, when they think of military drug use, instinctively (or cinematically) picture soldiers steeling their nerves before combat. One last drag before fixing bayonets. More typical, though, is the use of drugs to allay the boredom and fatigue inherent in military life. Cannabis smoking, for example, was not uncommon in the dull peacetime barracks of South African soldiers or among U.S. troops stationed in the Canal Zone in the 1920s and 1930s. Francisco Franco paid part of his Berber troops' wages in *kif*. The most important military drugs, however, have undoubtedly been alcohol and tobacco.[13]

From the siege of Troy, if not before, wine was part of the impedimenta of ancient armies. Alexander the Great and his officers drank heavily. One wine-drinking contest reportedly claimed 35 lives, including that of the 12-quart victor. The Romans, sensible of the necessity of moderation as well as the dangers of local water, carried wine with them on their many invasions. But wine was bulky. After the distilling revolution it gave way to spirits, which became the standard tipple in European armies and navies in the eighteenth century. British and American seamen received a half-pint of rum ("grog" in its watered version) as a daily ration. John Adams, who wrote the regulations for the Continental Navy, judiciously allowed more in times of engagement or for the performance of extra duties, a custom known as "splicing the main brace." Army practice was similar. One daring band of Continental soldiers earned a rum bonus for recovering incoming cannon balls, loaded into a 32-pounder and returned with interest to their former owners. For their part

British commanders often issued gills of rum before and after battle, in addition to the standard gallon-per-month ration.[14]

The use of liquor in the eighteenth-century British Army was neither unthinking nor unchallenged. "I am convinced Rum is the Bain [sic] of the English Army," wrote a lieutenant-colonel stationed near Montreal in 1761, "and Could wish there was none Allowed to Come into the Country whilst we remain in it." But other officers, while conceding the threat that drinking posed to health, morale, and discipline, regarded alcohol as a necessary evil. Taken in moderation, rum served as a medicine and water purifier. As a stimulus to labor it was indispensable; some troops refused to work without it. Officers could bribe soldiers who craved liquor into heavy labor with extra rations of "fatigue rum." Grog, summed up James Wolfe in 1758, was "the cheapest pay for work that can be given."[15]

The use of alcohol for fatigue duty persisted into the nineteenth century. Meriwether Lewis and William Clark rewarded their men with whiskey after a hard day's portage, at least until their supply ran out. Despite reformers' attempts to substitute coffee and sugar for spirits, alcoholic rations remained common during the Civil War. Union and Confederate soldiers seldom drank heavily before battle, but they did receive whiskey before undertaking such tasks as building bridges while waist-deep in cold water. Frontier garrisons were paid in the same liquid coin. Seventy-five enlisted men went through eight barrels of whiskey building Fort Cottonwood, situated where the North Platte joins the South.[16]

If any drug allayed anxiety during the Civil War and other nineteenth-century conflicts, it was tobacco. "Fear creates a desire for tobacco," Benjamin Rush perceptively observed. "Hence it is used in greater quantities by soldiers and sailors than by other classes of people. It is used most profusely by soldiers when they are picket guards, or centinels [sic], and by sailors in stormy weather." And by their anxious commanders. Louis Napoleon continuously smoked cigarettes, expertly rolled for him by an aide-de-camp, during the 1859 battle of Solferino. Common soldiers had to wait, though, until Duke's revolution before they had ready-made cigarettes of their own.[17]

World War I forged the decisive link between soldiering and cigarette smoking. Officers in all branches of the military, writes the historian Cassandra Tate, regarded tobacco rations, especially cigarettes, as a valuable aid to morale and discipline. Troops with smokes were easier to control—a belief underscored by reports that tobacco shortages had contributed to widespread mutinies by French soldiers in 1917. Aid workers made similar comments.

"Each man, when he got his cigarette, seemed to forget his troubles," wrote one YMCA volunteer. "He straightened up and became a man instead of a wearied drudge."

Relief organizations like the YMCA and the Red Cross routinely gave out cigarettes to fatigued and wounded men. Ernest Hemingway, who served with the Red Cross in Italy, suffered his celebrated shrapnel wounds while passing out cigarettes and chocolate on the Piave front. Mass distribution by respected humanitarian organizations legitimated and popularized what had been, at least in the United States, a controversial product. So did the actions of the U.S. War Department's Subsistence Division, which sent overseas some 16 billion cigarettes, either of the manufactured or the roll-your-own variety. By contrast, it shipped only 200 million of the more cumbersome cigars.[18]

Millions of young men were thus exposed to cigarettes under conditions of unparalleled physical and psychological stress. A horror of mutilation runs through the more candid letters and diaries. "Poor kids," wrote nurse Ethelyn Meyers, "I'd a thousand times rather be shot to pieces than gassed like some of these boys." An American sergeant, William von Kennell, suffered a recurring nightmare in which he saw himself lying on the ground, face gone, blood pumping from his dismembered body. Pilots not yet twenty looked forty, exhausted by the strain of high-altitude patrols and the fiery deaths of too many comrades. Practically everyone who could do so smoked cigarettes, the quickest and most convenient means of achieving nicotinic relief. "Cigarettes were as important as ammunition," recalled British machine gunner George Coppard. "A Tommy would ask for a fag when near death, as if it was some kind of opiate that relieved pain and soothed the path to oblivion. I've no doubt at all that it did."

Coppard got part of his precious supply from relatives in England. Officials frowned on shipments of other sorts of drugs, however. When Harrods and Savory and Moore offered morphine and cocaine gift packets (described without irony in a *Times* advertisement as a "useful present for friends at the front"), the firms found themselves in court. It was, the prosecutor said, exceedingly dangerous to provide soldiers with drugs like morphine, which might make them sleep on duty or otherwise endanger their safety. Cigarettes, when prudently smoked out of sight of the enemy, presented no such risk.

The biggest problem with cigarettes and other tobacco products during World War I was simply getting enough of them—and enduring the consequences when it proved impossible to do so. Men under orders to avoid lighting up suffered "like drug addicts," Coppard wrote, while a shortage of cigarettes provoked "sheer agony." Once he resorted to smoking dried tea leaves rolled in brown paper: "It was pretty horrible." Tobacco craving figures in many accounts of the war. Shortly after the Armistice, von Kennell came across a group of French and Italian soldiers set loose by the Germans. Ragged and shoeless, "they all wanted tobacco more than anything." He gave them his Bull Durham makings, "as we can get plenty of manufactured cigarets [*sic*] now. They were all very profuse in their thanks and wanted to give me in return little keepsakes and . . . the few German marks they had been paid for their slavery." A few days later the good sergeant gave an old man his pipe and smoking tobacco, "which I had brought from the states for an emergency which never arose. He threw several fits when he saw it. He had not had any real tobacco for four years."[19]

Von Kennell's story calls attention to an interesting paradox of total warfare. The need for tobacco and alcohol is often greatest among soldiers and civilians when these commodities are in shortest supply. Though war has historically stimulated the production of opium for analgesia and cannabis for fiber, it has had the opposite effect on alcohol: it has depressed production through a combination of grain and sugar rationing, higher taxes, labor shortages, blockades, and the destruction of crops, distilleries, and transportation facilities. German beer consumption, which stood at 102 liters per capita in 1913, fell to just 39 liters in 1918. Governments have often imposed bans on distilling, as Russia did during World War I. Wars have also cut tobacco availability, sometimes sharply Japanese adults, who smoked an average of more than four cigarettes a day in 1941, were reduced to less than two in 1945. Americans in uniform smoked thirty a day, sometimes more. Airborne troopers who landed behind the Normandy beaches each carried, along with sulfa tablets and morphine Syrettes, two or three cartons of cigarettes. Such abundance was an anomaly, as the United States was one of the few combatants able to privilege tobacco as an essential wartime material and grant military exemptions to its farmers.[20]

Nazi priorities and ideology—Hitler was a fanatical anti-smoker—were quite different. The regular cigarette ration for German troops was just six a day. However, local commanders issued extra cigarettes and alcohol under "special" circumstances, in both the literal and euphemistic senses of the term. One SS *Standartenführer* (colonel) gave each of his men a pack of cigarettes and a pint of cognac before their last-ditch defense of Paris. Soldiers

Alcohol and tobacco are the two great military drugs. During World War II the U.S. Army provided cigarettes in K-rations, but discouraged hard liquor among troops on duty. What happened unofficially was another matter. The 31st Infantry Division, a mostly southern outfit, included veteran moonshiners, some of whom appear here on Morotai Island. An enlisted man in a quartermaster company gave them sugar in exchange for a share of the liquor. They sold the rest to GIs or drank it themselves. A first sergeant, acting on orders, eventually destroyed their still. He did so with reluctance, as he was one of their customers.

and military police who took part in *Aktions* against Jews, shooting them at mass burial pits, earned supplementary rations of vodka. Sometimes the executioners became too drunk to shoot straight. SS doctor Johannes Paul Kremer noted in his Auschwitz diary that volunteers for execution details received a fifth of a liter of schnapps, five cigarettes, and 100 grams of salami and bread. "Because of the special rations," he added, "the men all clamor to take part in such actions."[21]

Drugs and Prostitution

Examples of this sort are by no means limited to the Holocaust. Drugs induce or facilitate all sorts of labors that men and women, in a sober frame of mind, would ordinarily spurn. To what extent this is due to the drug's effect on brain chemistry or to a given culture's rules about drug use (for example, drinking excuses misconduct) is debatable. The effect, nevertheless, is real and troubling.

Drinking has accompanied many unpleasant and dangerous tasks: informing, burying battlefield remains, dragging corpses out of slavers' holds. However, one of the commonest and most consistent associations has been with prostitution. In 1909 the Nebraskan Josie Washburn published a memoir of her long career as a madam. In it she described the many ways in which liquor was entwined with prostitution. Men did not just stroll into her brothel, she explained. They went first to the saloon, where they took a "personal liberty" bracer or two to work up their nerve. Once inside the parlor, they were plied with drink, beer going for as much as a dollar a bottle. It was by pushing drink that madams obtained their greatest profit. They expected their girls to drink with their customers. Considering the volume of the nightly traffic and the nature of the work, servicing drunks and listening to their smutty jokes, this was a sure route to alcoholism. Some prostitutes had tricks to reduce their intake: switching glasses or discreetly dumping wine into the nearest cuspidor. ("Men little realize how much money they spend to fill this vessel.") But in the end, Washburn judged, most of her girls became drunkards themselves. Or they became drug users. After a year a woman was either a hard case, "ready to take part in every kind of depravity," or was "stupefied with dope, lovers and more dope," or had come to her senses and made plans to get out.[22]

The drink-and-drug theme runs through nearly all accounts of prostitution from the late nineteenth century on. Opiates and cocaine became staples of prostitutes in societies as widely separated as India, France, and the United States. One 1941 Japanese police report, detailed to the point of obsession, described conditions among Chinese flophouse prostitutes in Harbin, a city in northern Manchuria. "Because they are exhausted from entertaining guests without a break; because they like to indulge in carnal pleasures; because of the pain of syphilis and gonorrhea, they are all addicted to morphine," the anonymous author observed. "Now, for instance, a woman will buy [a fifty-cent bag of morphine] and directly, in front of the patron's eyes, without hesitation she will rub the morphine into her genitals." A more recent study in Rio de Janeiro, a place with a unique sexual ecology and no social safety net, estimated that 91 percent of the city's small army of transvestite prostitutes had used alcohol, 76 percent cocaine, and 61 percent cannabis.[23]

Prostitutes have also put drugs to aphrodisiacal purposes, as in Cameroon, where they sometimes insert a mixture of cannabis, rock salt, and small stones into their vaginas to increase the pleasure of their customers. The most common use, though, is simply to help them get on with it. "I usually don't say no to a trade," one San Francisco masseuse reported, "but I usually try to get at least half cash and half coke. It depends on how desperate I feel I need to get coked out." Judging from other informants' accounts, kinky or degrading sex is more palatable when high. Drugs blot out memories as well as the physical pain. "When I was prostituting at the boarding house," one young Rio woman recalled, "my father would go there and want to pay me to have sex with him. I would never do it and every time he would leave, I would smoke a lot of marijuana to try and forget the things that he would say."[24]

Drugs have figured prominently in sexual bartering, a form of quasi-prostitution common in many cultures. Kola nuts in the central Sudan; beer in Papua New Guinea; cigarettes, coffee, and Coca-Colas in postwar Germany have all served as inducements for sexual favors. In American ghettos, illegitimate children of unknown paternity are sometimes called "staircase babies." The reference is to their place of conception by drug-dependent mothers who offer their bodies to men bearing marijuana and crack. Bartering has also occurred across cultures, most notoriously between European men and native women bribed with alcohol. "Thre is anothr thing that we do not like, & complain of vry much," runs a hasty transcription of a 1766 address by a delegation of Delaware Indians, "thre are some that do at times hire some of our Squaws to goe to Bed with them & give them Rum fr it[,] this thing is very Bad, & the squaws again selling the Rum to our people make them Drunk."[25]

Barter and Slaves

Europeans traded alcohol to Indians for a good deal more than sex. Consider the larger pattern of overseas expansion. Europeans established trading-post empires like Goa or Batavia; territorial empires like New Spain or Peru; true colonies settled by their own immigrants like Massachusetts or New Zealand; and plantation colonies like Haiti or Jamaica. The plantations were peopled mainly by unfree laborers from Africa or, after the abolition of slavery, Asia. For reasons of trade and agriculture, Europeans initially settled on arable islands and coastal plains. Beyond them lay a large though progressively shrinking interior domain under the control of natives, whom the Europeans variously viewed as potential enemies, allies, converts, laborers, concubines, and trading partners.[26]

Drug barter was the trump card in negotiations with these native peoples and, next to imported infections, the most important reason for their demographic and cultural ruin. What happened to the North American Indians happened also to natives throughout Siberia, the Pacific, and Central and South America. Nor has the process ended. Andean Indians are still selling coca leaves, a relatively benign and familiar drug, and using the proceeds to buy alcohol. The consequences have been as disastrous for them as for their distant ancestors.[27]

The British and the French provided rum and brandy to Indians because they were the surest means of obtaining furs. "It spurs them on to an unwaried application in hunting in order to supply the Trading Places with Furs and Skins in Exchange for Liquors," a group of Albany merchants coolly explained in a 1764 petition to the Lords Commissioners for Trade and Plantations. Nothing else worked as well, or was as lucrative. Traders offered guns and blankets, but such items were more expensive and durable than alcohol, which was quickly consumed and easily adulterated. The profit on watered rum could run as high as 400 percent. Better still, Indians who drank during negotiations made foolish trades, bartering their prime winter furs for more rum. "When I come to your place with my peltry," one Pennsylvania Indian rebuked a trader, "all call to me: 'Come, Thomas! here's rum, drink heartily, drink! it will not hurt you.' All this is done for the purpose of cheating me. When you have obtained from me all you want, you call me a drunken dog, and kick me out of the room." Indians who paid scarce cash fared little better. By the time of Jefferson's presidency, some were offering as much as two dollars for a pint of liquor. Farmland—once their land—sold for 25 cents an acre.[28]

The historical record is full of Indian braves who impoverished themselves and their families, ruined their health, and sold their women as prostitutes or their children into bondage for drink. And when they drank, they drank to achieve drunkenness, a heedless drunkenness in which they stumbled into fires, dropped off cliffs, or cut one another to pieces. British officials deplored the consequences. Their aim was to Christianize Indians and incorporate them into the empire, not to exterminate them or turn them into drunken menaces. Colonial and local governments therefore enacted laws forbidding the liquor trade with Indians. A 1689 Albany ordinance was typical: two months in prison without bail and a five-pound fine for anyone selling or giving spirits, or even beer, to Indians on any pretense whatever.[29]

All such laws failed. By 1770 British North America boasted 143 distilleries.

The colonists themselves drank an average of three pints of spirits a week. Rum was everywhere, and backwoods traders had no difficulty securing a supply. If they didn't provide liquor, Indian middlemen would. Imperial officials' efforts to suppress the traffic were halfhearted. They knew that acquiring furs and maintaining alliances would be difficult without the fiery waters the Indians craved. The French likewise failed to end the trade, despite pressure from missionaries. The Jesuits declared sales of brandy for intoxicating Indians a mortal sin and threatened excommunication of those who persisted in the sordid business. But they could not keep the *coureurs de bois* from selling brandy, nor the Indians from buying it. "The Savages no longer Think of hunting in order to clothe Themselves but only to get drink," an officer named Louis de La Porte de Louvigny reported in 1720. "Brandy is making them poor and miserable; sickness is killing them off; and they slay one another on very slight provocation. . . . They are all Furious and frantic in their intoxication, since when they can not stab one another, and when their weapons have been taken from them, they bite off one another's ears and noses."[30]

Indian leaders spoke out forcefully. "You Rot Your grain in Tubs," the Catawba chief Nopkehe complained in 1754. "You sell it to our young men and give it them, many times; they get very Drunk . . . [and] oftentimes Commit those Crimes that is offencive to You and us . . . it is also very bad for our people, for it Rots their guts and Causes our men to get very sick." A few Indian leaders tried to suppress the trade themselves, but they got no further than the colonial legislators. Indeed, the pattern of alcoholic exploitation established during the colonial period persisted into the nineteenth century, as the tide of booze rolled across the American plains. Adulterated whiskey replaced rum in the traders' arsenal, though otherwise the effects were the same: demoralized and dead Indians and a devastated ecosystem. Indians stepped up their quest for skins and choice meats to barter for whiskey. Once their hides and buffalo tongues were gone, they were left with little more than hangovers and empty bellies.[31]

Tobacco — "the wrath of the Red Man against the White Man, vengeance for having been given hard liquor," as Hitler ominously put it — seems like the opposite case. In fact, the white man's plantation tobacco quickly became a major item in the Indian trade. The Jesuits employed it, though not without mixed feelings, as a bribe to induce Indians to attend their sermons and destroy their own sacred objects. For reasons not entirely certain, but possibly stemming from the spiritual prowess imputed to distant goods, Indians preferred imported Brazilian tobacco. They also traded for burning mirrors, steels, and tinder boxes, which simplified smoking while traveling, and pipes of European manufacture. Around 1700 an unknown genius devised an iron-bladed tomahawk that featured a bowl above the blade and a hollow stem for smoking, conjoining war and peace in a single implement. Pipe tomahawks proved an irresistible trade good, becoming standard equipment of braves from the Atlantic to the Rocky Mountains. Tobacco pouches were furnished by the Indians, who sometimes severed and preserved the hands of their enemies for the purpose.[32]

By 1700 the tobacco and rum that Europeans supplied to Indians were largely produced by African slaves, who were fast replacing native laborers and indentured servants. Slave production had in fact become circular: rum and tobacco were commonly used to acquire more Africans, most of whom were bound for large tropical plantations. Tropical slavery was fundamentally a product of comparative immunological advantage. Black Africans who survived their childhood—and at least half did not—had typically acquired immunity to yellow fever, a mosquito-borne disease widely fatal to Europeans and Amerindians. They were also more resistant to malaria. Acquiring African slaves for Brazil and the Caribbean necessitated offering trade goods in return. Textiles were the most important, though fortified wine and, from about 1650 on, rum were also among the items commonly bartered for slaves. How commonly varied from region to region. The Portuguese and Brazilians seem to have been the most inclined to use alcohol for slave trading. The historian Jose Curto estimates that imported alcoholic beverages, mostly Brazilian rum, amounted to 27 percent of the value of the 1.6 million slaves exported from Luanda and Benguela during the period 1700–1830.

The great advantage of alcohol, apart from the fact that the Portuguese and Brazilians could produce so much of it in their vineyards and sugar plantations, was steady demand. The natives who drank it yearned for more. Palm wine and other beverages with which they were familiar were weak and spoiled quickly compared with what the Portuguese offered. Africans who developed a taste for imported alcohol sought out more captives for the trade, just as the Indians sought out more furs; sometimes they sold their own relatives. "What does it matter for us, if Africans in the backlands inebriate themselves [with our] . . . *vihno, aguardente,* and *cachaça* [low-quality rum]," Governor Almeida e Vasconcelos wrote in 1791 to Paulo Joze de Loreiro, director of the Kasanje *feira,* the largest of the slave markets in west central Africa.

"The more they acquire this taste, the more they will come to the slave markets with what to satisfy their appetite . . . One of [our] principal objectives is to attempt to please those with whom we live and from whom we wish to take advantage, making them successively more dependent and passionate for our booze."[33]

Brazilian merchants had another card to play. The Portuguese crown, anxious to reserve the best portion of the Brazilian tobacco crop for the European market, permitted traders to barter only inferior tobacco for slaves. Though in practice some superior tobacco was smuggled into African ports, most of the exports consisted of rolls of third-grade tobacco soaked in molasses. These were surprisingly popular on the Mina coast, so much so that foreigners competed to obtain cargoes for their own trading purposes. In 1777 the English merchant Richard Miles, writing during a temporary shortage, assured his correspondents that they could make a fortune if they could devise a way to directly ship Brazilian tobacco. It was, he reported, fetching more than four times its usual price.

The historian George Metcalf reviewed Miles's meticulous records. He found that tobacco and rum appeared in some 66 percent of his barters with the Akan peoples during the 1770s, though they collectively accounted for only 13.4 percent of the total value of the goods he traded. His and other quantitative studies suggest that, on a value basis, alcohol and tobacco did not loom as large in the British slave trade as in the Luso-Brazilian. Still, they were significant items, especially in the triangular trade among the New England colonies, West Africa, and the British sugar islands in the Caribbean. Rhode Island alone exported five million gallons of extra-proof "Guinea rum"—enough to fill the holds of 500 slavers—in the half century before the American Revolution. By the early 1770s nine out of every ten gallons of New England's rum exports went to Africa, whence slaves to the Caribbean, whence molasses to New England distilleries.[34]

A small portion of the alcohol went directly to the slaves. In Jamaica slaves received rum as well as sugar and molasses as part of their rations. Portuguese officials found it expedient to distribute rum as "wages" for laborers forced to work on construction projects in Luanda and its hinterland. They once dispatched a shipment of *cachaça* to African workers conscripted to build a church.[35]

Such incongruities were not lost on missionaries. Many spoke out against the liquor traffic, both before and after the abolition of the slave trade. By the

1880s "trade spirits" of Dutch and German manufacture were common along the West African coast. The completion of roads and railroads carried them into the interior, spreading alcoholism and crime, or so the missionaries claimed. Like the opium trade, to which they often compared it, missionaries and their sympathizers condemned the liquor traffic as incompatible with conversion and a blot on Christian civilization. "Mustn't the heathen consider us queer," ran one American prohibition song, "Sending them cargoes of Bibles and beer?"[36]

Those of a worldlier stripe engaged in alcoholic *realpolitik*. Colonial officials protested that the liquor duty was their best source of revenue. In Lagos, for example, duties on trade spirits produced well over half of all government income between 1892 and 1903. Apologists argued they could not govern without liquor taxes. Though a sharp decline in alcohol imports after 1914 would prove this argument false, it carried weight before the outbreak of World War I among those who sought empire on the cheap. Meanwhile merchants bartered spirits, watered after importation, for palm oil and other native goods. They and colonial officials understood that drink could be highly useful in negotiations with tribal leaders—a legacy of the days when slavers plied their trading partners with liquor.[37]

A notorious instance occurred in 1889. Dr. Leander Starr Jameson, Cecil Rhodes's friend and emissary, went to negotiate with Lobengula, the last king of the Ndebele and ruler of Matabeleland, which Rhodes coveted. Jameson was trying to keep Lobengula from reneging on a concession which gave Rhodes exclusive rights to all metals and minerals in his kingdom. During his second trip, in October, Jameson found the gouty king in ill health. He rummaged in his medicine chest and proceeded to work some white man's magic with an injection of morphine. "Things brightened up considerably," writes Rhodes's biographer Brian Roberts. "Freed from pain, and flattered by Jameson's banter, the king was easily coaxed out of his sulks. From then on all was sweetness and light."

The origins of Lobengula's gout attack are of some interest: he had brought it on by heavy drinking. Rival whites had supplied him with champagne and brandy. Like Rhodes, they had been angling for concessions.[38]

8

Taxes and Smuggling

THE NONMEDICAL USE of novel drugs provoked much disgust and repression during the first half of the 1600s, the great formative century of the psychoactive revolution. Officials directed their most spectacular campaigns against tobacco smoking, though other practices, notably the drinking of spirits, attracted their share of attention. By the end of the seventeenth century, however, suppression had almost universally given way to taxation. Peter the Great summed up the reasons in a 1697 *ukase* permitting the open sale and consumption of tobacco in Russia. Smuggling was ubiquitous, Peter complained, and all of it was untaxed. To gain his share he legalized the trade, establishing a high import duty and then a monopoly. Many other seventeenth-century monarchs, burdened with growing administrative and military costs (not to say ambitious building schemes and a taste for luxury), had already gone down the same road.

Even England's James I, though personally never reconciled to smoking, pragmatically acceded to its taxation. In 1608 he dropped the prohibitive impost for a more collectable one of a shilling per pound of tobacco. James's successors reduced it further, to twopence per pound in 1660, roughly equal to the price the planters received for it. The law also contained a mercantilist proviso, typical of the era, that Chesapeake tobacco had to be first shipped to England or another of its colonies by English or English colonial ships and crews. Despite the lower tax rate, the exploding volume of trade made tobacco an important source of revenue. During the 1660s duties on Maryland

and Virginia tobacco constituted fully a quarter of England's customs revenue and perhaps 5 percent of the government's total income.[1]

The Varieties of Taxation

Officials have subjected drugs to any number of taxes beyond simple import duties. They have taxed peasants on their opium crops, liquor distillers on their volume, coffee buyers on their religious beliefs. Under Suleiman the Magnificent, the Ottoman sultan from 1520 to 1566, Christians paid 25 percent more tax on their coffee purchases than Muslims. In 1783 the British government, impressed by the growing trade in proprietary (or "patent") medicines, imposed a stamp tax on them. Their purchasers, in a sense, paid double duty. An unknown but probably substantial percentage of eighteenth- and nineteenth-century proprietary medicines contained alcohol and other drugs. Consumers absorbed the price of the psychoactive ingredients, which was increased by excises and other taxes, as well as the cost of the stamp itself.[2]

Authorities also resorted to monopolies to derive revenue from psychoactive commerce. They were of two general types, those "farmed" to private interests in return for a fixed payment and those run directly by the government. The latter were uncommon until the nineteenth century, as most early-modern governments were unable or unwilling to administer the monopoly as a branch of the state. The more usual procedure was to auction the rights to import, manufacture, and/or sell drugs to one or more groups of concessionaires for a fixed period. Dutch colonial officials thoughtfully served champagne at pre-auction parties to loosen the purses of potential opium-farm bidders.[3]

Monopolies were both lucrative and controversial. To work effectively, they required unpopular regulations. These limited or forbade outright domestic production of drug crops, so that local farmers could not hold back a portion of their crop to sell at market price, undercutting the monopoly. Repeated applications of force were necessary to suppress illegal tobacco growing in seventeenth-century Europe. The conferral of monopolies provoked cries of favoritism or foreign influence. Lord North's attempt in 1773 to give the East India Company a monopoly on tea wholesaling in America, a blunder compounded by the retention of the hated Townshend duty, ignited protests all along the Atlantic coast. The foremost of these occurred on the moonlit evening of December 16, when patriots daubed with soot and paint unloaded three ships full of dutied tea into Boston Harbor. A crowd watched in quiet approval, their silence punctuated by the tattoo of hatchets breaking open the great chests of tea.[4]

The equivalent event in Iranian history occurred in 1890. Induced by bribes, Nasir ed-Din Shah sold tobacco monopoly rights to a British speculator named Major Gerald Talbot. He in turn sold them to a syndicate called the Imperial Tobacco Corporation of Persia. The deal guaranteed the Shah's government 15,000 pounds yearly plus a quarter of the net profits, less a 5 percent dividend to shareholders. For this the company gained the exclusive right to purchase, cure, and sell Iranian tobacco. London investors rubbed their hands: some enthusiasts projected Imperial's net annual profits at more than 50 percent of its capital. But the peasants who grew the tobacco, the petty merchants who sold it, the mullahs who controlled agricultural land, and the nationalists and intellectuals who despised Nasir ed-Din were appalled. No other measure could have been as successful in uniting the opposition. The mullahs decreed a tobacco boycott in 1891. It was popular and effective, spreading even to the royal household. (Not a small group, consisting as it did of some 1,600 wives, concubines, and eunuchs.) In early 1892 Nasir ed-Din backed down and canceled the concession. After the boycott was lifted, his subjects gratefully returned to their water pipes. The event, however, had lasting consequences. Humiliated by the success of the boycott, the Shah never retrieved his position. Four years later an assassin ended his greedy reign with a bullet through his heart.[5]

Whether or not they bore the taint of foreign association, private monopolies had certain inherent problems. These were most obvious in the opium farms. Having paid large sums to secure the rights, the successful bidders naturally wanted to maximize consumption and profits. That meant, for example, expanding retail outlets. In 1848 Singapore had 45 opium shops; in 1897 it had 500. Concessionaires subverted periodic government attempts to limit popular use. In Java Chinese opium farmers, allotted a fixed amount by Dutch officials, simply smuggled in additional shipments.

Confronted with such abuses, and facing growing nationalist and humanitarian pressure to suppress the opium traffic, colonial officials throughout Asia largely abandoned the farm system by 1910. They replaced it with state-run monopolies, which they rationalized in the name of controlling opium use and restricting its spread. How they operated in practice was another matter. In Singapore the state monopoly actually proved more efficient in extracting profits from the opium trade, which still provided 46 percent of the government's revenue in 1920. After that the percentage steadily declined, though more for reasons of demography than bureaucratic self-restraint. Singapore's large Chinese population was changing—fewer immigrants, more women, more family life—in ways that reduced the demand for opium. A similar dynamic in the United States would turn the few surviving Chinatown opium dens into anachronisms by the 1930s.

Though gradually diminishing, opium tax revenues remained important throughout Southeast Asia well into the twentieth century. In 1920 they made up 13 percent of the Dutch East Indies' budget, 14 percent of French Indochina's, 17 percent of Brunei's, and 29 percent of Hong Kong's. (The British gained twice: they supplied their Asian retail monopolies with opium from their own production monopoly in India.) Such revenue streams would have been impossible without substantial numbers of opium smokers. Estimates for Hong Kong run as high as one adult male in four in 1924. The managers of the state monopolies knew that if they discouraged use too vigorously they would lose both revenue and customers to illicit suppliers, among them those who dealt in hard narcotics. For all their defects, the opium monopolies' legal supply at least provided an alternative to black-market morphine and heroin—drugs increasingly available in East Asia in the early twentieth century.[6]

Tax Addiction

The retreat of colonialism, the defeat of the Japanese (drug monopolists par excellence) in 1945, and steady opposition from the United States led to the eventual demise of the opium monopolies. But other forms of monopoly persisted, notably in tobacco and alcohol production. Like the lottery and legal gambling monopolies they closely resembled, drug monopolies acted as lucrative but regressive taxes that generated serious externalities. High-minded critics condemned them as the worst sort of parasitism, providing profit at the expense of the people's welfare.

The farms, monopolies, and other schemes that flourished during the golden age of drug taxation, from the seventeenth through nineteenth centuries, made a perfect target for those fond of satirizing royal greed. The English diarist John Evelyn remarked that Charles II's government so depended on revenue from "Smoke, and exotic Drinks" that it would have "sunk in all appearance" had the people been as temperate as Christianity obliged. The gibe might have come from the pen of any wit in any European monarchy. The Russian crown was especially voracious. In 1859 rye that fetched 2 rubles on the open market brought 64 when, distilled, taxed, and watered, it was finally sold in taverns. "The alchemists would have envied a process that transmuted grain so readily to gold," David Christian has written. He adds that, for all its fiscal importance, vodka drinking posed chronic problems of law and order for the Russian government.[7]

Many twentieth-century officials had second thoughts about profiting from psychoactive commerce. The growing political feasibility of progressive alternatives like income taxes or death duties encouraged their doubts. Yet drug taxes and monopolies remained important sources of revenue, especially during periods of national emergency. So reliable was tobacco revenue that the French government used it as collateral, pledging post–World War I proceeds to secure loans which foreign bankers might not otherwise have granted. The United States, a latecomer to that war, boosted tobacco revenue by half in the space of a single year, 1917 to 1918. The final nail in the coffin of Prohibition (1920–1933) was the desperate need for revenue during the Depression. If Prohibition were repealed, "the income tax would not be necessary in the future, and half of the revenue required for the budget . . . would be furnished by the tax on liquor alone," argued the industrialist Pierre du Pont, not without self-interest, in a 1932 radio address. When the government permitted legal distilling, federal taxes escalated quickly from about a dollar per gallon in 1933 to three dollars in 1940 to nine dollars in wartime 1944. This last sum represented eight times the cost of production.[8]

Governments have a way of becoming dependent on drug taxes. Like addiction itself, this dependence is in the nature of a chronic, relapsing disorder. Confronted with catastrophic levels of popular abuse—for example, alcoholism in the Soviet Union in the 1980s—an enlightened leader—Gorbachev—and his associates may decide that enough is enough, and sacrifice revenues in the interest of sharply curtailing consumption. Despite the gains in productivity, health, and public morale that initially follow such campaigns, two forces continuously tempt governments to "relapse." These are social costs generated by the black market, which are seized upon and given wide publicity by prohibition's ideological opponents, and the need, most acute in times of fiscal duress, to restore the revenue from drug taxes. The classic illustration is America's repeal of Prohibition, though the same forces are even more transparently at work in modern India.

Prohibition and nationalism were always closely linked in India. Nationalists, as well as many western reformers, charged that British greed had spread alcoholism among the poor. Excise taxes, inaugurated by the East India Company in 1790, and subsequently a farming system gave the government and its liquor dealers every incentive to maximize consumption. By 1900 liquor revenues were running ahead of those from the notorious opium excise.[9]

Mahatma Gandhi, the apostle of self-rule, was an especially sharp critic of alcohol and drug use. "We must understand thoroughly what self-purification means," he said in 1921. "Give up drinking alcohol, smoking ganja, and eating opium." Tobacco, too. Though its evil effects were not so obvious, it was as addictive as opium and wasteful of money the poor could ill afford. But the worst evil was liquor, which sapped the vitality of the people and undermined the cause of independence. Gandhi preached that unreformed drunkards should be lovingly but firmly ostracized: no eating or drinking with them, no marriage connections with their families. Under no circumstances should the state profit from the liquor trade, which was as bad as thieving and prostitution, and the mother of them both. Liquor vendors' shops should be closed; they should take up carding, spinning, and weaving. At one meeting in Bombay a nervous dealer politely protested that the liquor business had been going on for thousands of years. Surely it could not cease all at once. On exactly what date did the great soul expect to see sales stopped? "From today," Gandhi replied to laughter and cheers.[10]

The 1928 draft of the Constitution of Free India, which called for prohibition to save the people from "the evil and temptation of alcoholic liquor and intoxicating drugs," made Gandhi's proposal explicit. The prohibition was to be total and quickly implemented by the Commonwealth of Indian States after independence. The language of the actual constitution of 1947 was a good deal weaker: individual states "shall endeavor" to bring about prohibition of nonmedical use of alcohol and injurious drugs. National politicians passed the buck to their state counterparts, a situation not unlike that of American alcohol regulation after 1933.[11]

Outside Gandhi's own state of Gujarat, prohibition went nowhere, mainly because of government dependence on liquor revenue. Indeed, state policies often made the situation worse. Government stills produced arrack, a clear, potent liquor made from palm sap, molasses, rice, or other base ingredients. Flavored with red chili pepper, arrack sold in plastic packets for 6 to 8 cents, cheap enough for landless rural workers who earned as little as 40 cents a day. They drank, as Gandhi had foretold, to forget the misery of lives lived on small wages. In some villages as many as 90 percent of the men reportedly developed serious alcohol problems, with all that entailed for their battered wives and hungry children.

In the early 1990s women in the southern state of Andhra Pradesh began a sustained campaign to end the trade in cheap spirits. The spark for this effort was a reading assignment in a government literacy program. It told the story of a heroine who mobilized the women of her village to close a liquor shop where feckless husbands were squandering all their pay, a plot no less effective for being fictional. Seeing themselves all too clearly in the story, the real village women moved from discussion to organization to confrontation with liquor industry thugs, lathi-wielding police, and male politicians newly keen on censoring the reading list. They denied drunken husbands cooking, washing, and sex, the last tactic straight out of Aristophanes. The campaign was revolutionary on at least two counts: it was the first in India's history led by poor rural women, and it got results. In October 1993 Andhra Pradesh banned outright the sale of government-distilled arrack. Sales of all other forms of liquor were forbidden on paydays for agricultural workers.

Enter now N. T. Rama Rao, actor turned politician. The aging but ruggedly handsome star of more than 300 movies, beloved for his portrayal of Lord Krishna and other Hindu gods, Rama Rao knew a winning issue when he saw one. Combining a pledge for near-total prohibition with rice subsidies, another popular cause, he and his Telugu Desam party swept to power in December 1994. Andhra Pradesh went dry the following month.

The dramatic events in Andhra Pradesh inspired long-suffering women in other Indian states to launch their own reform efforts. The most spectacular success—and failure—came in Haryana, a northern state of 17 million that nearly surrounds the capital of New Delhi. Haryana men had long had a reputation for hard drinking. A disproportionate share of them had soldiered for the Raj or, later, the Indian army, where they had acquired a taste for strong drink. Haryana's liquor shops were open around the clock. Lorry drivers went about their rounds drunk. Wives were beaten until they collapsed. "I have lived all over India and I have never seen as much domestic violence as there was in Haryana," recalled General J. M. Vohra. "The maidservants would come to work late or not turn up at all because they had been beaten. A large percentage of village men were alcoholics."

In 1996 the long-suffering women of Haryana voted for Bansi Lal, another populist who ran on a platform of total prohibition. As the state's chief minister, Lal engineered an unusually strict law. It provided stiff fines and prison terms of up to three years for the manufacture, transportation, sale, and consumption of liquor, whether publicly or privately produced. The statute was, by comparison, much stricter than America's Volstead Act, which permitted private consumption and home brewing.

What ensued was both tragedy and farce. Nervous middle-class residents, fearful of servants who might blackmail them, waited until late at night to drink their whiskey and water. The value of their houses dropped 20 percent, as thirsty Delhi commuters shied away from Haryana real estate. Couples moved their wedding receptions out of state. One hundred and fifty thousand liquor industry employees were reportedly out of work, though doubtless many quietly continued their trade as members of the "liquor mafia," outfitted with souped-up cars and cellular phones. Bootlegging flourished. The unwary were poisoned. Sixty died. Ninety thousand liquor cases backlogged the courts. Police officers, when not operating their 3,000 new breath analyzers, took bribes and liberated seized stock. Risks and bribes translated into higher prices. A seven-ounce pouch of "spicy country liquor" sold for triple the customary rate. The Haryana government, desperate for lost excise revenues, increased utility, gasoline, and other taxes, with broadly inflationary consequences. Higher prices squeezed the families of men who continued to drink black-market liquor. "People don't change overnight," conceded one politician. Stung by an electoral backlash, the government reversed course and repealed prohibition in the spring of 1998. The liquor dealers went back into business, gleefully installing string beds for drunks outside their barred cinder-block premises.[12]

By then Andhra Pradesh had also repealed prohibition. The ban had cost the state the equivalent of 400 million U.S. dollars per year, roughly a quarter of its revenue. Rama Rao stayed the dry course, but in August 1995 he was ousted in an intra-party coup worthy of one of his movies. He died of a heart attack the following January. His successor and son-in-law, N. Chandrababu Naidu, was of more pragmatic bent. Naidu staked his chances on getting a 3.5 billion dollar loan from the World Bank to restructure the state's finances and modernize its infrastructure. Bank officials made it clear that money would not be forthcoming unless the state's revenue flow improved, which for all practical purposes meant reimposing the liquor tax. Naidu found himself caught between the bank's conditions and the threat of possibly violent protests by angry women's groups and underground Maoist parties demanding continued prohibition. But, on the scales of power, rural women and Maoists do not balance the World Bank. In February 1997 the government announced it would repeal the ban on the sale of alcohol. "State-sponsored liquor addiction for the masses is the name of the game," lamented one activist. "Nothing but bowing down to pressure from the World Bank," was the scornful verdict of another.[13]

The High-Low Problem

The trade-off between revenue and public welfare is not the only dilemma inherent in drug taxation. Finding the right level of taxation is also a serious problem. Taxes can be either too high or too low. The latter encourages widespread use: for example, domestic gin in early eighteenth-century England, or cigarettes in America after the 1883 tax cut. Governments can always ratchet up taxes to discourage consumption, as the British attempted to do with cannabis in India in the early twentieth century. But if they peg the rates too high, whether to control prevalence or increase revenue or both, they will face widespread bootlegging and smuggling. When the United States government elected to keep liquor taxes at unprecedented levels after 1945, moonshiners immediately scaled up their operations, previously limited by wartime shortages of base materials. By 1949 revenue agents were seizing 19,000 stills a year, representing a producing capacity of over half a million gallons *per day*. Assuming, conservatively, that their owners averaged three months of full-capacity operation before discovery, the combined federal-state excise loss amounted to a half-billion dollars a year.[14]

The best illustration of tax-avoidance smuggling is Britain in the eighteenth and the first half of the nineteenth centuries. Though British officials often resorted to drug farms and monopolies in their colonies, they imposed excise and customs duties in the home islands. In 1685 James II persuaded Parliament to raise the tobacco duty from two- to fivepence per pound. Chesapeake prices were then in the trough of a prolonged depression, averaging only about a penny a pound. The equivalent ad valorem (percentage of value) rate, 500 percent, was highly attractive to smugglers. They could sell contraband at half the price of taxed tobacco and still earn a large profit. High profit margins made it easy to bribe customs officials, some of whom boldly ran their own loads of contraband tobacco in His Majesty's ships.[15]

Imported tea, gaining rapidly in popularity in eighteenth-century Britain, also bore a heavy duty. It stood at four shillings a pound in 1740. Smugglers could purchase tea in Holland or other countries, evade customs, and then sell it for two or three shillings below the prevailing "legal" price. Far from interfering with their operations, continental officials proved quite hospitable to the smugglers. Contraband was a handy weapon against economic and military rivals in the eighteenth century. Domestic customers were equally cooperative. "Andrews the Smuggler brought me this night about 11 o'clock a bagg of Hysson tea 6 Pd weight," Parson James Woodforde wrote matter-offactly in his diary. "He frightened us a little by whistling under the Parlour Window just as we were going to bed. I gave him some Geneva [gin] and paid him for the tea at 10/6 per Pd."[16]

Another gambit involved the free cargo space the East India Company customarily allotted to its captains, which they filled with the finest quality tea they could find. They resold it to smugglers who swarmed about them in small craft as they sailed up the English coast, then paid off their crews to assure their silence. The clandestine nature of such transactions makes it impossible to know how much tea actually entered Britain, to the frustration of economic historians trying to pin down consumption levels. William Pitt the Younger, who came to power in 1784, judged that his countrymen consumed 13 million pounds of tea annually, but that only 5.5 million yielded duty. By then the trade in smuggled tea was so well organized that it threatened the survival of legal importers and wholesalers. Pitt solved the problem by slashing the levy from 119 percent ad valorem to 12.5, effectively ending the illicit traffic.[17]

Spirits and tobacco smuggling flourished in the eighteenth and early nineteenth centuries. Duties on these commodities, unlike that on tea, remained appreciable after 1784. Alcohol and tobacco smugglers were numerous, well organized, and more than willing to employ violence, including torture and terrorism, to protect their covert trade. Despite harsh penalties — smugglers could be transported, or worse — the British government had no hope of suppressing the traffic. With so many continental ports nearby, 6,000 miles of coast to guard, and an army and navy spread thin by constant warfare, it could not seriously challenge smugglers — not, at any rate, until Napoleon was firmly planted on St. Helena. Compounding the problem was the fact that its citizens were more likely to act as sympathetic customers than as informers. Like most Europeans, the average Briton was fed up with taxes and glad of the chance to lay in the odd pipe or hogshead at a bargain price. "To pretend to have any scruple about buying smuggled goods," Adam Smith wrote with his usual acuity, "though a manifest encouragement to the violation of the revenue laws, and to the perjury which almost always attends it, would in most countries be regarded as one of those pedantic pieces of hypocrisy which, instead of gaining credit with any body, serve only to expose the person who affects to practise them, to the suspicion of being a greater knave than most of his neighbors."[18]

What finally ended large-scale smuggling was the triumph of free trade under the ministry of Sir Robert Peel, who engineered a general reduction in

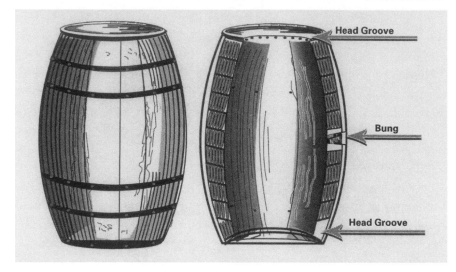

Head Groove

Bung

Head Groove

Though tea smuggling into Britain abated after duties were lowered in 1784, a lively traffic in alcohol and tobacco continued until tariffs came down in the mid-nineteenth century. Given the risk and space limitations, smugglers preferred to carry high-value items like cognac, snuff, or cigars. One tactic was to secrete cigars between the walls of a cask and an inner tin lining. Such Trojan devices required talented cooperage, a skill much in demand among professional smugglers.

tariffs by 1846. Though customs continued to intercept some concealed shipments of spirits and tobacco after that date, smugglers no longer numbered in the tens of thousands or devoted whole fleets to the "gainful and exciting pursuit of defrauding the government." The traffic declined with the incentive.[19]

How High Is Too High?

How much incentive do professional smugglers need to ply their trade? Is it a tax equivalent to 25 percent ad valorem? Or 50 percent? Or 100? No simple answer to this question is possible, in part because of what economists call cross-border effects. A tax, figured as a percentage of a legal commodity's value, may seem high in the abstract. However, if taxes in surrounding areas are equally steep, there is little incentive to smuggle—or, conversely, to go to where the drugs are. Eighteenth-century Parisians often did their weekend drinking in *guinguettes*, suburban cabarets where they could dodge the city's high taxes on wine. Efforts to extend the tax boundary just before the Revolution provoked riots.[20]

Smuggling to avoid taxes works best when drugs or other compact merchandise can be bought cheaply, transported short distances, and sold quickly. In 1995, when the Virginia cigarette tax was just one-thirteenth of that in the District of Columbia, Washingtonians needed no more than a Metro farecard to exploit the price difference. If cheap supplies are unavailable nearby, long-distance smuggling is still a possibility, though it is costlier, riskier, and less tempting. So government officials, in thinking about how high they can safely push their own taxes, must be aware of those of their neighbors. "How high is too high?" is geographically relative.[21]

Take, for example, the tax on salt, one of history's most durable sources of revenue. Salt is habit-forming. Its regular use makes the taste of unsalted, natural foods seem insipid and unappetizing. The strong taste for added salt—some historical epidemiologists have called it an addiction—created a fiscal opportunity. Chinese emperors, the British in India, and various princes and monarchs of the old regime all exploited it. *La gabelle*, the French salt tax, was particularly oppressive. Peasants might spend an eighth of their yearly income on salt, with most of the price representing the tax. But what made *la gabelle* so infuriating, and its avoidance so tempting, was its lack of uniformity. The price of salt varied as much as tenfold across provincial and national borders. French officials caught men, women, children, and trained dogs smuggling the cheaper salt. Penalties included whipping, branding, condemnation to the galleys, and death upon the wheel. When the Terror came, officials of the Farmers-General, the corporation that collected the salt tax, found themselves riding to the guillotine. Among them was Antoine Lavoisier, who had used the proceeds from tax farming to finance his pioneering chemical research.[22]

What salt taxes were to the eighteenth century, cigarette taxes were to the twentieth. After 1965 most American state legislatures, responding to health concerns and sensing a politically painless way to raise revenues, passed cigarette tax increases. They did not, however, raise them evenly. Some, mainly in the Northeast, imposed much higher taxes, making cigarettes that much more costly. By 1975 the same package of cigarettes that sold for 36 cents in North Carolina cost 54 cents in New York State. The price was higher still in New York City because of a local levy. It added 8 cents a pack in 1976—as much as the entire federal tax.

Thus was born an opportunity to buy cheap and sell dear. Those who bought in volume at North Carolina prices and sold at New York (or Connecticut, or Massachusetts) prices realized a substantial profit. By the mid-1970s net revenue losses ran well over 300 million dollars a year. Much of this went to organized criminals, who were at one point responsible for a quarter of the cigarettes sold in New York State and half of those sold in New York City. Their methods—truck fleets, concealed cargoes, dummy corporations, fortress-like warehouses, bribery, hijacking, assault, and murder—closely resembled those used by Prohibition bootleggers.[23]

Large-scale cigarette smuggling spread to Canada after its government hiked taxes in 1989 and again in 1991. Cartons selling in Canada for 45 dollars apiece cost half as much south of the border. Smugglers stuffed cigarettes into boats, kayaks, snowmobiles, and inside the bodies of cars and vans, in the manner of narcotics traffickers. They exported Canadian brands in volume (export cigarettes bore no tax) and then snuck them back across the border, allegedly with the knowledge and assistance of tobacco company executives. Professional criminals became involved. Violence erupted. The strategically situated town of Cornwall, Ontario, acquired the name "Dodge City East." Canadian citizens, apostles of peace, order, and good government, showed themselves to be every bit as contemptuous of high tobacco taxes as their English and French forebears. By 1994 an estimated one-third of the cigarettes in Ontario and two-thirds of those in Quebec were contraband, purchased from defiant merchants who kept double inventories and sold from below the counter. The government, citing a frightening growth in criminal activity and a breakdown in respect for Canadian law, announced large tax cuts in February of that year. Cigarette seizures promptly declined as Canadian smugglers shifted their attention to liquor, guns, illicit drugs, illegal immigrants, and other, more traditional forms of contraband.[24]

Cigarette smuggling was by then flourishing worldwide. Trade figures from the early 1990s show that global exports annually exceeded imports by some 280 billion cigarettes. This represented 5 percent of total cigarette production and 30 percent of all cigarettes in international trade. Allowing for a small lag due to transport time, smuggling is the obvious explanation for the discrepancy. In Colombia the illegal sale of Marlboros alone cost the country's leading cigarette manufacturer 300 million dollars a year by 1996. In Italy two organized criminal groups took in 600 million dollars a year from the sale of Marlboros and other smuggled cigarettes. In 1992 the Italian government, accusing Philip Morris of collusion with the smugglers, prohibited Marlboro cigarettes outright. This only increased the smuggling of the popular brand, so the government rescinded the ban. The gangs promptly went back to smuggling Marlboros for the customary reason, to avoid Italy's high tobacco taxes.[25]

The story has a moral. The idea that the black market is the result of some-thing called "prohibition" is the central premise of the liberal view of drug history and the basis for the affiliated proposal of controlled legalization. Licit, taxed sales of drugs like marijuana, cocaine, and heroin to adults could, theoretically, end the evils attendant to the black market while provid-ing revenue for state-sponsored prevention and treatment programs. The catch, apart from increased addiction due to increased exposure, is that re-taining taxes (and restrictions like no sales to minors) means retaining, to some degree, the black market. Light taxes and few restrictions would make the black market a minor nuisance, but would increase the amount of com-pulsive use. Heavy taxes and many restrictions would mean fewer new ad-dicts, but would create incentives for illicit manufacturing, smuggling, diver-sion, and violence. The high-low problem still applies.

When most people hear the phrase "drug trafficking," they think of crimi-nals scheming to bypass strict prohibitions on nonmedical sales and use. Viewed in historical terms, this sort of activity is a peculiarity of modern times. From about the mid-seventeenth century to the late nineteenth, the world's governing elites, with a few notable exceptions, were concerned with how best to tax the traffic, not how to suppress it. Prohibition would have struck them as futile and wasteful, had they thought of it at all.

9

About-Face: Restriction and Prohibition

During the late nineteenth and early twentieth centuries political elites had second thoughts about the consequences of the growing drug trade, and showed a growing willingness to criminalize the nonmedical sale and use of at least some drugs. In fact, as the historian Alan Block has observed, they did something unprecedented. They created an international control regime designed to shrink a prosperous industry, narcotics manufacturing, by regulating every detail from the point where the raw materials entered the factory to the final delivery to legitimate consumers. Looked at strictly in terms of revenue and power, this and other attempts to curtail psychoactive commerce are puzzling.[1]

Or so it seemed to me when I began sorting out winners and losers. The early modern phase of the psychoactive revolution occurred with the speed that it did, and on the scale that it did, because it served the interests of the wealthy and powerful. The elites most responsible for promoting drug cultivation and use were European. They could not have overspread the world so rapidly, nor brought it so completely under their dominion, without the large-scale production of alcohol and the cultivation of drug and sugar crops, the latter commonly used in, or made into, potent drinks. With these psychoactive products they paid their bills, bribed and corrupted their native opponents, pacified their workers and soldiers, and stocked their plantations with field hands. Despite scattered opposition from physicians and clergy, who warned against excessive and nonmedical use, the drug trade proved indispensable to planters, merchants, investors, slave traders, labor creditors, military officers, colonial bureaucrats, finance ministers, and others who were strategically placed to promote, protect, and profit from it.

Cannabis was an exception, in that imperial powers encouraged its growth for fibrous rather than psychoactive purposes. Cannabis as a drug was an affair of common folk, slaves and peasants, who spread the ganja complex in the wake of European expansion. Wine, spirits, tobacco, coffee, tea, chocolate, opium, and, later, coca and kola were different. Global production and commerce were closely tied to their uses as drugs. Their medical, hedonic, habituating, social, and, in some cases, nutritional properties made them ideal products and reliable sources of profit. Drugs meant money, and money meant power. Tobacco financed the American Revolution and helped underwrite Europe's dynastic conflicts. Sugar and rum sustained transatlantic slavery; opium subsidized imperialism in Asia. The alcohol-and-fur trade created great family fortunes and capital for industrial investment; the coffee boom stimulated railroad construction and drew a million impoverished immigrants to Brazil. In these and countless other ways drug production and commerce shaped the emerging modern world and its power relationships. By the early 1800s the new forces of habit were remaking the global environment itself.

Ironies abound. Today western political elites struggle against popular drug use. In the early modern world they promoted it by their collective decisions and by their own conspicuous consumption. This is not to say that the psychoactive revolution was strictly a top-down affair. The common people popularized any number of drugs, diverting novel medicines like *aqua vitae* to their own purposes. Still, elites made the key political and economic decisions: to tax rather than ban; to subsidize production with colonial land grants; to cover entire islands with sugar and drug plantations, expanding supply and driving down prices. They profited handsomely from those decisions. Then, during the nineteenth century, elites gradually became more concerned with drug abuse, more willing to implement restrictions and prohibitions, despite sometimes substantial revenue losses. A long-term trend rather than a specific event, it is hard to put an exact date on this collective shift in priorities. What can be said with certainty, though, is that it was a potent force in both domestic and international politics by the early 1900s, and that it represented one of history's great about-faces, however slowly and imperfectly executed.

Objections to Nonmedical Drug Use

Politically consequential opposition to nonmedical drug use stems from five basic concerns. The first is the direct harm users do to themselves and to others. Drinkers, for example, stand a much higher risk of accidental death. They succumb to everything from hypothermia to lions, who have learned to prey upon drunks staggering home at night from East African roadside bars. The personal health risks of intoxication most often prompt condemnation in nationalistic and totalitarian societies. "Has a man the right to destroy his own body by poisons?" the German physician Erich Hesse asked rhetorically in 1938. "No member of the national community has the right. On the contrary, everyone has the obligation to keep himself fit to the benefit of the community . . . which gives the individual his chance to live and to make a living."[2]

The same question might have elicited a very different response in, say, Australia in 1938: "It's my body, mate, and I'll do with it what I bloody well please." In individualistic societies, the dangers of harm to self and loss of social utility offer less compelling grounds for suppression, except in wartime. Personal drug use must affect others more directly, particularly those who wish to remain uninvolved. A drunken blow aimed at the occupant of the next barstool is less blameworthy than one aimed at a child cowering at home. Direct harm to innocent others is the most morally forceful argument against drug use, and one that cuts across all cultures. Opponents of tobacco had long stressed the annoyance that spitting, dipping, and smoking caused to nonusers. When medical research showed that environmental tobacco smoke was carcinogenic, the critics gained a decisive new weapon: "Mind if I give you cancer?" Bans on public indoor smoking soon followed in Britain and the United States. Other countries, including Australia, have adopted a variety of restrictions.[3]

Another common and politically influential objection is that nonmedical drug use inspires criminal violence. "Many crimes of blood are committed under the pathological influence of marijuana," proclaimed Mexico City's *Excélsior* in 1936, a charge echoed in Canada, Jamaica, and the United States. Critics made similar claims about alcohol, heroin, cocaine, and amphetamine—the last was sniper Charles Whitman's drug as he picked off campus bystanders from the University of Texas tower. How drugs trigger violence, and to what extent they are actually responsible for it, are complex questions, compounded by prejudice and propaganda. Yet appearances have a political reality. Reports of drug-inspired crimes, true or otherwise, increase support for restriction and prohibition.[4]

The second source of opposition is concern over social costs. The Enlightenment and its legacy of secular philosophies such as utilitarianism, with its imperative to pursue the greatest good for the greatest number, gave rise to a simple but very powerful idea. It was that private gains, however large, might entail unacceptably high and morally indefensible public costs. The costs, moreover, could be estimated with reasonable precision. If alcohol abuse leads to more sickness and premature death, it translates into fewer days worked, which equal so many dollars less in productivity, wages, and taxes. If it causes more crime and accidents, it raises police and medical costs, passed on to others as higher taxes and insurance premiums. Heavy drinking becomes everyone's business when a liver transplant costs close to a quarter of a million dollars.

To be complete and logically consistent, arguments involving social costs should net out economic benefits, such as savings on uncollected pensions. But even when their proponents attempt to do so, the computational problems are daunting. How do you quantify and subtract the coronary benefits of moderate drinking from the liver damage of heavy drinking? The difficulty of accurately estimating net social costs has not kept critics from trying, however, or from publicizing their efforts. Claims that abuse of this or that drug costs so many billions of dollars, pounds, or rubles implicitly justify further restrictions. Drug abuse beggars thy neighbors.[5]

The third source of opposition to nonmedical drug use is religious disapproval. Though hallucinogens form a part of many tribal rituals, they and other forms of chemical intoxication are regarded with disfavor in the world's major religions. Prayer, fasting, meditation, and exercise are the preferred means of transforming consciousness. Drugs transiently mimic only the feeling, not the disciplined knowing, of true mystical experience. They are false religions, chemical idols that distract the faithful and lead them down the path of self-destruction. Hence the unequivocal condemnations of drug abuse in the Catholic catechism, the Buddhist *sila*, and other basic moral codifications.

But what of *bhang* use by Hindu holy men, or hashish by Muslims who protest their innocence of wrongdoing? These exceptions should be understood in the context of underlying suspicion and disapproval. Tradition permits the use of cannabis in connection with the worship of Shiva. Hindu scriptures nevertheless condemn alcoholic intoxication, and later writings at-

THE BAD HUSBAND.

Dry propaganda, like this 1870 Currier and Ives print, stressed the harm that immoderate drinking did to innocent others, always an emotionally powerful appeal. The suffering of the innocent was also the theme of Lydia Sigourney's "The Intemperate," the 1834 story from which this illustration derived. The heroine, Jane Harwood, loses both her son and her drunken husband, ending as an impoverished widow. Other anti-liquor arguments were less sentimental: almshouses, jails, and asylums to house the intemperate ran up taxpayers' bills.

tack tobacco smoking. The Koran pairs wine drinking with gambling and deplores them both as ruinous vices (Sura II, 219; V, 90, 91). But did "wine" refer only to alcoholic beverages, or did it extend to all intoxicating drugs? Disagreement over this question created an opportunity—some say a pretext—for the use of cannabis in sects and among the masses. The Prophet, after all, did not explicitly forbid it. Most Islamic clergy, however, have consistently condemned nonmedical cannabis use, along with opium smoking and qat chewing. The controversy is not unlike that over artificial contraception in the Catholic Church. Birth control is a widespread practice, though one carried on in defiance of the Magisterium and shunned by the most orthodox and pious adherents.[6]

Resistance to drugs is likewise strongest among the true believers, those who suspect all forms of self-indulgence and fear anything that might undermine their assiduously cultivated self-control. "Pharmacological Calvinism" is a common trait of evangelical Christians, orthodox Jews, purity-conscious Brahmins, and mullahs who hustle dealers off to the gallows. Antipathy to drugs also has a practical aspect in this context. Joseph Westermeyer, a medical anthropologist, points out that addicts are functional agnostics: they neglect their shrines and temples, drop out of church affairs. Recovered addicts, by contrast, are often devout and enthusiastic participants. Proselytizers of all denominations thus automatically target addiction and abuse.[7]

The fourth source of opposition is the association of a particular drug with deviant or disliked groups. If, as one writer remarked, Viagra had originated in a clandestine inner-city drug lab and had been sold under the street name "Hardy Boy," its possession and use might well be illegal. Owing to its pluralistic character, American history is particularly rich in such cases. Liquor was associated with lower-class Catholic immigrants; opium smoking with Chinese laborers; heroin with big-city delinquents; and cocaine with out-of-control black men. In every instance, prohibitive legislation followed. Prejudice alone did not cause the bans. Nevertheless, as the sociologist Patricia Erickson observes, the smaller and lower-status the target population, the easier it is to enact such legislation—and the easier it is to keep it in place.[8]

The fifth source is the perception that drug use endangers the future of the group, whether the tribe, the nation, or the race. Native American opponents of the liquor traffic often voiced fears of collective destruction. Japanese critics called tobacco *binbōsō* ("poverty plant") and worried that its cultivation would crowd out grain production. Anxieties about drugs and collective well-being are most intense in times of international conflict, as are allegations of trafficking by foreign enemies. In the 1930s and 1940s Harry Anslinger accused the Japanese of promoting the narcotics traffic to gain revenue, corrupt western nations, and enslave peoples whose lands they had invaded or marked for invasion. During the Cold War he pointed his finger at the Chinese Communists—charges echoed in *Pravda* following the 1964 Sino-Soviet split, and in 1972 by the wary Taiwanese. In the 1980s Ayatollah Khomeini accused the United States *and* the Soviet bloc of conspiring to distribute heroin in Iran.[9]

Anxieties about drugs and collective survival are often intertwined with concerns about the young. Richmond Hobson, an American temperance figure who became an international antinarcotics gadfly in the 1920s, hammered at this theme. Drugs, he said, were a deadly contagion, blighting young lives and turning society's natural defenders into criminal menaces. Youthful drug abuse threatened the future of the nation, the race, and hu-

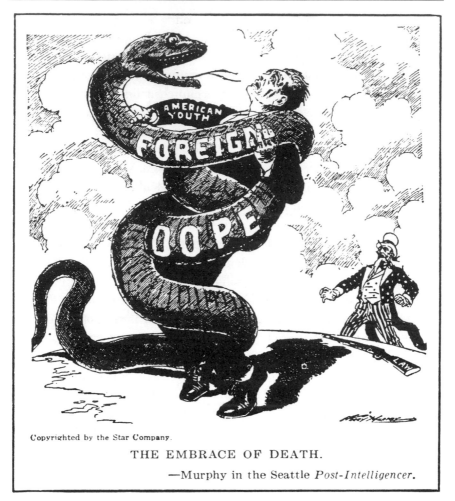

THE EMBRACE OF DEATH.

—Murphy in the Seattle *Post-Intelligencer.*

This cartoon accompanied a 1922 *Literary Digest* article which asserted that criminals found opium a tonic, that drug injection and addiction were spreading in all regions and social classes in the United States, and that there might be as many as five million addicts in the country. All these claims were wrong; the last was preposterous. But the public has always tended to believe the worst about drugs, especially when they affect the younger generation.

manity itself. Protestations scarcely less overwrought greeted the surge of cannabis and heroin use in Europe in the 1970s. "This horrible 'scourge' which is afflicting especially the youth . . . is mushrooming in an 'American' fashion," proclaimed Rome's *L'Unita* in 1976. The West German government, alarmed by the burgeoning youth drug culture, strengthened its narcotics law in 1971 and again in 1981. Across the Atlantic the Venezuelans did the same, adding a revealing proviso: sales to minors extended prison terms by a third. One black militant in the United States went further: "They should kill every dope pusher in Harlem," she told an interviewer. Many African-American activists had come to see narcotics in genocidal terms by the early 1970s.[10]

These five categories are not mutually exclusive. Direct harms, social costs, sinful conduct, deviant groups, and anxieties about the collective future can figure simultaneously in the rhetorical mix—witness the gin scare in early eighteenth-century England, or crack in late twentieth-century America. Nor are the categories entirely distinct. Net social costs, if heavy and sustained, would eventually raise concerns over the security of the state. But models are meant to be useful rather than tidy. This one can help us understand how world-historical developments after 1800 generated increased regulatory pressure from several independent sources. That pressure varied from country to country and from drug to drug. Highlighting recurring problems and concerns in the international literature does not "explain" every case of restriction and prohibition, each of which arose in a unique political and institutional context. Still, the exercise is necessary for understanding the global drift toward restriction and prohibition as something more than the happenstance accumulation of independent national decisions.

Drugs in an Industrial World

If the single most important fact about the early modern world was the expansion of oceangoing commerce, that of its modern successor was industrialization. During the nineteenth century psychoactive discoveries and innovations—the isolation of alkaloids, the invention of hypodermic syringes and safety matches, the creation of synthetic and semisynthetic drugs—were married to new techniques of industrial production and distribution. Factories did for drugs what canning did for vegetables. They democratized them. It became easier, cheaper, and faster for the masses to saturate their brains with chemicals, making a lasting impression on their most primitive pleasure and motivational systems. In a world in which the most downtrodden coolie in Singapore could purchase a morphine injection for four cents, the possibility of addiction was obviously much greater.[11]

The same was true of alcoholism. Between 1802 and 1815 the United States government issued no fewer than 100 patents for distilling devices, or more than 5 percent of all patents granted. Farmers who used the new equipment and distilling methods discovered that they could get 3.5 gallons of superior whiskey out of a bushel of corn, rather than the 2 gallons to which they were accustomed. Their collective efforts produced a river of cheap whiskey and helped bring about what one historian has dubbed "the alcoholic republic." The French experience might just as aptly be called one of alcoholic republics. Mass production and marketing lifted annual per capita adult consumption from 18 liters of pure alcohol in 1840 to 30 liters (about 7 gallons) by 1914, sharply increasing problem drinking. Though the trend pleased distillers and tax collectors, physicians, hygienists, and social reformers warned of grave consequences. They reduced their message to a slogan: "Alcohol: national wealth; alcoholism, national peril."[12]

If industrialization made drug abuse more likely and more visible, prompting increasing concern, abuse threatened the industrial process itself. As work moved indoors, tobacco became more of a nuisance and a fire risk. Even those tobacco users who did not smoke interfered with continuous production. Benjamin Rush calculated that a snuff taker who stopped work every 20 minutes wasted 5 days of every year. The key issue, though, was alcohol. Drinkers fouled things up, sometimes spectacularly. After Japan was opened to foreign trade, so many crewmen failed to make it back on board from the Yokohama bars that they disrupted sailing schedules. Employers everywhere became increasingly wary of on-the-job imbibing and of hiring drinking men. Missteps could lead to serious accidents, wrecked machinery, and lost lives or profits.[13]

In antebellum Massachusetts, a state undergoing rapid industrialization, manufacturers banned drinking on their premises, voted for revoking liquor licenses, and backed temperance candidates. These same candidates were opposed by merchants, grocers, and tavern keepers with a direct stake in the liquor trade, as well as by Irish and German immigrants. Like most newcomers to nineteenth-century America, the Irish and the Germans came from preindustrial communities where drinking was traditional and uncontroversial. Their culture as well as their religion differed from those of the "drys," who grew up in a modernizing Protestant society that emphasized individual achievement, self-discipline, and thrift. Yankee manufacturers, as well as a growing number of skilled native workers, came to regard drinking as a prolific source of human and financial waste. Thus were sown the seeds of history's most protracted controversy over prohibition, a conflict fed by wave after wave of peasants entering a nation that was becoming progressively more industrial, efficiency-conscious, and anxious about the social order.[14]

Clergymen and evangelical reformers, the latter increasingly numerous and active in the nineteenth century, had their own, religious reasons for supporting temperance. Yet it is striking how often and how seamlessly they combined concern for individual salvation with alarm over the social and economic consequences of drinking, particularly among uprooted workers freed from the traditional controls of church and rural gentry. "Temperance Societies are most instrumental in raising tens of thousands from degraded profligacy to virtuous and industrial habits, and converting sinners from the ways of vice to those of religion," the Bishop of Norwich wrote in 1837, conjoining the two sentiments in a single sentence. Those who combined evangelical piety with concern for industrial efficiency—John D. Rockefeller, Sr. comes immediately to mind—were particularly keen supporters of temperance. "Boys, do you know why I never became a drunkard?" Rockefeller asked his Sunday school class. "Because I never took the *first* drink." As if to demonstrate his point, the abstemious Rockefeller amassed an unprecedented industrial fortune and lived to a spry 97. He had hoped to make 100 [15]

Everywhere new industrial realities clashed with old customs. South Africans had long used tobacco and alcohol to recruit native laborers. By the nineteenth century the practice had become institutionalized in the "tot" or "dop" system. Alcohol-dependent field hands, who received part of their wages in rations of cheap wine or brandy, toiled in the vineyards and wheat fields from sunrise to sunset. Their workday began, appropriately enough, with the ringing of the old slave bell. But when the mines began to compete with the farms for native labor, the situation changed. Mine owners, who regarded drunken laborers as a menace and a drain on productivity, supported controls over alcohol sales to African workers. Large farmers with substantial investments in machinery were also willing to abandon the tot system, paying higher wages or offering coffee instead of wine. Nevertheless, when a series of laws enacted between 1883 and 1898 restricted African access to liquor, legislators exempted the tot system because they deemed it too important to small farmers' livelihoods and labor supply. They effectively made the *kind* of work an African did the criterion of legal access to liquor.[16]

It would be a mistake, however, to view all restrictive or prohibitory regulations solely as efficiency measures that capitalists imposed on unwilling industrial workers. The more future-oriented workers and progressive union leaders also understood the debilitating and impoverishing consequences of drinking, and viewed abstinence, or at least moderation, as an important means of achieving self-respect and independence. "As soon as a man has spent all his money for drink," summed up one railroad employee, "he becomes a slave to the corporation." Sentiments like these translated into growing support for temperance campaigns and, in some cases, legal restrictions and membership bans. The Knights of Labor denied admittance to saloon keepers, whom they classed with bankers and lawyers as social parasites.[17]

Saloon keepers admittedly had their champions, and most regulars persisted in viewing their establishments as benign institutions. Drug use has always had a strong social dimension, and saloons, taverns, and public houses served as the "great good places" in many workers' lives. But their centrality and social attractiveness declined as fraternal lodges and trade unions began providing alternatives for after-work association. Amusement parks, music halls, and movie theaters offered affordable entertainment. In Britain the expression "go to the local" acquired a double meaning, to visit the cinema as well as the pub. The competition implied by the ambiguity may help explain why British alcohol consumption declined during the 1920s and 1930s, the same years when Britons were becoming avid moviegoers. The larger point is that workers and their families were beginning to have attractive, inexpensive alternatives to traditional drinking establishments. The urban-industrial transformation not only put a premium on sobriety, it spawned competing forms of association and recreation.[18]

Businessmen often made common cause with concerned workers, especially in the Protestant, spirits-drinking societies where temperance movements were strongest. In Holmsund, a Swedish port and sawmill town, the money, land, and building materials for the Good Templar lodge came directly from the company's management. Like most progressive initiatives, this one sprang from mixed motives, from both care and control. The aim was to encourage a quiet, proper, and diligent way of life. Abstinent workers were more industrious—though also, as it turned out, more politically active once they ceased to be anesthetized by drink.[19]

Labor's growing political influence increased pressure for welfare services. Germany led the way, providing compulsory health insurance for industrial workers in 1883. As traditional two-party health care evolved into three-party systems—patient, provider, and public or private insurer—the incentive to curtail abuse increased. Insurance costs were passed on to taxpayers, as were those of care in almshouses, charity hospitals, and other public institutions. "Drinking subjects the society to the burden of high taxes," complained Justice Tek Chand, a prominent Indian prohibitionist. "Large sums have to be spent on the ravages wrought on account of drinking." The more complex, interdependent, and mechanized society became, the larger were those sums and the greater the risks of intoxication.[20]

The more threatening, too, seemed the connections between drugs and foreign groups. Industrialization was accompanied by—indeed, required— revolutionary changes in transportation and communication. Regional markets grew into national markets, and national ones into international, knit together by cable, rail, and steamship. People and ideas moved faster and less expensively. Cheaper travel and mass emigrations spread novel drug practices; steam presses and penny newspapers broadcast the alarming news about them. Diaspora opium smoking especially provoked the nativists, and provided a godsend for adjectivally-minded journalists:

> Smoked in the vilest dens of Mongol depravity, breathed upon by the fetid breath of hideous leprosy-stricken wretches, holding the pestilential exhalations of the loathsome victims of venereal plague, catching the noisome salival drippings of coolie bawds in dens shut out from air and sunlight, this polluted mass [of opium] is again mixed in a festering compound and is put to the lips of Christian imitators of a fatal pagan vice. These are the cold, unyielding facts. The English language cannot adequately portray the situation.

It was, however, sufficient to proscribe the practice in American statute books. Opium prepared for smoking, though milder and less addictive than morphine, was the first narcotic banned outright by local, state, and federal legislation. The same thing happened in Australia, whose not especially temperate citizens were heavy consumers of narcotic-laced patent medicines. What made the difference in both cases was the association of opium smoking with coolies, consensus that it lacked therapeutic value, and fear that it would spread beyond the Chinese. This last point also deeply concerned Meiji officials. They banned opium smoking in 1868, and in 1870 threatened Chinese residents in Japan with severe punishment should they indulge. Habitual smokers faced deportation. The British outlawed the practice in 1916, while simultaneously tightening access to other types of opiates and cocaine.[21]

The date, 1916, is significant. Industrialization changed the nature of warfare. Equipping and sustaining large, mechanized forces required unprecedented civilian productivity. Anxieties about the effects of alcohol and other drugs deepened, particularly during World War I. America's entry into the conflict in 1917 allowed the Anti-Saloon League to recast prohibition as a war issue, catalyzing national legislation. Britain's omnibus Defense of the Realm Act stopped short of prohibition, though it forbade supplying intoxicants to soldiers to make them drunk or disabled. Hard drinking by war workers, flush with overtime pay, was another sore point. It lowered their productivity, if their governors are to be credited, by up to 30 percent. In 1915 David Lloyd George, Britain's minister of munitions, remarked that settling with German militarism meant first of all settling with drink. His government drastically reduced opening hours and raised taxes, measures that cut consumption by more than half. George V himself took the King's Pledge to abstain for the duration, though, on his doctor's advice, he occasionally indulged in private.[22]

The journalist Samuel Hopkins Adams thought upper-class hypocrisy provided an important clue to the nature of prohibition. Manufacturers believed their employees would be happier and more productive if they did not drink. Bankers and merchants thought they would receive funds that had formerly passed through the bartender's hands. Labor leaders anticipated larger membership and dues paid on time. Yet few of these worthies intended to give up their own drinking, which they judged controlled and harmless. What prohibition amounted to, consciously or unconsciously, Adams wrote, was class legislation. Though his formulation was too pat, and discounted popular support for the reform too sharply, Adams had nevertheless hit upon something important. Industrialization created influential groups for whom unregulated commerce in intoxicating drugs was *not* profitable, and these groups acted as a counterweight to those for whom it was still lucrative.[23]

Herein lies the historical logic of discouraging the consumption of valuable and heavily taxed merchandise. Drug commerce was straightforwardly profitable for early modern commercial and political elites. Whatever moral reservations they may have entertained, they found that they could live with nonmedical drug use by the common folk who prepared their meals, harvested their crops, and fought their wars. The odd bender was less disruptive in traditional cultures with undisciplined pastimes and work settings. As the social environment changed, becoming more rationalized, bureaucratized, and mechanized, the distribution of cheap intoxicants became more troublesome and divisive. A drunken field hand was one thing, a drunken railroad brakeman quite another. While the consumption of drugs might keep workers on a treadmill, over time and in certain industrial contexts it rendered their labor worse than useless. The growing cost of the abuse of manufactured drugs turned out to be a fundamental contradiction of capitalism itself.[24]

The Medical Indictment

This contradiction was not, however, the only source of restrictive pressure. Developments in pharmacy, medicine, and public health shrank the officially recognized scope of intoxicating drugs and heightened fears about their inherent dangers. Pharmaceutical innovation affected psychoactive commerce in a paradoxical way. It introduced seductive new drugs like cocaine, but also safer therapeutic equivalents like novocaine. By 1912, declared one Colorado official, cocaine's value in dentistry had become trifling, hardly worth the risk of forming a demoralizing habit. The drug was inessential, he said, in contrast to morphine, which still numbered among humanity's greatest blessings. Alcohol's therapeutic stock likewise fell during the nineteenth century. "While it is indicated in medicine," one physician advised a temperance lecturer in 1901, "in every case there are other drugs more reliable and none so dangerous." Patent medicines loaded with alcohol and other drugs were particularly deadly, for they might mask the symptoms of diseases like tuberculosis, delaying competent professional diagnosis and treatment.[25]

Those who escaped illness did not require drugs, self-administered or otherwise. Rates of sickness and death from infectious diseases declined sharply in the second half of the nineteenth and the first half of the twentieth century, particularly in industrializing nations. Tuberculosis, which took the life of 1 of every 200 Europeans in 1845, claimed only 1 in 2,000 by 1950. The widespread use of opiates might be imperative in lands plagued by fever and famine, as the old Asia hands claimed; it was less tenable in countries where improved living standards and public health reforms, rationalized by bacteriology, were slashing morbidity and mortality. Thus the necessity of narcotics was declining, even as the risks, magnified by hypodermic injection and the attendant possibility of infection, were increasing.[26]

Western physicians became more statistically minded in the nineteenth century. Though their techniques were still primitive, doctors began to quantify the risks of drug use, particularly those of alcohol. Samuel Cartwright, a young physician who settled in Natchez, Mississippi, in 1823, followed the careers of his colleagues over the next thirty years. He found that 76 percent of the abstaining doctors were still living in 1853, compared with just 12 percent of the nonabstainers. Hospital admissions of European soldiers serving in the Madras army in India told a similar tale. Heavy drinkers were four times as likely to die in the hospital as abstainers, moderate drinkers twice as likely. Not to be outdone, Victorian teachers devised their own empirical demonstration, bidding their charges to observe the effects of sprinkling one potted plant with whiskey, another with water.[27]

As biostatistics matured, yielding more elegant and accurate means of demonstrating risk, public awareness of the harmful effects of drug use increased. In 1930, for example, New Zealand prohibitionists could tell audiences precisely how much excess mortality moderate drinkers could expect between the ages of 40 and 50. They backed their claim with the authority of the British Institute of Actuaries. Mounting international evidence—eight studies linking smoking to cancer had appeared in Germany, Holland, the United States, and Britain by the end of the year 1950—was crucial in changing attitudes toward tobacco. Despite the industry's determined rearguard action, smoking came to be regarded as a prolific source of illness and death. Specialists cashed out the risks, claiming, for example, that a fifth of Medicaid's hospital expenditures derived from abuse of tobacco, alcohol, and other drugs. The combination of chronic disease epidemiology and social-cost analysis turned drugs into morally loaded "risk factors," dangerous for users and bad for the public purse.[28]

Advocates of restriction and prohibition seized upon another emergent medical idea, that addictive behavior was a progressive disease brought on by sustained exposure to the drug itself. This understanding began crystallizing around alcohol in the late eighteenth and early nineteenth centuries; specialists had extended it to nearly all psychoactive drugs by the beginning of the twentieth. Some Anglo-American writers dubbed the phenomenon "inebriety." Its roots lay in drugs' pathological action on the nervous system, not simply in the moral defects of weak-willed individuals. Those with frail nervous constitutions were particularly susceptible. Normal persons, however, could fall victim to inebriating drugs, as could their children. Physicians deplored the "doping" of infants and narcotic use during pregnancy. Dependent newborns faced catastrophic outcomes. "Death, weakness or mental stunting in the child are not uncommon results of continued morphia taking by the mother during the period of gestation," one specialist observed in 1881. He cited cases of children who were near-idiots or unable to speak and walk at the age of five.[29]

The harm caused by drug use, including a tendency to inebriety, could be passed on to children. Alcohol and other drugs supposedly damaged germ cells, working their degenerative mischief across generations. They were "racial poisons," a phrase that had great resonance in an age of nativist fears and intense international rivalries. Some eugenicists, such as Britain's Caleb Saleeby, urged that the state prevent drunkards from procreating. Though ideas about the heritability of acquired traits declined after 1910, concern about fetal damage persisted and was eventually vindicated by research in the late 1960s and early 1970s.[30]

Victorian-era investigations of the toxic and habit-forming properties of drugs had at least two important political effects. The first was to reinforce the determination of the progressive physicians, pharmacists, and health bureaucrats to restrict access to opiates and cocaine through prescription laws and refill limits. Regulations of this sort appeared first in European nations, later and more unevenly in America. (Lack of effective regulation was one likely reason the cocaine epidemic hit first and hardest in the United States.) The second effect was to hand prohibitionists a very big rhetorical stick. A few of the religiously minded did not care for the materialist cast of inebriety theories—one clergyman denounced them as infidel efforts to dignify vice— but the majority married their traditional morality to the newer medical insights. John B. Gough summed up this attitude when he said that he considered drunkenness a sin, but also a disease: "It is a physical as well as a moral evil." Medicine explicitly linked the two. Drug abuse always eroded the brain's moral faculties. Scratch an inebriate, find a liar. Even the crimes of the Communards were laid at the feet of nicotine and alcohol. Tobacco's fumes had numbed them to humanity. Drink had drowned their reason.[31]

The biggest challenge the medical findings presented to evangelical temperance advocates was scriptural. Norman Kerr, a British authority on inebriety, put it thus: "To teach that Christ made, and that the Bible sanctioned the social use of, a poisonous narcotic beverage, is . . . a proposition which seems to me to carry with it its own condemnation." Kerr and others suggested that the original scriptures referred to two sorts of wine: the bad, fermented sort and the good, unfermented variety that Jesus blessed at Cana. The different terms for vinous beverages had been carelessly conflated into "wine." Thus was contradiction swept under the rug of mistranslation.

The grape-juice hypothesis provoked hoots of derision. "Special pleading without any adequate foundation," wrote one Cambridge don, adding that fermentation was bound to occur under ancient Near Eastern hygienic conditions. Scripture condemned intemperance, not drinking. Evangelical resistance to this conclusion—the controversy spawned commentaries of unbelievable density, some of which enjoyed large sales—is a clue to how pathologized alcohol had become during the nineteenth century. Drinking caused drunkenness. Moderate drinkers of good character were in peril of their lives and souls. Biblical endorsement of evil was impossible. The dissonance could be resolved only by the mistranslation gambit—an unsound tactic, though one that was stubbornly defended.[32]

China: Nationalists and Internationalists

If statistical and medical inquiries provided opponents of drug commerce with scientifically plausible arguments, the deterioration of China served as their great object lesson. Missionaries, who penetrated into every part of the country after 1860, kept up a barrage of criticism. Saving souls in an opium-besotted land was a fool's errand, the opium trade the height of hypocrisy. "Its history is a Christian sin, a Christian shame," wrote one. "Take away this abnormal, this unnatural ally of heathenism, and we can meet the enemy without doubt of the final outcome." Medical missionaries documented the more corporeal harms of opium smoking, and energetically challenged apologists for the practice. Their writings reinforced anxieties that western countries, with their own sprouting dens and morphine fiends, were headed down the same road to degeneration and national enfeeblement.

The missionaries aimed their complaints primarily at the British government and public, among whom opposition to the trade was growing. They had less impact on the Chinese, who needed no sermons to convince them of the problem. Nationalists like Chang Chih-tung, governor of Shansi province, led the attack. "The real calamity in Shansi is . . . the opium," he wrote to a friend in 1881. "Sixty percent of the country folk, 90 percent of the city dwellers, and 100 percent of the officials, clerks, and troops are addicts." While these figures were exaggerated, the sense of crisis was real enough. Patriotic contemporaries shared Chang's belief that talk of a sovereign country was futile until something was done about opium. That meant ending domestic production, upon which the provincial and imperial governments depended for revenue, as well as the India trade, so redolent of barbarian domination. (The Chinese called opium "foreign mud," among other earthy epithets.) Students returning from Japan and abroad were particularly critical of the status quo. They had seen at first hand what stricter controls could accomplish.[33]

The Ch'ing court finally acted in 1906. The opium poison had permeated the whole of China, it decreed. Smokers were wasting their time, ruining their health, impoverishing their families, and undermining the Empire. The government would therefore suppress cultivation over a period of ten years. Chinese officials simultaneously began negotiating to end shipments from India. The timing was propitious. Their British counterparts were beginning to acknowledge, however belatedly, the threat that opium posed to Chinese national integrity. Britain enjoyed more trade with and investment in China than any of its imperial rivals; these interests would be jeopardized if China suffered collapse and partition. Moreover, the India-China opium trade had been declining for many years, as Chinese domestic production took its place. From providing 14 percent of the Indian government's revenues in 1880–1887, it had fallen to just 7 percent by 1905.[34] Finally, the Liberals—a party disproportionately middle-class, temperance-minded, nonconformist, and hostile to the opium traffic—came into power after the 1906 election.

That same year the United States began sounding out other governments about the possibility of an international meeting on the opium question, which was eventually held at Shanghai in 1909. American diplomats had two essential goals, to preserve Chinese sovereignty and to open China's markets to American exports. Widespread opium use meant less political stability and less demand for American products. With no significant financial stake in the Asian opium traffic, reform was a no-lose proposition for the United States. The State Department's initiatives pleased the Chinese government and American business interests, as well as politically influential temperance advocates and missionaries, now also concerned about the opium situation in America's newly acquired Philippine colony.

In 1907 British and Indian officials reached an agreement with the Chinese. They would phase out exports at a rate of 10 percent a year, provided the Chinese eliminated their own production at the same rate—which, to the surprise of many observers, they did. Though the campaign generated strong resistance in the interior provinces, and produced uneven results, nationalist officials made some headway. Enough, at any rate, that the British inspectors pronounced themselves satisfied. Indian officials agreed to end exports ahead of the ten-year schedule. The last licit shipment of opium bound for China left India in 1913.

By then the Chinese were beginning to falter. The collapse of the Manchu dynasty in 1911, the weakness of the succeeding republic, the descent of the country into warlordism and civil war, the expansion and export-mindedness of the Japanese pharmaceutical industry, and the parasitism of the *ronin*—Japanese soldiers of fortune who dealt vast quantities of narcotics—all contributed to history's most spectacular relapse. ("Opium is a terrible poison," shrugged Nitan'osa Otozō, a leading Japanese cultivator, "but the drain of gold"—Japan's trade deficit—"is also very deplorable.") Though reformers continued to mount sporadic campaigns against use and cultivation in the 1920s and 1930s, their efforts uniformly failed. Opium revenue was simply too important for the various parties vying for control of China. Mao's dictum, that all power flows from the barrel of a gun, presupposes the means to buy the gun and to pay the soldier who wields it. Trafficking flourishes wherever private armies, endemic conflict, proxy warfare, and weak states are found. The generalization applies as well to the Golden Triangle or Afghanistan as it does to China before 1949. It was not until the Communists eliminated all internal opposition and mounted a sustained campaign of suppression and reeducation that addiction came under control. The revival of cross-border traffic from Burma (Myanmar) in the 1980s and the recrudescence of scattered poppy cultivation would prove even that success transient.[35]

All this lay in the future, however. Reformers drew two immediate lessons from the dramatic events of 1906–1911. The first was that drug control was a matter of national will. States that were really serious about imposing effective restrictions, observes the historian William McAllister, could apparently do so in short order. The Chinese government, off to a good start, might have succeeded had it been able to maintain power. Other nations, blessed with greater stability, could surely put their own houses in order and circumscribe the global traffic. Diplomatic precedent favored the enterprise. International treaties covered the mails, tariffs, waterways, battlefield casualties, and prisoners of war. Why not drugs?

The second lesson, inspired by the success of the India-China agreement, was that supply reduction offered the likeliest means of success. Eliminate production that was not medically essential, eliminate the problem of abuse. Though far simpler in theory than in practice, this strategy became the cornerstone of the international system that evolved after 1911. Despite protectionist haggling, world war, political intrigue, and lobbying by pharmaceutical companies, a coterie of diplomats managed to cobble together a series of compromise treaties. The most important of these were the 1925 International Opium Convention and the more comprehensive 1931 Limitation Convention. These agreements created a permanent, if not quite watertight, regulatory system designed to limit what had been a highly profitable,

Arise, comrades, and smite opium. Sun Yat-sen's anti-opium message leads the strike force; other slogans urge narcotic education, rehabilitation hospitals, and opium investigation. Though nationalist campaigns against narcotic use continued into the 1920s—this poster is from 1928—political weaknesses negated their effectiveness. Contending warlords were more interested in extracting revenue from the opium crop than suppressing it.

heavily taxed, and globally expansive industry. Subsequent United Nations treaties and amendments rationalized the system's administration and brought "psychotropics"—manufactured drugs such as amphetamines or barbiturates—under international control.[36]

By 1933, the year enough nations had ratified the Limitation Convention for it to take effect, the whole landscape of psychoactive commerce had changed. Unregulated trade was increasingly rare. Laws forbade the sale of cigarettes to minors, of alcohol after hours, of narcotics without prescriptions, and of some drugs altogether. International treaties limited not only the opium traffic but the spirits trade in the African interior. Allowing for significant national policy differences—the United States, for example, prohibited narcotic maintenance, while most European, Latin American, and Asian nations did not—the overall trend was toward restriction and selective prohibition. That trend was, as historians say, overdetermined; it was a manifestation of modernity itself. Some form of stricter regulation was inevitable as the world became more industrialized, calculating, easily traversed, medically informed, and impatient of the imperial yoke.

10

LICIT AND ILLICIT DRUGS

MODERN REGULATORY REGIMES divide psychoactive drugs into seven categories. These categories, illustrated with current American examples, appear in the table on the following page. They form a continuum of legal access, ranging from outright prohibition to unrestricted availability. This continuum intersects with another, taxation, to form a simple graph. The tax axis runs from zero to prohibitory. The point of origin — universal access, zero tax — is the free market. Movement away from the free market along either axis, toward stricter regulations or heavier taxes, prompts illicit activity. What to do about such activity requires choices along a third policy axis, strength of sanctions. These range from warnings to fines to institutionalization to execution. The Chinese shoot heroin traffickers in the back of the head, or sometimes in the heart, if the police happen to have sold the corneas for transplantation, rather than the kidneys. They then send a bill for the bullet to the condemned man's family.[1]

The Chinese do not, however, shoot the merchants of tea or whiskey or cigarettes. Despite the worldwide trend toward increased regulation, higher taxes, and stronger sanctions during the twentieth century, caffeine, alcohol, and tobacco have remained more legally accessible than opiates, cannabis, cocaine, and most synthetics. American Prohibition, a seeming exception to this generalization, was neither pure nor prohibition. The Volstead Act permitted sacramental use and limited home brewing, as well as alcoholic prescription. Bonded warehouses, guarded by dogs and electric alarms, held thousands of barrels of medicinal whiskey. It was perfectly legal, if sometimes obtained by means of forgery. Big-city taxi drivers offered counterfeit prescription orders for two dollars apiece.[2]

REGULATORY CATEGORIES FOR PSYCHOACTIVE DRUGS

Pure prohibition. No manufacture, sale, or use allowed, e.g., heroin.

Prohibitory prescription. Prohibited except for narrow therapeutic purposes unrelated to addiction, and then only if administered by health-care professionals, e.g., cocaine.

Maintenance. Prescription allowed for relief of addiction, but only under supervision, e.g., methadone.

Regulatory prescription. Unsupervised self-administration allowed for those holding a valid prescription, e.g., Valium.

Restricted adult access. No prescription required, though availability is legally limited, e.g., alcohol sold only to unintoxicated persons during certain hours.

Unrestricted adult access. Sufficient age the sole criterion of purchase, e.g., tobacco.

Universal access. Available to any individual, e.g., caffeinated beverages.

Easier access to alcohol, tobacco, and caffeine is plainly a global, not just a western, pattern. Alcohol is even legally available in many Islamic nations, though its status is controversial and fluctuates with the political fortunes of the local fundamentalists. Why, then, did these three drugs, all of which have toxic properties and all of which can lead to dependency, fare so much better than other drugs in the regulatory era? What objections have arisen to their liberal treatment? Is the distinction between licit and illicit drugs likely to persist?

The Harmfulness of Licit Drugs

Caffeine's privileged status is the easiest to explain. Though medical authorities from Paulli on have warned of the effects of caffeinated drinks, their cautionary tales have typically featured heavy consumers—the "nerve-wrecked slaves," as one authority called them. Nineteenth-century French devotees of coffee ("strong enough for any man to walk on that has Faith as Peter had") produced some of the most spectacular cases. However, moderate use, while not without adverse effects, has yet to be convincingly linked to life-threatening illness. Caffeine lacks the equivalent of cirrhosis or lung cancer. Nor is there any connection to crime or violence. Coffee, as John McCann puts it, intoxicates without inviting the police. Intravenous caffeine is another matter, but this mode of administration, apart from adulterated street drugs, is rare. Small oral doses of a drug, especially when integrated into daily life, are always less dangerous than injecting alkaloids.[3]

Caffeine, to extend the metaphor, keeps the police away. Its antidepressant properties have prevented suicides; its awakening effects have prevented nighttime driving accidents. It has drawn little in the way of official or, with the exception of the Mormons, religious opposition. Caffeine is kosher. Coca-Cola ads aimed at Israel's Orthodox community simply replace scantily clad models with nice boys in side curls. Protestants have long approved of caffeinated beverages as benign alternatives to alcohol. Buddhists have relied on tea to ward off the "the devil of sleep." Catholic priests have sipped tea to get through all-night marathons in the confessional. Caffeine cuts across all social classes, provides employment for tens of millions of people, and is popular with elites. Ninety percent of Dutch parliamentarians drink coffee, half of them five or more cups a day. No chance of a ban there.[4]

Alcohol is a very different matter. In 1958 Maurice Seevers published addiction liability ratings for different drugs in a standard pharmacology textbook. He assigned points for their ability to produce tolerance, emotional dependence, physical dependence, physical deterioration, antisocial behavior during administration, and the same during withdrawal. The maximum score was 24, or 4 points in each category. The highest actual score was for alcohol, at 21 points. Barbiturates earned 18 points; heroin 16; cocaine 14; marijuana 8; and peyote 1. A glance at these numbers shows that the degree of danger was conspicuously out of sync with the prevailing regulations. Alcohol, Seevers's worst drug, was among the most available. Lawrence Kolb, the leading U.S. expert on narcotic addiction, made a similar point in the privacy of a 1957 letter. "Marihuana intoxication is less dangerous than alcoholic intoxication," he wrote. "[It] is a mixture of pleasant and fantastic symptoms likely to lead to reverie and contemplation rather than to the fury, irresponsibility, and foolish activity so commonly associated with alcoholic intoxication."[5]

Tobacco's easy availability also defies straightforward medical explanation. While not intoxicating in the same sense as alcohol, tobacco's use has long been recognized as addictive and unhealthful. Well before the lung-cancer research, critics blamed it for enslaving users, heightening mortality, impairing vision, corrupting youth, and encouraging intemperance. Had Seevers applied his criteria to nicotine—and it is interesting that, in 1958, he did not—it undoubtedly would have merited a 14 or 15 on his addiction liability scale, about the same as cocaine. Caffeine would have scored 4 or 5.

However measured, the dangers of licit drugs have prompted endless charges of hypocrisy and irrationality. An entire genre of drug literature, of which Edward Brecher's *Licit and Illicit Drugs* (1972) is the progenitor, assesses the relative harms of different drugs and then professes dismay at their misalignment with policy. Alcohol and tobacco are exhibits A and B.[6]

Drug Realpolitik

The campaigns against alcohol and narcotics that quickened in the late nineteenth century were rhetorically very similar. The charges leveled at the one—racial poison, moral corrosive, pauperizer—were leveled at the other. Alcohol, as Norman Kerr put it, was a "narcotic poison." Yet it outlived all attempts at national prohibition. It was never a serious candidate for global regulation. Until recently, few described or treated it as a "drug."

The most obvious reason for alcohol's privileged status was the industry's size and fiscal importance in the western nations that dominated the world's economic and diplomatic affairs. Counting all the producers, retailers, shippers, and cork makers, the early twentieth-century French alcohol industry affected the livelihoods of 4.5 to 5 million people, or roughly 13 percent of the French population. At the same time, alcohol taxes—then yielding the Russians, for example, an amount equivalent to their entire military budget—remained a bedrock of western finance. The same was true for many colonial governments in Africa and Asia. Alcohol taxes were crucial in both the "core" and "peripheral" regions of the modern world system. Opium, by contrast, was gradually declining in importance, at least within the British empire. The India-China opium trade was shrinking in the late nineteenth and early twentieth centuries, simplifying Britain's shift from chief protector of the traffic to advocate of international control.[7]

Proceeds from the alcohol industry supported high culture as well as state bureaucracies. When he died in 1887, the Danish brewing magnate J. C. Jacobsen bequeathed his Old Carlsberg Brewery to a foundation for the promotion of the arts and humanistic and scientific research. The effect was subtly co-optive. To this day most Danes consider beer-drinking (a custom in which they lead all Scandinavian nations) to be a benign, patriotic activity. What's good for Carlsberg is good for Denmark—or at least for its academic and artistic establishments, heavily dependent on the Carlsberg Foundation for funding.[8]

The scale and location of alcohol production were also significant. Viticulture, brewing, and distilling flourished in Europe and throughout much of the non-Islamic world. Narcotic production, by contrast, was more confined. Poor nations and colonies in southern Asia grew most of the opium. Two places, Peru and Java, accounted for most of the coca. A handful of industrial nations manufactured cocaine and morphine. Germany, the most important of these, initially resisted control efforts. Its narcotic manufacturing capacity threatened the entire international regulatory enterprise, first laid out in the 1912 Hague Opium Convention. But then Germany lost World War I. The British and American delegations to the Paris conference insisted that the treaties imposed on the Central Powers include the Hague Opium Convention. Germany and Turkey, another recalcitrant nation, had to agree to export controls, now under the supervision of the League of Nations. Though Hitler took Germany out of the League in 1933, Berlin quietly continued to cooperate with its drug-control authorities. The Nazis consistently, and strictly, opposed illicit trafficking.[9]

The tobacco story closely resembles that of alcohol. The industry's economic impact and breadth of operations conferred a measure of immunity, as did the sheer number of addicted smokers. The cigarette revolution, with all it entailed for expanded consumption, deepened dependency, and heightened profitability, occurred *before* the most damning cancer evidence emerged. Had the U.S. government vigorously attempted to restrict smoking in the wake of the 1964 Surgeon General's report, Richard Kluger observes, the move would have affected upwards of 70 million smokers and 2 million stockholders, farmers, factory workers, retailers, publishers, broadcasters, and others in some measure financially dependent on tobacco. That was hardly a realistic prospect. (Nor would the United States—the tail wagging the world's drug control dog in those years—have acquiesced to international export controls.) As cultivation and consumption spread in developing nations, tobacco's economic stake grew progressively larger. By 1983 world production and distribution provided more than 18 million full-time jobs. Factoring in workers' family members plus part-time and seasonal laborers, something like 100 million people depended on tobacco for their livelihoods.[10]

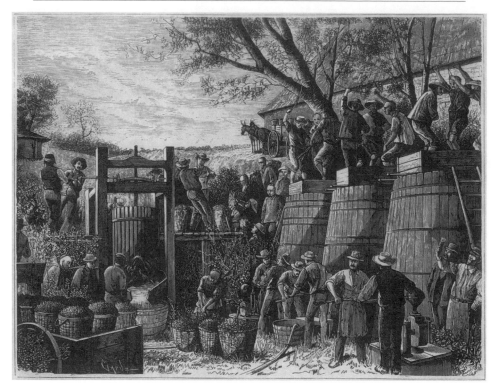

Viticulture was a far-flung enterprise by the late nineteenth century; workers tended vines on every continent except Antarctica. The California labor force was the most heterogeneous, employing Anglo-American, Native American, Latin American, European, and Asian workers, some of whom are shown here bringing in baskets of grapes and treading them out over redwood vats. The economic and fiscal importance of viticulture, together with brewing and distilling, made alcoholic beverages more resistant to prohibition efforts than other intoxicating drugs.

Production and revenue on this scale conferred great co-optive power on the multinational tobacco companies. They were not loath to use it, whether through public relations campaigns, subornation of the media, political donations, arts endowments, sports sponsorships, or the purchase of lobbyists, expert witnesses, and lawyers. Philip Morris and R. J. Reynolds even provided 90 percent of the funding for the American Civil Liberties Union's workplace privacy task force, which campaigned, among other things, for employees' smoking rights.[11]

Pharmaceutical companies also proved adept at lobbying to protect endangered products. In fact, they managed to delay a comprehensive international treaty on psychotropic drugs until 1971, extracting several concessions in the process. They had a similar impact on domestic regulations. Lester Grinspoon, a physician and drug historian, explained how the companies worked. While waiting to testify on the therapeutic use of cannabis before the Bureau of Narcotics and Dangerous Drugs (the chief federal enforcement agency from 1968 to 1973 and predecessor of the DEA), he listened in on another administrative hearing. It concerned the fate of pentazocine (Talwin), a Winthrop Pharmaceuticals product for which there was considerable evidence of addiction, overdose, and abuse:

> Six lawyers from the drug company, briefcases in hand, came forward to prevent the classification of pentazocine or at least to ensure that it was placed in one of the less restrictive schedules. They succeeded in part; it became a Schedule IV drug. In the testimony on cannabis, the next drug to be considered, there was no evidence of overdose deaths or addiction—simply many witnesses, both patients and physicians, who testified to its medical utility. The government refused to transfer it [from Schedule I, the most restrictive] to Schedule II. Might the outcome have been different if a large drug company with enormous financial resources had a commercial interest in cannabis?[12]

Cannabis as drug—or, more precisely, as folk and countercultural drug—never had the international corporate backing or fiscal influence that alcohol and tobacco enjoyed. This fact, along with its officially described links to crime and deviance (and, more recently, its status as a culture-war football), made it highly vulnerable to prohibitive pressure.

Follow the Leaders

The more liberal treatment of alcohol and tobacco also reflects the personal habits of influential leaders and celebrities. Historically, these have often worked to undermine drug strictures. It was Peter the Great, tutored abroad in the ways of smoking, who rescinded the Russian ban on tobacco. The snuff-taking Pope Benedict XIII performed similar offices for the Church. (The Vatican opened its own tobacco factory in 1790.) Leaders' vices had a way of becoming the official vices, the devil's corollary of *cujus regio, ejus religio*. If not legally sanctioned, they were at least more likely to be tolerated. The Chinese campaign against opium, for example, made less progress in areas where key officials themselves indulged.[13]

The personal use of alcohol and tobacco, as well as caffeine, was extremely widespread among western politicians in the first half of the twentieth cen-

·THE FALL OF THE DESERT SHEIK·

Resistance, American style: lynching the Prohibition bluenose. The cartoon correctly predicts the demise of Prohibition as a result of the 1932 election.

tury. Picture Churchill, Roosevelt, and Stalin seated together at Yalta: hardly a crew to do battle against alcohol and tobacco. Harry Anslinger, who smoked and drank Jack Daniels ("cheers you up on a bad day"), ended up with a cane and an oxygen tank. The professional classes were hardly more abstemious, particularly with respect to tobacco. So long as ministers, teachers, businessmen, captains of industry, and socialites promoted smoking by their example, Harvey Wiley complained, "the habit will not be regarded as a moral obliquity."[14]

As for doctors, they had trouble seeing the lantern-slide images through the clouds of smoke at their meetings. Richard Doll was a pioneer of lung cancer epidemiology. He observed that, if anything, there was less concern about the health effects of cigarettes when he began his researches in 1948 than there had been a half-century before. Heavy smoking had dulled the collective sense of danger, both within and outside of the profession. (Asked if he were surprised by his own findings, Doll replied "very.") If exemplars like physicians were smoking, remarks the historian John Burnham, how could the public take seriously claims that the habit was harmful?

Burnham calls attention to another important trend, the use of alcohol and tobacco by celebrities. The decanter and cigarette were ubiquitous props in Hollywood films, which rarely depicted other forms of drug use. The first all-talking movie, *Lights of New York* (1928) was about bootlegging. By 1930 four-fifths of all American films depicted at least some drinking. (I have found no comparable estimate for the European cinema, though alcohol and tobacco were hardly absent from the works of René Clair, Jean Renoir, and their contemporaries.) One M-G-M director, Clarence Brown, remarked that the movies, by showing the immense role liquor played in American life despite Prohibition, helped change public opinion on the question. At a minimum, movie stars' smoking and drinking valorized tobacco and alcohol use, undermining Victorian scruples and allaying doubts about their healthfulness.[15]

Popular Resistance: The Case of the Soviet Union

Elite conduct, in short, reinforced and perpetuated the alcohol/tobacco double standard for most of the twentieth century. But what happened when elite practice and ideology ran against, rather than with, the grain of popular custom? The Soviet experience with alcohol control provides an excellent example—actually, two—of how popular resistance can frustrate official attempts to limit consumption even in a command economy.

When the Bolsheviks came to power in 1917, they attempted to close wine and spirits factories and forbade the manufacture and sale of beverage alcohol. "We shall never go back to vodka," boasted Nikolai Semashko, commissar for health, who envisioned prohibition on American lines. Drunkenness, like the state itself, would wither away. In 1923 Leon Trotsky declared that the

Bolshevik ban on vodka was one of the "two big facts" that had "set a new stamp on working-class life," the other being the eight-hour day.

By the late 1920s the government had ended prohibition and restored the *monopol'ka*, or state liquor outlet. Prisons, police, and threats of execution had all failed to overcome the Russian thirst for liquor. Partly it was a matter of cultural inertia. Drinking, especially binge drinking, was entrenched in all classes and both sexes to a degree unmatched in Europe. Partly it was a matter of survival. Peasants, desperate for income, diverted their harvests to making *samogon* (home brew). And partly it was a matter of revenue. Better to finance socialism through the vodka monopoly, Nikolai Bukharin reasoned, than drown in an ocean of *samogon*. In September 1930 Stalin ordered officials to "aim openly and directly for the maximum output." They did. By 1940 more shops in the Soviet Union sold drink than sold meat, fruit, and vegetables.[16]

And so alcoholism and public drunkenness became as much facts of life under the Communists as they had been under the Romanovs. Alcohol consumption, including both state-produced beverages and *samogon*, increased 4.4 percent per year during the postwar era. Per capita consumption of absolute alcohol quadrupled between the 1940s and the early 1980s, by which time upwards of 15 percent of the population were alcoholics. The government covered up these trends, dropping vodka production from its statistical yearbook in 1963. It neglected, however, to omit the consumption of sugar, the preferred base ingredient for *samogon*. Annual per capita consumption rose from under 62 pounds in 1960 to over 94 in 1979. Most of the increase went into stills.

Under Leonid Brezhnev, the Soviet Union effectively became a government of drunks, by drunks, and for drunks. Politicians and diplomats were afraid to drink with the premier, whose capacity for vodka was legendary. The one man who could match him, Konstantin Chernenko, died of cirrhosis of the liver. Once Brezhnev was driving back from the Zavidovo hunting lodge, Andrei Gromyko at his side. Gromyko was complaining that drunkenness had reached a catastrophic level; it was affecting every aspect of Soviet life. Brezhnev patiently listened to Gromyko's arguments, then abruptly said, "But you know, Andrei, a Russian cannot do without it . . ." Gromyko immediately dropped the subject.

But he had been right to raise it. Drunkenness was by then a society-wide calamity, increasing premature mortality, divorce, mental retardation, road deaths, industrial accidents, crime, and accidental fires. Ground crews drained the de-icing fluid from military aircraft, distilled it, drank the alcohol, and replaced it with water to disguise the theft. Pilots who had to use their de-icing tanks at high altitudes were in serious trouble. Researchers estimated that an alcoholic worker was 36 percent less efficient than an abstemious one, a figure equivalent to 93 lost workdays a year. Miniaturization and computerization worsened the problem. Drunk and hung-over workers could not make or maintain complex electronic systems. In 1985 a group of scientists added up the social costs of alcoholism and came up with an annual figure of 180 billion rubles, about four times the sum derived from the sale of drink.[17]

The reform-minded Mikhail Gorbachev was a moderate drinker. He was advised and influenced by people (not least his wife, Raisa) who thought alcoholism a national curse. In 1985 the government launched a campaign aimed at progressively restricting the supply of alcohol: less production, diminished hours, fewer retail outlets. The city of Chelyabinsk went from 150 wine shops to only 4 in just two years. Officials ordered vineyards destroyed, liquor factories closed. Crime, absenteeism, and accidents decreased. Total per capita consumption, including bootlegging, fell nearly one-quarter, an unprecedented decline.

Yet by 1988 the campaign was dead. The restrictions had produced long lines—the average Muscovite was spending 90 hours a year waiting to buy liquor—as well as widespread bootlegging and poisoning. Those who drank lacquer polish turned a violet hue. Some 11,000 died of methanol and related poisonings in 1987, a figure nearly equal to Soviet deaths in the Afghanistan War. Samogon, which accounted for perhaps a third of total consumption before 1985, now accounted for two-thirds. Gorbachev's policies prompted growing criticism, freely voiced in the era of glasnost. "I personally think the measures are too much," complained Vladimir Yamnikov, manager of the giant Kristall distillery. "Nature is against emptiness."[18]

A few Soviet officials still championed the cause. Yegor Ligachev, an ardent dry, thought abandoning the restrictions and reverting to a high-tax policy—by 1989 the state was taking in more than it had in 1984—was tragic and immoral. He likened the surge in licit liquor consumption after 1988 to a "slow Chernobyl." Gorbachev, derided as the "Mineral Water Secretary," also defended the campaign, though he admitted to errors in its implementation. One problem was ambiguity. Neither the political leadership nor the new national temperance society ever decided whether abstinence or moderate drinking was the correct line. Though such equivocation was hardly with-

Resistance, Russian style: "Bring back the good old Brezhnev days!" The translation obscures a pun: *prezhnie vremena* ("good old times") has become *Brezhnie vremena*. The motto on the flag is "vodka." 1989 poster by D. Oboznenko.

out precedent in Russian history—Nicholas II's finance ministry had used monopoly profits to finance both distilleries and temperance societies—it had the fatal result of allowing local bureaucrats to set their own agendas. Some imposed the new regime too enthusiastically. Others ignored the central directives, content to mind the still in the party headquarters' basement. Charges of hypocrisy dogged the campaign.

So did a sense of unfairness. Millions of ordinary citizens drank to combat the boredom and sterility of life in a communist state. Their masters wanted them to stay sober and work harder, but for whose benefit? The stores were bare of consumer goods. The promised sports and cultural amenities had not appeared. Life was bleak. Honest, sober labor to enrich those who were neither was a form of slavery, as one worker put it. "Who needs socialism without beer?" jeered another.[19]

Or who needed a bankrupt, *Mafiya*-riddled republic? Boris Yeltsin's government, chronically short of revenue, continued the high-tax policy of the last Gorbachev years. Bootlegging flourished, though for the traditional tax-avoidance motive. Resurgent consumption, binge drinking, and widespread alcohol poisoning, combined with heavy smoking, drastically affected Russian mortality. Male life expectancy, which had been increasing during the dry era, declined more than six years between 1990 and 1994. Yet neither the mounting casualties nor the publicity surrounding them deterred Russian drinking. "Many citizens," summed up one psychologist, "consider alcohol use a cultural characteristic of the Slavic people bordering on a birthright."[20]

What happened in the Soviet Union was the collision of a seemingly irresistible historical force, rationalization, with a seemingly immovable object, Russian drinking. The object won, showing that a pattern of drug use can become so entrenched in a culture that it is impossible to permanently suppress and delegitimate it. A clue to this is the near-absence of minority scapegoats in the mid-1980s anti-alcohol campaign. Although a few pointed accusing fingers at Jews for "alcoholizing" Soviet society, the drys lacked the credible equivalent of drunken immigrants or Chinese opium smokers. The socially, ethnically, and ideologically privileged class, male Slavic workers, was the one most given to intoxication.

Illicit Drugs: The Politics of De-escalation

The opposite is true of the users of cannabis, cocaine, and other illicit drugs. They make for politically softer—indeed, attractive—targets. Despite the vogue among some affluent youth in the mid-1960s through early 1980s, illicit drug use remains concentrated among street children, dropouts, petty criminals, prostitutes, the jobless, and other socially marginal groups. Half of Pakistan's heroin addicts come from the poorest 20 percent of the population. Ninety percent of Bombay's ragpickers are reportedly addicted to "brown sugar." Most Chinese heroin addicts are male, young, single, and poorly educated. About half are unemployed when they enter treatment.[21]

Addicts to heroin and other illicit drugs are caught in a social trap. They tend to stay unemployed because employers, reasonably, want nothing to do with them. An interview with a 31-year-old heroin addict, who worked for the federal government in the bygone days of the IBM Selectric typewriter, shows why:

> I working for the Department of Energy, in all kind of big old government buildings. My ID get me through the door so I just flash my ID on the guard. Walk past him and usually the door be open in the building. . . . I know a guy that buys IBM typewriters. The ball that goes around. You don't have to steal the whole typewriter. You just gotta be patient and get them balls. . . . Take fifty of them and the dude gives you four dollars a ball. So that's fifty times four, that two hundred dollars.

And 1,300 dollars for the government to replace them. Theft, accidents, and legal liability give employers every incentive to avoid illicit drug users, and urine tests give them the means of their detection. Those who fail or avoid the tests stay jobless and poor, and in their desperation keep using drugs—or trafficking in them. Lower-class users have long been the mainstays of illicit retail sales, with plenty of assistance from nonusing sociopaths. ("Wrong? What's wrong? . . . I ain't using the shit, I just sell drugs.") This fact, paradoxically, both strengthens the consensus for prohibition and makes it practically impossible to accomplish. For every peddler or body-packer arrested, there are several desperate or greedy enough to take his place. The prisons silt up. Taxes increase. DEA agents tape pictures of Pancho Villa above their cubicles and soldier on.[22]

The inconsistency, expense, violence, corruption, adulteration, accidental overdoses, and needle-transmitted infections attendant to an illicit drug policy have created an ongoing controversy, spawning referenda, polemics, and polls from Bolivia to Switzerland. The controversy has been most intense in the United States, site of history's costliest drug war. Though officially declared in 1986, the origins of the American drug war date to the mid-1970s, when methadone maintenance and other therapeutic priorities of the Nixon administration fell into disfavor. Beginning with Nelson A. Rockefeller, who was maneuvering for a thrice-denied Republican presidential nomination, American politicians discovered that angry, anxious voters preferred get-tough measures like long minimum sentences—and that they were willing to foot the bill. By the mid-1990s, however, the drug war was consuming up-wards of 35 billion dollars a year. That sum equaled more than two-thirds the volume of illicit sales, then running about 50 billion dollars a year. Four hun-dred thousand persons were in prison or jail on drug charges. Yet heroin and cocaine remained cheap and available. Doubts about the wisdom and justice of such a campaign inevitably provoked a backlash.[23]

The most extreme form of the backlash has been the call for legalization. A form of reactionary libertarianism, combining elements of left- and right-wing ideology, legalization would reset the policy clock by more than a hun-dred years. Heroin, cannabis, and other prohibited drugs would be legally available to adult purchasers, just as laudanum, patent medicines, and coca wines were in the nineteenth century. Fears that adult access, however re-stricted, would lead to excessive addiction and diversion have so far stymied the proposal, both in the United States and elsewhere. One 1997 survey, taken in Vienna, showed only 6 percent in favor of legalization, 84 percent opposed.[24]

The less extreme form of the backlash has been the advocacy of harm re-duction. Often attacked as a haven and stalking horse for legalizers, the harm-reduction movement is in fact historically antecedent to the modern legalization campaign. Rooted in the marijuana and methadone wars of the 1970s, it draws its adherents and ideas from many sources. Advocates differ over particular issues, such as the cost-effectiveness of heroin maintenance, but share certain common tendencies. They stress demand reduction over supply reduction. They urge the depoliticization of drug abuse and the sub-stitution of treatment programs for criminal sanctions, which are considered inappropriate and unduly expensive. They favor sterile injection equipment for those who will not remain abstinent, and indefinite methadone mainte-nance. (No more missing typewriter balls.) They are resolutely non-judgmental, skeptical of absolute prohibitions, and tolerant of medical pre-scription and decriminalization experiments. They would reschedule canna-bis and perhaps other drugs from the top restrictive categories.

The harm-reduction agenda has provoked only slightly less controversy than legalization. Conservatives who believe that scriptural injunctions and moral outrage are sufficient grounds for prohibitory legislation reject it out of hand. "Knowledge that an activity is taking place," as Robert Bork put it, "is a harm to those who find it profoundly immoral." These feelings are not confined to zealots. Certain practices—Michael Massing offers the example of handing sterile needles to a visibly pregnant woman, no questions asked—

might give pause to anyone. Harm reduction saves lives, but it is also a moral eyesore.[25]

And thus it is politically vulnerable. Mainstream politicians have been quick to make common cause with moral and religious conservatives on drug policy. The harder the line, the better. "Drug education and treatment have gained a name as a wimp activity," Representative John Conyers explained. "If you favor these things, you're a softy. When these proposals come up in Congress, most members want to know, before they vote, which one is the toughest. It's sort of, 'I don't know if this is going to work, but nobody is going to blame me for not being tough.'" One South Australian politician dramatically cast his tie-breaking vote in favor of a marijuana de-criminalization bill, only to be greeted with cries of "Shame! Shame!" George Soros, the international financier who has spent millions trying to steer drug policy in the direction of harm reduction, admits that few politicians have dared to stand up. "If they touch the issue, it's like touching a third rail."[26]

Much of the electricity in the third rail is supplied by middle-class parents, politically important constituents who are concerned with the danger to their children posed by cannabis and other illicit drugs. Drug prohibitions may produce heavy social costs, but they do so only in the aggregate. The heaviest burdens fall on poor communities where the users, dealers, and police street sweeps are concentrated. Affluent and suburban voters see aggressive enforcement as protecting their own families. In supporting firm sanctions against trafficking and use they consider themselves to be acquiring a kind of insurance, the costs of which are absorbed by people who shouldn't be behaving like that anyway.[27]

Not all opposition to harm reduction is the product of resentment, political calculation, and class interest. Secular hawks, drug-abuse experts like Robert DuPont, have challenged harm reduction on its own public-health grounds. Decriminalization and needle exchange send the wrong signals to young people, they claim, heightening the chances of experimental use. Cannabis is still a dangerous gateway drug, and a harder drug than its apologists concede. Heroin and cocaine are highly seductive, difficult to control, and likely to lead to addiction. De-escalation of the war against these chemical enemies is tantamount to surrender.[28]

Against this formidable opposition, harm-reduction advocates have one big weapon: AIDS. Intravenous users, fearful of detection and short of cash, share injection equipment and drugs. In Vietnam they gather in slum rooms without running water or sanitary facilities, where a dealer mixes opium or heroin solution in a communal pot. Using the same needle and syringe, he injects up to 50 customers from a single batch, with no cleaning in between. Drug injectors made up 70 percent of Vietnam's officially diagnosed HIV cases in 1997. Shooting-gallery conditions and HIV rates were not much different in Malaysia, Myanmar, and the southwest Chinese provinces.

Recognition that intravenous drug use was a prolific source of HIV infection galvanized public health officials around the world. Robert Haemmig, a Bern physician, noted that although the Swiss had geared treatment toward abstinence in the early 1980s, the lethality of AIDS forced them to rethink the policy. People shooting drugs might very well quit in the future, but there would not be much of a future if they contracted HIV. Getting them out of the public toilets and into more hygienic surroundings was imperative, both for their own health and to prevent the spread of HIV to the general population. By 1990 sterile needles and syringes were widely available, not only in Switzerland but in Britain, Canada, Denmark, Germany, Italy, Holland, and Norway. They were available on a more limited basis in France, Spain, and Sweden. Among the western industrial nations only the United States, its drug policy hostage to its culture war, officially barred such practices. Harm-reduction guerillas carried them out anyway.[29]

Licit Drugs: The Politics of Escalation

If schemes to de-escalate the war on illicit drugs have caused controversy, so have efforts to escalate it against licit drugs. This is the other side of the great policy debate of the last three decades. Many public health authorities and drug-abuse experts have argued that the government should increase the regulatory burden on alcohol and tobacco. Consumption of these "underscheduled" drugs is bad for the collective health and conducive to other forms of drug abuse. (Children's unrestricted access to caffeine has also begun to draw scrutiny.) Officials, in this view, should recognize tobacco and alcohol for what science shows them to be, dangerous psychoactive drugs. They should adjust their positions on the axes of policy—regulation, taxes, and penalties—to better reflect actual risk and social costs. Ban ads. Run counter-ads. Raise excises. Lower the legal blood alcohol content for drivers. Fund more treatment. Reduce alcohol consumption. Engineer a smoke-free future.

Proposals of this sort are incompatible with the libertarian strain of legalization. They are not, however, incompatible with harm reduction. In fact, many harm-reducers have called for intensified efforts against licit drugs. In the lingo of drug policy, they are "owls," as opposed to criminalizing "hawks" and legalizing "doves." The owls seek a convergent public health policy, one that treats licit and illicit drugs more evenhandedly: no more convenience-store signs declaring "this is a drug-free workplace." Owls believe that a policy of convergence, adjusted for local conditions and priorities, offers the most sensible approach to managing what has plainly become an intractable social problem.

That does not mean it will happen. The inertial forces—too often discounted by public-health rationalists, impatient like all children of the Enlightenment—are very strong. Of late, however, the reformers have had some luck with tobacco: ad bans and restrictions, tax increases, multi-billion-dollar legal settlements, and a string of embarrassing disclosures about industry dissimulation. The World Bank, which loaned 1.5 billion dollars for tobacco development projects between 1974 and 1988, has reversed course and no longer invests in tobacco production. Smoke-free environments have gone global. At the insistence of nonsmokers, the Tupac Amaru hostages, seized in Lima in December 1996, sorted themselves into smoking and nonsmoking sections. "The Japanese really smoked a lot," one remembered, "but they were all in a room together so it was not so bad." Desk-bound Americans lack their own room for smoking. They puff away in the wintry out-of-doors, consigned to localized Siberian exile.[30]

The tobacco siege is very much a reversal of fortune. In the first half of the twentieth century alcohol, not tobacco, was the most controversial licit drug. Alcoholics Anonymous, founded in 1935 as a fellowship for the rescue and renewal of alcoholics, simply disregarded smoking. Its co-founders, Bill Wilson and Dr. Bob Smith, both smoked heavily and died of cigarette-related illnesses. As late as 1955 one physician—of all things, a Park Avenue pediatrician—protested that there were "no scientific grounds for believing smoking harmful. All I can say is, if I had a spare $2,000 kicking around, I would still invest it in cigarette stock." No more. Epidemiological and scientific evidence has established beyond any reasonable doubt that smoking is the most widespread and lethal form of addiction in the world. No precautions can eliminate the danger. Cigarettes, as the trial lawyers say, are deadly hazards when used as intended.[31]

Alcohol presents a more complicated picture. Compared with tobacco, it has several liabilities: intoxication, slurred speech, lost balance, impaired visual acuity. Worry if your airline pilot has been drinking, Thomas Schelling

By the 1920s and 1930s cigarette smoking, sexy, slinky, and the height of fashion, was catching on with growing numbers of middle-class men and women. Late in the century the process reversed itself, as cigarette smoking became increasingly *déclassé* in health-conscious western societies. Drawing by Russell Patterson, sometime in the 1920s.

observes, not if he has been smoking.[32] Alcohol as a drug of the many, as opposed to alcoholism as a chronic disease of the few, has attracted increasing scientific scrutiny since 1975. Renewed concerns about drinking's social harms, such as car crashes, have fueled a "new temperance movement"—a more narrowly secular enterprise than its nineteenth-century predecessor, which tended to conflate salvation and rationalization. Yet, despite these developments, alcohol is less vulnerable to regulatory escalation than tobacco. It will likely remain so in western societies in the near future.

One reason is that *moderate* drinking, such as a glass of wine with a daily meal, may lower the risk of coronary heart disease. It may also give protection against stroke, adult-onset diabetes, osteoporosis, and rheumatoid arthritis, among other illnesses. Whether it is the beverage itself or the healthy lifestyle of the moderate drinker that confers these benefits is not clear. What is clear is that many people can drink moderately with little fear of serious health consequences. The same cannot be said of smoking—a key distinction in aging western societies grown increasingly health-conscious and risk-averse.[33]

Humanity also has long experience of alcohol, and has evolved all manner of rules and taboos to reduce the harmfulness of drinking. Civilized men drink diluted wine. Don't drink on an empty stomach. Some cultures, such as the Italian and Jewish, have been conspicuously successful in integrating drinking in salubrious ways into everyday life and ritual. (Others, such as the Russian, have been conspicuously unsuccessful.) Cultural norms can likewise mitigate some of tobacco's harms. Don't smoke in bed. Don't smoke if it annoys others. Yet it now appears that tobacco is so intrinsically toxic as to defy safe integration. Even Philip Morris publicly admitted as much about cigarettes in 1999.[34]

Tobacco, finally, is becoming a losers' drug. Alcohol continues to be broadly popular outside the Islamic world, particularly in western Europe, where three-quarters of the adults drink. Smoking, however, has visibly declined among the educated classes in the United States, Britain, and other western countries. It persists as a "culturally normal activity"—as the historian Virginia Berridge puts it—mainly among the poorest elements of society, those most resistant to public health sanctions and appeals. Lower-class concentration has increased the political vulnerability of tobacco, much as it did for narcotics a century ago.[35]

Convergence, then, seems to be a more realistic prospect for tobacco than for alcohol. The days of prescription sale may not be far off. But this should be taken only as a summation of current trends, not a prediction. Technological change has a way of reshuffling the drug-policy deck. The development of safer nicotine-delivery devices would alter the situation, just as a vaccine for AIDS might take the steam out of harm reduction.

One thing, however, is not likely to change. It is the political awareness of the dangers of exposing people to psychoactive substances for which, it is increasingly clear, they lack evolutionary preparation. Psychoactive technology, like military technology, has outstripped natural history. The question is what to do about it. The answer, whatever it may be, is not a return to a minimally regulated drug market. The movement toward restrictive categorization was fundamentally progressive in nature. Like most reforms, it was partly motivated by self-interest, tainted by prejudice, and imperfect in its execution. But its basic premise was both correct and humane. The drive to maximize profit—individual, corporate, and state—underlay the explosive global increase in drug use. Checking the increase meant restricting commerce and profits, which meant regulatory laws and treaties. The task now is to adjust the system, eliminating its worst concomitants and plugging its most conspicuous gaps.

Plugging those gaps will not be easy, particularly in consumer societies. Pleasure is to consumerism what winning is to sports: an imperative pursued by all means short of cheating with certain chemicals. Even if policymakers (or athletic governing bodies) succeed in scheduling drugs more rationally, they cannot avoid the fundamental contradiction. The emergent global capitalist system—McWorld—depends heavily on the commercial exploitation of innate drives, such as sex or the taste for sweet and fatty foods. Its products are often dangerous, yet individuals are free to ignore, assume, or work around the risks. Advertisers systematically encourage them to do so for the sake of transient pleasures. The very essence of modern culture, as Daniel Bell remarked, is that of sovereign individuals "ransacking the world storehouse," casting aside traditional restraints in pursuit of self-fulfillment.[36] So why should certain drugs be off limits? Be happy and partake, except of the forbidden fruit, has always been a hard message to swallow. Genesis tells us that Adam and Eve could not abide by it in the old Eden. It is hard to imagine that our prospects are much better in today's new one.

BIBLIOGRAPHIC NOTE

ABBREVIATIONS

NOTES

ILLUSTRATION CREDITS

INDEX

Bibliographic Note

READERS WHO WISH to learn more about drugs in world history can consult several pioneering books and anthologies. A good place to begin is Wolfgang Schivelbusch's *Tastes of Paradise: A Social History of Spices, Stimulants, and Intoxicants*, trans. David Jacobson (New York: Pantheon, 1992). The book is lavishly illustrated and crisply written; its chief limitation is that it has little to say about the twentieth century. Paul B. Stares's *Global Habit: The Drug Problem in a Borderless World* (Washington, D.C.: Brookings Institution, 1996), is just the reverse: it offers much on drug trafficking and policy in the twentieth century, but nothing on the origins of the problem in the early modern period. Rudi Matthee, "Exotic Substances: The Introduction and Global Spread of Tobacco, Coffee, Cocoa, Tea, and Distilled Liquor, Sixteenth to Eighteenth Centuries," in *Drugs and Narcotics in History*, ed. Roy Porter and Mikuláš Teich (Cambridge: Cambridge U. Press, 1995), 24–51, is good on early developments but stops at 1800. Another 1995 anthology, *Consuming Habits: Drugs in History and Anthropology*, ed. Jordan Goodman, Paul E. Lovejoy, and Andrew Sherratt (London: Routledge, 1995), contains several fine contributions. However, except for Sherratt's introduction and essay and a brief afterword by Goodman and Lovejoy, these deal *seriatim* with particular drugs in particular countries or regions.

Lewis Lewin's still valuable *Phantastica: A Classic Survey on the Use and Abuse of Mind-Altering Plants*, trans. P. H. A. Wirth (Rochester, Vt.: Park Street Press, 1998; first pub. 1924) is organized on an encyclopedic, drug-by-drug basis. Gregory A. Austin's *Perspectives on the History of Psychoactive Substance Use* (Rockville, Md.: National Institute on Drug Abuse, 1978) lacks an integrated narrative, though it offers a useful chronology and bibliography. Richard Rudgley's *Essential Substances: A Cultural History of Intoxicants in Society* (New York: Kodansha International, 1993) takes an anthropological approach and focuses on drug use in traditional and prehistoric cultures, with some attention given to global psychoactive commerce in the last chapter. Rudgley's *The Encyclopedia of Psychoactive Substances* (New York: St. Martin's Press, 1999) is also geared toward traditional societies; it excludes alcohol for reasons of space. Kenneth Pomeranz and Steven Topik devote the third chapter of *The World That Trade Created: Society, Culture, and the World Economy, 1400–the Present* (Armonk, N.Y.: M. E. Sharpe, 1999) to the "economic culture of drugs," though they likewise omit alcoholic beverages. Norman Taylor's *Plant Drugs That Changed the World* (New York: Dodd, Mead, 1965); Edward Hyams's *Plants in the Service of Man: 10,000 Years of Domestication* (Philadelphia: J. B. Lippincott, 1972); and Henry Hobhouse's *Seeds of Change: Five Plants That Transformed Mankind* (New York: Harper and Row, 1986) are all global in scope and deal with transformative themes, but do not focus on psychoactive plants per se. Neither does Walter Sneader's *Drug Discovery: The Evolution of Modern Medicines* (Chichester: Wiley, 1985), though it provides a wealth of detail on the discovery, development, and chemistry of important drugs.

Researchers particularly interested in tobacco should visit the Special Collections Library (SCL) of Duke University, home of the Tobacco Collection, Duke Papers, and J. Walter Thompson Co. Archives, as well as the State Historical Society of Wisconsin, which houses the Hill Papers. The College of Physicians of Philadelphia Library (CPPL) offers an outstanding collection of rare books, international journals, and medical trade ephemera. Located in Arlington, Virginia, the Drug Enforcement Administration (DEA) Library—once used by Timothy Leary—has a large, internationally oriented collection of government documents and drug books, reflecting both official and critical views. It maintains a superb vertical filing system with thousands of reports, articles, speeches, intelligence summaries, clippings, and translations of hard-to-come-by foreign newspaper and periodical sources. The Kremers Reference Files (KRF) at the F. B. Power Pharmaceutical Library, Madison, Wisconsin, are even more voluminous. Though broadly devoted to the history of pharmacy rather than to psychoactive drugs, they offer a wealth of visual and printed material in several languages. Like the DEA files, they are periodically updated, well organized, and readily accessible. For more on this unique resource see Gregory J. Higby and Elaine C. Stroud, "Pharmaco-

Historical Resources in Madison, Wisconsin," part 3, *Pharmacy in History* 30 (1988): 157–162.

Though most of my research was of the lone-scholar-in-the-stacks variety, I found Lexis-Nexis Academic Universe to be a convenient source of information. Its large database provided access to a range of international documents, periodicals, and newspapers that no single library could match. However, the page numbers of the electronic version did not always correspond to those of the original text, whose pagination was often omitted or incomplete. To avoid confusion, I have used the abbreviation "LN" instead of page numbers for Lexis-Nexis sources. For electronic documents other than those from Lexis-Nexis I have simply cited the URL (Internet address) and given the date of access.

Works on drug history and policy, like drugs themselves, are increasingly available through the Internet. The Media Awareness Project Drug Links Page, *http://www.mapinc.org/dpr.htm*, 6 October 1999, conveniently lists several dozen relevant sites. Like much else on the Internet, these vary greatly in quality and ideology.

Abbreviations

AA	*Ashes to Ashes: The History of Smoking and Health,* ed. S. Lock et al. (Amsterdam: Rodopi, 1998)
BJA	*British Journal of Addiction*
BN	*Bulletin on Narcotics*
BP	Bruce Barton Papers, State Historical Society of Wisconsin, Madison
CC	*Cannabis and Culture,* ed. Vera Rubin (The Hague: Mouton, 1975)
CH	*Consuming Habits: Drugs in History and Anthropology,* ed. Jordan Goodman et al. (London: Routledge, 1995)
CPPL	College of Physicians of Philadelphia Library
DEA	Drug Enforcement Administration
DNH	*Drugs and Narcotics in History,* ed. Roy Porter and Mikuláš Teich (Cambridge: Cambridge U. Press, 1995)
G.P.O.	Government Printing Office
HP	John W. Hill Papers, State Historical Society of Wisconsin, Madison
IJA	*International Journal of the Addictions*
J.	Journal
JAMA	*Journal of the American Medical Association*
JWT	J. Walter Thompson Co. Archives, SCL
KP	Lawrence Kolb Papers, History of Medicine Division, National Library of Medicine, Bethesda, Maryland
KRF	Kremers Reference Files, Pharmacy Library, University of Wisconsin, Madison
KSHS	Kansas State Historical Society
LC	Library of Congress
LN	Lexis-Nexis Academic Universe

MTE   Medical Trade Ephemera, CPPL

NEJM   *New England Journal of Medicine*

NYT   *New York Times*

PMCAB   *Production, Marketing and Consumption of Alcoholic Beverages since the Late Middle Ages*, ed. Erik Aerts et al. (Leuven: Leuven U. Press, 1990)

SCL   Special Collections Library, Duke University, Durham, North Carolina

SUM   *Substance Use and Misuse*

U.   University

VF   Vertical Files, Drug Enforcement Administration Library, Arlington, Virginia

Notes

Introduction: The Psychoactive Revolution

1. Case records of the Philadelphia Committee for the Clinical Study of Opium Addiction (TS, 1925–1929), vol. 5, CPPL. "Anthony" is an alias.
2. John Parascandola, "The Drug Habit: The Association of the Word 'Drug' with Abuse in American History," in *DNH*, 163–164.
3. Francis B. Thurber, *Coffee: From Plantation to Cup. A Brief History of Coffee Production and Consumption* (New York: American Grocer Publishing Association, 1881), 53–59, 240.
4. Robert Ardrey, *The Social Contract: A Personal Inquiry into the Evolutionary Sources of Order and Disorder* (New York: Athencum, 1970), 93.
5. *Statistical Abstract for the United Kingdom*, no. 32 (London: Eyre and Spottiswoode, 1885), 9, 12.

1. The Big Three: Alcohol, Tobacco, and Caffeine

1. Tim Unwin, *Wine and the Vine: An Historical Geography of Viticulture and the Wine Trade* (London: Routledge, 1991), chs. 1–6; *The Origins and Ancient History of Wine*, ed. Patrick McGovern et al. (Amsterdam: Gordon and Breach, 1995), intro. and part IV; Charles B. Heiser, Jr., *Seed to Civilization: The Story of Food*, new ed. (Cambridge, Mass.: Harvard U. Press, 1990), 192 (Bible count).
2. George Vernadsky, *Kievan Russia* (New Haven: Yale U. Press, 1948), 307–308; D. B. Grigg, *The Agricultural Systems of the World: An Evolutionary Approach* (Cambridge: Cambridge U. Press, 1974), 164; Andrew Sherratt, "Alcohol and Its Alternatives: Symbol and Substance in Pre-Industrial Cultures," in *CH*, 17–18, 20–24.
3. Stephen Braun, *Buzz: The Science and Lore of Alcohol and Caffeine* (New

York: Oxford U. Press, 1996), 34–35; Bert L. Vallee, "Alcohol in the Western World," *Scientific American* 278 (June 1998): 80–85.

4. Henry Hobhouse, "New World, Vineyard to the Old," in *Seeds of Change: A Quincentennial Commemoration*, ed. Herman J. Viola and Carolyn Margolis (Washington, D.C.: Smithsonian Institution Press, 1991), 60–69; Unwin, *Wine and the Vine*, 216–219, 245–248, 250–252, 296–304; Thomas Pinney, *A History of Wine in America: From the Beginnings to Prohibition* (Berkeley: U. of California Press, 1989), chs. 1, 9–13; C. Louis Leipoldt, *300 Years of Cape Wine* (Capetown: Tafelberg, 1974), 1–5.

5. Lucille H. Brockway, *Science and Colonial Expansion: The Role of the British Royal Botanical Gardens* (New York: Academic Press, 1979); Sam McKinney, *Bligh: A True Account of Mutiny Aboard His Majesty's Ship Bounty* (Camden, Maine: International Marine Publishing, 1989), 16–17, 71, 182.

6. C. Anne Wilson, "Water of Life: Its Beginnings and Early History," in *"Liquid Nourishment": Potable Foods and Stimulating Drinks*, ed. C. Anne Wilson (Edinburgh: Edinburgh U. Press, 1993), 142–164; John J. McCusker, "Distilling and Its Implications for the Atlantic World of the Seventeenth and Eighteenth Centuries," in *PMCAB*, 7–19; Unwin, *Wine and the Vine*, 236–237; Rudi Matthee, "Exotic Substances: The Introduction and Global Spread of Tobacco, Coffee, Cocoa, Tea, and Distilled Liquor, Sixteenth to Eighteenth Centuries," in *DNH*, 44; Mark Keller et al., *A Dictionary of Words about Alcohol*, 2nd ed. (New Brunswick: Rutgers Center of Alcohol Studies, 1982), 62, 111, 126–127.

7. Fernand Braudel, *Civilization and Capitalism, 15th–18th Century*, vol. 1: *The Structures of Everyday Life: The Limits of the Possible*, trans. Siân Reynolds (New York: Harper and Row, 1979), 231–249; Edward Kremers, "Agricultural Alcohol: Studies of Its Manufacture in Germany," *Bulletin of the U.S. Department of Agriculture*, no. 182 (1915): 1–17; L. K. Gluckman, "Alcohol and the Maori in Historic Perspective," *New Zealand Medical Journal* 79 (1974): 554.

8. Ian M. Ball, *Pitcairn: Children of Mutiny* (Boston: Little, Brown, 1973), 111; Francis X. Hezel, *The First Taint of Civilization: A History of the Caroline and Marshall Islands in Pre-Colonial Days, 1521–1885* (Honolulu: U. of Hawaii Press, 1983), 130 ("skill").

9. Gluckman, "Alcohol and the Maori," 555; "Use of Narcotics in Siam," *Boston Medical and Surgical Journal* 31 (1844): 341.

10. Gregory A. Austin et al., *Alcohol in Western Society from Antiquity to 1800: A Chronological History* (Santa Barbara: ABC-Clio, 1985), xvi–xxv, 207; Hans

Jurgen Teuteberg and Jean-Louis Flandrin, "The Transformation of the European Diet," in *Food: A Culinary History from Antiquity to the Present*, ed. Flandrin et al., trans. Clarissa Botsford et al. (New York: Columbia U. Press, 1999), 453 (dilution); David Christian, "Alcohol and Primitive Accumulation in Tsarist Russia," in *PMCAB*, 33.

11. Stephen J. Kunitz and Jerrold E. Levy, "Changes in Alcohol Use among the Navajos and Other Indians of the American Southwest," in *DNH*, 134–135; Ruth C. Engs, "Cycles of Social Reform: Is the Current Anti-Alcohol Movement Cresting?" *J. of Studies on Alcohol* 58 (1997): 223–224; Wolfgang Schivelbusch, *Tastes of Paradise: A Social History of Spices, Stimulants, and Intoxicants*, trans. David Jacobson (New York: Pantheon, 1992), ch. 5; Craig MacAndrew and Robert B. Edgerton, *Drunken Comportment: A Social Explanation* (Chicago: Aldine, 1969).

12. This sketch of tobacco's diffusion relies on Jordan Goodman, *Tobacco in History: The Cultures of Dependence* (London: Routledge, 1993), chs. 3–4, 6; C. M. MacInnes, *The Early English Tobacco Trade* (London: Kegan Paul, 1926), 15–33; Mac Marshall, "An Overview of Drugs in Oceania," in *Drugs in Western Pacific Societies*, ed. Lamont Lindstrom (Lanham, Md.: U. Press of America, 1987), 31–32; Euan M. Scrimgeour, "Cigarette Smoking in Papua New Guinea," *New York State J. of Medicine* 85 (1985): 420; O. Comes, *Histoire, Géographie, Statistique du Tabac* (Naples: Typographie Coopérative, 1900), ch. 3; J. W. Purseglove, "The Origins and Migrations of Crops in Tropical Africa," in *Origins of African Plant Domestication*, ed. Jack R. Harlan et al. (The Hague: Mouton, 1976), 296, 302; Matthee, "Exotic Substances," 26; and Braudel, *Structures of Everyday Life*, 261–264. "About 1590": Tobacco was not cultivated in Japan until 1605, but may have been introduced as a trade item much earlier. See Ernest M. Satow, "The Introduction of Tobacco into Japan," *Transactions of the Asiatic Society of Japan* 6 (1878): 68–84.

13. Allan Kulikoff, *Tobacco and Slaves: The Development of Southern Cultures in the Chesapeake, 1680–1800* (Chapel Hill: U. of North Carolina Press, 1986), 31–32; Jacob M. Price, "The Tobacco Adventure to Russia: Enterprise, Politics, and Diplomacy in the Quest for a Northern Market for English Colonial Tobacco," *Transactions of the American Philosophical Society*, n.s. 51 (1961): 1–120.

14. Count [Egon Caesar] Corti, *A History of Smoking*, trans. Paul England (New York: Harcourt, Brace, 1932), 101 (Gustavus Adolphus); Jan Rogoziński, *Smokeless Tobacco in the Western World, 1550–1950* (New York: Praeger, 1990), ch. 3; C. Stefanis et al., "Sociocultural and Epidemiological Aspects of

Hashish Use in Greece," in *CC*, 315; Giel van Brussel, "Methadone Treatment by General Practitioners in Amsterdam," *Bulletin of the New York Academy of Medicine* 72 (1995): 349.

15. Corti, *History of Smoking*, chs. 5–10; L. Carrington Goodrich, "Early Prohibitions of Tobacco in China and Manchuria," *J. of the American Oriental Society* 58 (1938): 648–657; V. G. Kiernan, *Tobacco: A History* (London: Hutchinson Radius, 1991), remark on p. 227.

16. Goodman, *Tobacco in History*, chs. 4–5; Rogoziński, *Smokeless Tobacco*, chs. 5–6.

17. Rogoziński, *Smokeless Tobacco*, 83, 112; Francis Dowling, "The French Government Tobacco Factory at Issy, Near Paris," *JAMA* 53 (1909): 1171–73.

18. U.S. Senate, Committee on Commerce, *"Titanic" Disaster: Subcommittee Hearings*, 62nd Congress, 2nd session (Washington, D.C.: G. P. O, 1912), 424–425; Cassandra Tate, *Cigarette Wars: The Triumph of "the Little White Slaver"* (New York: Oxford U. Press, 1999); *Tobacco Industry Annual Review, 1930* (New York: Charles D. Barney, 1930), quotations on pp. 11, 21.

19. *A Short History of the R. J. Reynolds Tobacco Company* (Winston-Salem: R. J. Reynolds, 1961), 3 (15,000 a second); U.S. Department of Agriculture, Foreign Agricultural Service, Tobacco Division, "World of Tobacco" [map] (Washington, D.C.: G. P. O., 1957), n.p. (tonnage and production breakdown); *Agrarwirtschaftsatlas der Erde in Vergleichender Darstellung*, ed. Bruno Skibbe (Gotha: Hermann Haack, 1958), 50–51 (export flows); Elizabeth Marshall Thomas, *The Tribe of Tiger: Cats and Their Culture* (New York: Simon and Schuster, 1994), 153 (Bushmen); World Health Organization, "The Tobacco Epidemic: A Global Public Health Emergency," *http://www.who/int/inf-fs/en/fact118.html*, 29 June 2000 (prevalence data, 5.5 billion); Tom Stevenson, "BAT Draws on Massive Third World Craving," *The Independent*, 7 March 1996, LN (pack a week).

20. Kenneth Silverman and Roland R. Griffiths, "Caffeine," *Encyclopedia of Drugs and Alcohol*, vol. 1 (New York: Simon and Schuster/Macmillan, 1995), 183; E. N. Anderson, *The Food of China* (New Haven: Yale U. Press, 1988), 138. Calling cacao a caffeine plant is a slight misnomer. Its chief alkaloid is theobromine, with only traces of caffeine present. However, theobromine is similar in molecular structure and stimulating effect to caffeine, of which it is essentially a milder version. (Theobromine differs from caffeine only in the replacement of the $-N-CH_3$ group by $-N-H$.) It therefore does no great harm to include cacao under the heading of plants that yield caffeinated beverages or foods.

21. *Coffee: The World Cup* (Washington, D.C.: International Coffee Organiza-

tion, 1979), 10 (trailed only oil); Ralph S. Hattox, *Coffee and Coffeehouses: The Origins of a Social Beverage in the Medieval Near East* (Seattle: U. of Washington Press, 1985); Rudi Matthee, "Coffee in Safavid Iran: Commerce and Consumption," *Journal of the Economic and Social History of the Orient* 37 (1994): 1–32; William H. Ukers, *All About Coffee*, 2nd ed. (New York: Tea and Coffee Trade Journal, 1935).

22. O. Guelliot, "Du Caféisme Chronique," *Union Médicale et Scientifique du Nord-est* 9 (1885): 238 ("most illustrious"); Simon Schama, *Citizens: A Chronicle of the French Revolution* (New York: Knopf, 1989), 382 (Desmoulins).

23. Jean Leclant, "Coffee and Cafés in Paris, 1644–1693," in *Food and Drink in History: Selections from the Annales Economies, Sociétés, Civilisations*, vol. 5, ed. Robert Forster and Orest Ranum, trans. Elborg Forster and Patricia M. Ranum (Baltimore: Johns Hopkins U. Press, 1979), 89–91; Richard M. Gilbert, *Caffeine: The Most Popular Stimulant* (New York: Chelsea House, 1986), 77.

24. Jordan Goodman, "Excitantia: Or, How Enlightenment Europe Took to Soft Drugs," in *CH*, 126 (poundage estimates); G. J. Knaap, "Coffee for Cash: The Dutch East India Company and the Expansion of Coffee Cultivation in Java, Ambon, and Ceylon, 1700–1730," in *Trading Companies in Asia, 1600–1830*, ed. J. Van Goor (Utrecht: HES Uitgevers, 1986), 33–49.

25. Michel-Rolph Trouillot, "Motion in the System: Coffee, Color, and Slavery in Eighteenth-Century Saint-Domingue," *Review* 5 (1982): 341; Steve Mirsky, "Coffee Talk," *Scientific American* 276 (May 1997): 30 (44 percent).

26. Winfred Blevins assisted by Ruth Valsing, *Dictionary of the American West* (New York: Facts on File, 1993), 9 ("don't"); *Coffee: The World Cup*, 22 (astronauts).

27. Ukers, *All About Coffee*, 102–103, 520–521; Robert Hewitt, Jr., *Coffee: Its History, Cultivation, and Uses* (New York: D. Appleton, 1872), 95–96 (duties); Mark Pendergrast, *Uncommon Grounds. The History of Coffee and How It Transformed Our World* (New York: Basic Books, 1999), chs. 2, 3, consumption stats on p. 46; Erik Aerts and Richard Unger, "Brewing in the Low Countries," in *PMCAB*, 96.

28. "3¢ Coffee Pays Off," *Drug Topics* clipping, 9 June 1969, in "Fountains, Soda—1966–1969," *Drug Topics* collection, KRF; *Coffee: The World Cup*, 6, 7 (30 seconds); William H. Ukers, *The Romance of Tea: An Outline History of Tea and Tea-Drinking through Sixteen Hundred Years* (New York: Knopf, 1936), 91 ("prenatal").

29. Ukers, *Romance of Tea*, 3–51; Elin McCoy and John Frederick Walker, *Coffee and Tea*, 3rd ed. (New York: Raines and Raines, 1991), chs. 8, 15; Sen

Sōshitsu XV, *The Japanese Way of Tea: From Its Origins in China to Sen Rikyū*, trans. V. Dixon Morris (Honolulu: U. of Hawaii Press, 1998), chs. 4–5; Carole Shammas, "Changes in English and Anglo-American Consumption from 1550 to 1800," in *Consumption and the World of Goods*, ed. John Brewer and Roy Porter (London: Routledge, 1993), 183–185; John Burnett, *Liquid Pleasures: A Social History of Drinks in Modern Britain* (London: Routledge, 1999), 65 (cup equivalency).

30. C. R. Harler, *The Culture and Marketing of Tea*, 2nd ed. (Oxford: Oxford U. Press, 1956), chs. 15–16 (stages); *China: Imperial Maritime Customs*, vol. 2, spec. ser. no. 11, *Tea, 1888* (Shanghai: Inspector General of Customs, 1889), 1–6, 110–120; John C. Evans, *Tea in China: The History of China's National Drink* (Westport, Conn.: Greenwood Press, 1992), 128–129; Burnett, *Liquid Pleasures*, 62 (Lipton).

31. Harler, *Culture and Marketing of Tea*, 218 (47 million); *Agrarwirtschaftsatlas*, ed. Skibbe, 54 (geographic distribution); Louis Lewin, *Phantastica: A Classic Survey on the Use and Abuse of Mind-Altering Plants*, trans. P. H. A. Wirth (Rochester, Vt.: Park Street Press, 1998), 229–235 (competition); Heiser, *Seed to Civilization*, 191 (20 million).

32. Sophie D. Coe and Michael D. Coe, *The True History of Chocolate* (London: Thames and Hudson, 1996), chs. 2–8, 1991 percentages on p. 201, De Sade quotation on p. 234; Schivelbusch, *Tastes of Paradise*, ch. 3; *Cocoa and Chocolate: A Short History of Their Production and Use*, new ed. (Dorchester, Mass.: Walter Baker, 1899), 7 (100 million estimate); Allen M. Young, *The Chocolate Tree: A Natural History of Cacao* (Washington: Smithsonian Institution Press, 1994), 38–41 (spread to Africa).

33. Paul E. Lovejoy, "Kola Nuts: The 'Coffee' of the Central Sudan," in *CH*, 103–125; Kristof Glamann, *Dutch-Asiatic Trade, 1620–1740* (Copenhagen: Danish Science Press, 1958), 193.

34. *Power in a Nutshell* (quotation, p. 5) and *Vino-Kolafra* (New York: Brunswick Pharmacal, ca. 1900), pamphlets in MTE; Monroe Martin King, *Dr. John S. Pemberton, Originator of the Formula for Coca-Cola: A Short Biographical Sketch* (Douglasville, Ga.: Pemberton Archives, 1986); J. C. Louis and Harvey Z. Yazijian, *The Cola Wars* (New York: Everest House, 1980), 15–16 (quotation), 34–35, 265–266.

35. Benjamin T. Ludy, Jr., "Coca-Cola, Caffeine, and Mental Deficiency: Harry Hollingworth and the Chattanooga Trial of 1911," *J. of the History of the Behavioral Sciences* 27 (1991): 42–55; Harvey W. Wiley, "The Alcohol and Drug Habit and Its Prophylaxis," *Proceedings of the Second Pan American Scientific Congress*, vol. 9 (Washington, D.C.: G. P. O., 1917), quotation on p. 146, and

Wiley, *Beverages and Their Adulteration* (Philadelphia: P. Blakiston's Son, 1919), 106–115.

36. Mark Pendergrast, *For God, Country and Coca-Cola* (New York: Charles Scribner's Sons, 1993), ch. 12; "The Sun Never Sets on Cacoola," *Time* 55 (15 May 1950): 32 ("long").

37. *Address by Hon. James A. Farley . . . October 25, 1955* (Washington, D.C.: G. P. O., 1956), 5; Rajendar Dara, *The Real Pepsi, The Real Story* (New Delhi: the author, 1991), 16–17; Lovejoy, "Kola Nuts," 107.

38. Braun, *Buzz*, 108–109; Benjamin R. Barber, *Jihad vs. McWorld* (New York: Times Books, 1995), 61–62, 69–70.

39. Sidney W. Mintz, *Sweetness and Power: The Place of Sugar in Modern History* (New York: Viking, 1985), 19, 25 ("Koran"), 67, 73, 143, 174, 186; Alain Huetz de Lemps, *Histoire du Rhum* (Paris: Éditions Desjonquères, 1997), 12; Henry Hobhouse, *Seeds of Change: Five Plants that Transformed Mankind* (New York: Harper and Row, 1986), 43–91 ("addicted" on p. 82), and Henry Hobhouse, "New World, Vineyard to the Old," 60; Woodruff D. Smith, "From Coffeehouse to Parlour: The Consumption of Coffee, Tea and Sugar in North-western Europe in the Seventeenth and Eighteenth Centuries," in *CH*, 148–164, and Woodruff D. Smith, "Complications of the Commonplace: Tea, Sugar, and Imperialism," *J. of Interdisciplinary History* 23 (1992): 259–278.

40. Thomas Short, *Discourses on Tea, Sugar, Milk, Made-wines, Spirits, Punch, Tobacco, &c: With Plain and Useful Rules for Gouty People* (London: T. Longman and A. Millar, 1750), 77; Braudel, *Structures of Everyday Life*, 258; Mintz, *Sweetness and Power*, 109 (quotation), 248 n. 85; *Henry IV, Part I*, act 2, scene 4; R. J. Forbes, *Short History of the Art of Distillation* (Leiden: E. J. Brill, 1948), 95; Ralph A. Austen and Woodruff D. Smith, "Private Tooth Decay as Public Economic Virtue: The Slave-Sugar Triangle, Consumerism, and European Industrialization," in *The Atlantic Slave Trade: Effects on Economies, Societies, and Peoples in Africa, the Americas, and Europe*, ed. Joseph E. Inkori and Stanley L. Engerman (Durham, N.C.: Duke U. Press, 1992), 183–203, quotation on p. 198.

41. Sweetened cannabis: Marie Alexandrine Martin, "Ethnobotanical Aspects of Cannabis in Southeast Asia," in *CC*, 71; James R. Rush, *Opium to Java: Revenue Farming and Chinese Enterprise in Colonial Indonesia, 1860–1910* (Ithaca: Cornell U. Press, 1990), 30, 31. Sweetened tobacco: Thomas C. Sullivan, *Notes on the Culture, Cure, Manufacture, Inspection and Preservation of Tobacco* (Washington, D.C.: [U.S. Subsistence Department], 1867), 5–6; André Provost, *Technique du Tabac: Généralités—Tabacs coupés—Cig-*

arettes (Lausanne: Héliographia, 1959), 192–196. The recipe is in the Edward James Parrish Papers, box 7, SCL.

42. Jacob M. Price, "Tobacco Use and Tobacco Taxation: A Battle of Interests in Early Modern Europe," in *CH*, 177 (ropes); Mark Edward Lender and James Kirby Martin, *Drinking in America: A History* (New York: Free Press, 1982), 30; Robert William Fogel and Stanley L. Engerman, *Time on the Cross: The Economics of American Negro Slavery* (Boston: Little, Brown, 1974), ch. 1.

2. The Little Three: Opium, Cannabis, and Coca

1. Tens of millions: According to the United Nations' International Drug Control Programme, annual prevalence in the 1990s was 8.0 million for heroin and other opiates; 13.3 million for cocaine; and 141.2 million for cannabis. "Annual prevalence" refers to the number of people who used these drugs nonmedically at least once during a given year. *Special Session on the World Drug Problem, New York, 8–10 June 1998*, information sheet no. 2 (1998), 7.

2. Mark David Merlin, *On the Trail of the Ancient Opium Poppy* (London: Associated University Presses, 1984); Mark Nathan Cohen, *Health and the Rise of Civilization* (New Haven: Yale U. Press, 1989); John Scarborough, "The Opium Poppy in Hellenistic and Roman Medicine," in *DNH*, 4–23; Thomas W. Africa, "The Opium Addiction of Marcus Aurelius," *J. of the History of Ideas* 22 (1961): 97–102; Paul Haupt, "Alcohol in the Bible," *J. of Biblical Literature* 36 (1917): 80–81.

3. Glenn Sonnedecker, "Emergence of the Concept of Opiate Addiction," *J. Mondial de Pharmacie*, no. 3 (1962): 278–279; J. F. Richards, "The Indian Empire and Peasant Production of Opium in the Nineteenth Century," *Modern Asian Studies* 15 (1981): 59–82; Donald MacLaren [and William Moore], "Opium Eating and Smoking," *Medical Brief* 35 (1907): 506–507; Sami Hamarneh, "Pharmacy in Medieval Islam and the History of Drug Addiction," *Medical History* 16 (1972), Al-Bīrūnī quotation on pp. 230–231; John Uri Lloyd, "Opium," *Pharmaceutical Era* 39 (1908): 76–80 (peasant labor).

4. Jonathan Spence, "Opium Smoking in Ch'ing China," in *Conflict and Control in Late Imperial China*, ed. Frederic Wakeman, Jr., and Carolyn Grant (Berkeley: U. of California Press, 1975), 143–173; R. K. Newman, "Opium Smoking in Late Imperial China: A Reconsideration," *Modern Asian Studies* 29 (1995): 765–794. Newman's 16.2 million figure includes terminally ill users smoking opium as a palliative; his adult population includes working adolescents. His ingenious method has much to commend it, but his revisionist tone—opium smoking was not such a big problem after all—invites skeptical comment. To the extent that his supply-based estimate leaves out contraband trade, whose full size he admits he does not know (771 n. 17), it is low. And

the possibly low figure of 3.6 percent is still extremely high compared to contemporaneous western societies. It is, for example, an order of magnitude greater than the maximum possible rate in turn-of-the-century America, which had the worst opiate addiction problem among industrial nations.

5. David Edward Owen, *British Opium Policy in China and India* (Hamden, Conn.: Archon, 1968 reprint ed.), vii (one-seventh); John Newsinger, "Britain's Opium Wars," *Monthly Review* 49 (October 1997): 35–42 (Matheson); "Lews Castle," *http://www.scotland-inverness.co.uk/lewis.htm*, 14 June 2000; Jacques M. Downs, "American Merchants and the China Opium Trade, 1800–1840," *Business History Review* 42 (1968): 432 (Perkins); Geoffrey C. Ward with Frederic Delano Grant, Jr., "A Fair, Honorable, and Legitimate Trade," *American Heritage* 37 (Aug.-Sept. 1986): 49–64, "fair" on p. 55, "gloury" on p. 60. Import figures: Michael Greenberg, *British Trade and the Opening of China, 1800–1842* (Cambridge: Cambridge U. Press, 1969 reprint ed.) appendix I.D.2, and Newman, "Opium Smoking in Late Imperial China," 770. Greenberg and Newman give the 1839 and 1879 figures in "chests" of opium. Following Owen, *British Opium Policy*, 373, I am using a conversion factor of 160 pounds per chest.

6. Newman, "Opium Smoking," 770–771; S. A. M. Adshead, "Opium in Szechwan, 1881–1911," *J. of Southeast Asian History* 7 (Sept. 1966): 93–99, "nowhere" on p. 94; Lynn Pan, *Sons of the Yellow Emperor* (Boston: Little, Brown, 1990), 43, 84–90, 118–120; G. William Skinner, *Chinese Society in Thailand: An Analytical History* (Ithaca: Cornell U. Press, 1957), 29–30, 125 (virtues/vices).

7. O. P. Coats, *The System of Cure for the Opium-Morphine or Cocaine Habit* (Kansas City, Mo.: n.p., ca. 1890), MTE, 4–5 ("If it were possible"); David T. Courtwright, *Dark Paradise: Opiate Addiction in America before 1940* (Cambridge, Mass.: Harvard U. Press, 1982).

8. Rudolf Schmitz, "Friedrich Wilhelm Sertürner and the Discovery of Morphine," trans. Brigitte Gretenkord and David L. Cowen, *Pharmacy in History* 27 (1985): 61–74; "The Merck Tradition," *Medical Times* 86 (1958): 1308–1309.

9. James Harvey Young, *Pure Food: Securing the Federal Food and Drugs Act of 1906* (Princeton: Princeton U. Press, 1989), 9, 12, 21, 41; Norman Howard-Jones, "A Critical Study of the Origins and Early Development of Hypodermic Medication," *J. of the History of Medicine and Allied Sciences* 2 (1947): 201–249.

10. Jean-Jacques Yvorel, *Les Poisons de l'Espirit: Drogues et Drogués au XIXe Siècle* (Paris: Quai Voltaire, 1992), 101–102, 312, 317–318; Paul Crestois, "Jules Verne et la Morphine," *Revue d'Histoire de la Pharmacie* 27 (1980): 128.

11. P[aul] Brouardel, *Opium, Morphine et Cocaïne* . . . (Paris: J.-B. Baillière, 1906), 55–56; Paul Butel, *L'Opium: Histoire d'une Fascination* (Paris: Perrin, 1995), 364 (Boulanger).

12. Otto Pflanze, *Bismarck and the Development of Germany*, vol. 3: *The Period of Fortification, 1880–1898* (Princeton: Princeton U. Press, 1990), 100–102, 186, 303; *The Holstein Papers*, vol. 2: *Diaries*, ed. Norman Rich and M. H. Fisher (Cambridge: Cambridge U. Press, 1957), 362.

13. *Drugs in the Western Hemisphere: An Odyssey of Cultures in Conflict*, ed. William O. Walker III (Wilmington, Del.: Scholarly Resources, 1996), 57–80, 133–134; Rensselaer W. Lee III, "Global Reach: The Threat of International Drug Trafficking," *Current History* 94 (1995): 207 (70 to 80 percent); Joseph B. Treaster, "Colombia's Drug Lords Add New Product: Heroin for U.S.," *NYT*, 14 January 1992, LN; United Nations, *Special Session*, 1; Alfred W. McCoy, *The Politics of Heroin: CIA Complicity in the Global Drug Trade* (New York: Lawrence Hill, 1991), 389–390.

14. This account of cannabis's spread draws on *CC*, part 1; Richard E. Schultes, "Man and Marijuana," *Natural History* 82 (Aug.-Sept. 1973): 59–65, 80–82 (Iran on p. 63); Joe Zias et al., "Early Medical Use of Cannabis," *Nature* 363 (1993): 215; Ernest L. Abel, *Marihuana: The First Twelve Thousand Years* (New York: Plenum, 1980), part 1; Lester Grinspoon and James B. Bakalar, *Marijuana, the Forbidden Medicine* (New Haven: Yale U. Press, 1993), ch. 1; and I. C. Chopra and R. N. Chopra, "The Use of Cannabis Drugs in India," *BN* 9 (Jan.-March 1957): 4–29. The Herodotus passage is in *Histories*, IV.74–75.

15. *CC*, 4 (Rubin quotation), 5–6, 81–116, 147–183, 293–302; *The Works of Hubert Howe Bancroft: History of California*, vol. 2 (San Francisco: History Company, 1886), 177–181; Vera Rubin and Lambros Comitas, *Ganja in Jamaica: A Medical Anthropological Study of Chronic Marijuana Use* (The Hague: Mouton, 1975), 8–38, 48–59, 127, 171 (editorial); Sidney W. Mintz, "The Caribbean as a Socio-cultural Area," in *Peoples and Cultures of the Caribbean: An Anthropological Reader*, ed. Michael M. Horowitz (Garden City, N.Y.: Natural History Press, 1971), 31 (half a million).

16. Aviva Chomsky, *West Indian Workers and the United Fruit Company in Costa Rica, 1870–1940* (Baton Rouge: Louisiana State U. Press, 1996), 42–45; Michael L. Conniff, *Black Labor on a White Canal: Panama, 1904–1981* (Pittsburgh: U. of Pittsburgh Press, 1985), 3–4; J. F. Siler et al., "Mariajuana [*sic*] Smoking in Panama," *Military Surgeon* 73 (1933): 269–280, quotation on p. 271.

17. Carey McWilliams, *North from Mexico: The Spanish-Speaking People of the*

United States (Westport, Conn.: Greenwood Press, 1990 rev. ed.), 152; Richard J. Bonnie and Charles H. Whitebread II, *The Marijuana Conviction: A History of Marijuana Prohibition in the United States* (Charlottesville: University Press of Virginia, 1974), 46 (Chicago); J. R. Stock to H. B. Greeson, 17 March 1934, and Greeson to H. J. Anslinger, 24 March 1934 (Louisiana), file 0550-1, DEA Records, RG 170-74-12, National Archives II, College Park, Md.; Harry L. Freedman and Myron J. Rockmore, "Marihuana: A Factor in Personality Evaluation and Army Adjustment," *Clinical Psychopathology* 8 (1946): 225 (Tennessee), 232 ("rather have weed"); "Marijuana: New Federal Tax Hits Dealings in Potent Weed," *Newsweek* 10 (14 August 1937): 22 (San Quentin); "Marijuana Menace," *Literary Digest* 125 (1 January 1938): 26–27 (price, NYC seizures); Jill Jonnes, *Hep-Cats, Narcs, and Pipe Dreams: A History of America's Romance with Illegal Drugs* (New York: Scribner, 1996), ch. 7; David Courtwright et al., *Addicts Who Survived: An Oral History of Narcotic Use in America, 1923–1965* (Knoxville: U. of Tennessee Press, 1989), 85, 132–133 (Mezzrow).

18. Eli Marcovitz and Henry J. Meyers, "The Marijuana Addict in the Army," *War Medicine* 6 (1944): 382–391, quotation on p. 383.

19. Charles Baudelaire, *Artificial Paradise: On Hashish and Wine as Means of Expanding Individuality*, trans. Ellen Fox (New York: McGraw-Hill, 1971), 17; *CC*, 535–536 (McGlothlin quotation); "Survey of Drug Use Among Michigan Students," *Public Health Reports* 84 (1969): 1084.

20. National Institute on Drug Abuse, "Drug Abuse Statistics 1979: Preliminary Population Projections" (TS, n.d.), VF "Addiction—Incidence, 1976–1979"; Malcolm C. Hall, "Illicit Drug Abuse in Australia—A Brief Statistical Picture," *J. of Drug Issues* 7 (1977): 311–318; *CC*, 327, 499, 506–507; Yuet W. Cheung and James M. N. Ch'ien, "Drug Use and Drug Policy in Hong Kong: Changing Patterns and New Challenges," *SUM* 31 (1996): 1589; D. Mohan et al., "Prevalence and Pattern of Drug Abuse Among Delhi University Students," *Indian J. of Medical Research* 66 (1977): 627–634; Cesarea Goduco-Auglar, "A Note on Drug Abuse in the Philippines," *BN* 24 (April-June 1972): 43; J. A. Ward, "The Drug Scene in Scotland," *Scottish Medical J.* 16 (1971): 377; L. Sanchez, "The Drug Problem in Venezuela" (TS, 1971) and "FRG Report . . ." (TS, 1971), both in VF, "Addiction—Incidence; Countries [to] 1973;" Merete Watt Boolsen, "Drugs in Denmark," *IJA* 10 (1975): 505, 509; J. C. Ball et al., "Changing World Patterns of Drug Abuse, 1945–1974," *International J. of Clinical Pharmacology* 12 (1975): 109–113; "Western Europe's Latest Worry: A Growing Army of 'Junkies,'" *International Drug Report* 18 (1977): 9–13.

21. Eric Hoffer, *The True Believer: Thoughts on the Nature of Mass Movements* (New York: Harper and Row, 1966), 103; Donald J. Bogue, *Principles of Demography* (New York: John Wiley and Sons, 1969), 48, 71–72, 155.

22. S. Taqi, "The Drug Cinema," *BN* 24 (Oct.-Dec. 1972): 19–28; Todd Gitlin, "On Drugs and Mass Media in America's Consumer Society," in *Youth and Drugs: Society's Mixed Messages*, ed. Hank Resnik et al. (Rockville, Md.: Office for Substance Abuse Prevention, 1990), 31–52; Christopher Lasch, *The Culture of Narcissism: American Life in an Age of Diminishing Expectations* (New York: Warner, 1979), 33.

23. Ravinder Singh, *I Was a Drug Addict* (New Delhi: Orient, 1979), 42–47, 58–59.

24. Mac Marshall, "An Overview of Drugs in Oceania," and R. Bruce Larson, "Marijuana in Truk," both in *Drugs in Western Pacific Societies*, ed. Lamont Lindstrom (Lanham, Md.: University Press of America, 1987), 38, 219–220 respectively.

25. Timothy Plowman, "Coca Chewing and the Botanical Origins of Coca (*Erythroxylum* Spp.) in South America," in *Coca and Cocaine: Effects on People and Policy in Latin America*, ed. Deborah Pacini and Christine Franquemont ([Ithaca, N.Y.]: Cultural Survival, 1986), 27–28; Andrew Weil, "The New Politics of Coca," *New Yorker* 71 (15 May 1995): 70–80; Henry H. Rusby, *Jungle Memories* (New York: Whittlesey House, 1933), 342 (old chewer).

26. Joseph Kennedy, *Coca Exotica: The Illustrated Story of Cocaine* (Rutherford, N.J.: Fairleigh Dickinson U. Press, 1985), chs. 1–8; Lester Grinspoon and James B. Bakalar, *Cocaine: A Drug and Its Social Evolution* (New York: Basic Books, 1976), ch. 2; Joseph F. Spillane, *Cocaine: From Medical Marvel to Modern Menace in the United States, 1884–1920* (Baltimore: Johns Hopkins U. Press, 2000), ch. 1; *Coca Erythroxylon (Vin Mariani): Its Use in the Treatment of Disease*, 3rd ed. (Paris: Mariani, 1884), iii (Grant).

27. Freud, *Cocaine Papers*, ed. Robert Byck (New York: Stonehill, 1974), quotation on p. 109; Rusby, *Jungle Memories*, 3–4, 99, 345, with additional material from Susan M. Rossi-Willcox, "Henry Hurd Rusby: A Biographical Sketch and Selectively Annotated Bibliography," *Harvard Papers in Botany*, no. 4 (1993): 1–29, and KRF A2: Rusby.

28. *Cocaine: Global Histories*, ed. Paul Gootenberg (London: Routledge, 1999), chs. 2, 3, 4, 6, 7; Spillane, *Cocaine*, ch. 3, coca export figures on p. 49, price data on p. 54.

29. Hans W. Maier, *Maier's Cocaine Addiction (Der Kokainismus)*, ed. and trans. Oriana Josseau Kalant (Toronto: Addiction Research Foundation, 1987), 31–67, 257; David T. Courtwright, "The Rise and Fall and Rise of Cocaine in

the United States," in *CH*, 206–214; Patricia G. Erickson et al., *The Steel Drug: Cocaine and Crack in Perspective*, 2nd ed. (New York: Lexington Books, 1994), ch. 1; V[ictor] Cyril and [E.] Berger, *La "Coco": Poison Moderne* (Paris: Ernest Fammarion, 1924), 17, 104; Louis Lewin, *Phantastica: A Classic Survey on the Use and Abuse of Mind-Altering Plants*, trans. P. H. A. Wirth (Rochester, Vt.: Park Street Press, 1998), 67.

30. Robert McG. Thomas, Jr., "Ernst Morch, 87, an Inventor and Leading Anesthesiologist," *NYT*, 18 January 1996, LN (hounds); Garland Williams to H. J. Anslinger, 9 February 1940, file 0120-9, DEA Records, RG 170-73-1, National Archives II, College Park, Md. (NYC quote); *Cocaine: Global Histories*, ed. Gootenberg, ch. 9 (Mexico).

31. David F. Musto, "International Traffic in Coca through the Early 20th Century," *Drug and Alcohol Dependence* 49 (1998): 145–156; Peter Reuter, "The Organization and Measurement of the International Drug Trade," and Rensselaer W. Lee III, "Trends in the Evolution of Narcotics Industries: Problems of Influence and Legitimacy," both in *Economics of the Narcotics Industry* (TS proceedings of November 1994 conference, U.S. State Department and Central Intelligence Agency), n.p.; Courtwright, "Rise and Fall," 217 219.

Musto's theory best describes highly toxic drugs like cocaine, heroin, and the amphetamines. Drugs like alcohol and cigarettes do not fit the generational learning model as well, possibly because it can take years or even decades before significant problems become evident.

32. James A. Inciardi and Hilary L. Surratt, "Children in the Streets of Brazil: Drug Use, Crime, Violence, and HIV Risks," *SUM* 33 (1998): 1461–1480.

3. The Puzzle of Distribution

1. Oliver Sacks, *The Island of the Colorblind and Cycad Island* (New York: Knopf, 1997), 86–89, 224–225 n. 41; quotations on pp. 87–88.

2. Richard Rudgley, *Essential Substances: A Cultural History of Intoxicants in Society* (New York: Kodansha International, 1994), 151–161; E. J. H. Corner, *The Natural History of Palms* (Berkeley: U. of California Press, 1966), 282 (Haldane); Edward Hyams, *Plants in the Service of Man: 10,000 Years of Domestication* (Philadelphia: J. B. Lippincott, 1972), 138; Louis Lewin, *Phantastica: A Classic Survey on the Use and Abuse of Mind-Altering Plants*, trans. P. H. A. Wirth (Rochester, Vt.: Park Street Press, 1998), 192–201.

3. Andrew Weil, "The New Politics of Coca," *New Yorker* 71 (15 May 1995): 70 (Vespucci); Joseph Westermeyer, *Poppies, Pipes, and People: Opium and Its Use in Laos* (Berkeley: U. of California Press, 1982), 264 (damaged teeth).

4. The vigilance of the DEA in this matter is attested by the thickness of the

"Khat" vertical files, whence this information is drawn. Representative sources are World Health Organization, "Medical Aspects of the Habitual Chewing of Khat Leaves," WHO/APD/127 Rev. 1 (TS, 1964); John G. Kennedy et al., "Qat Use in North Yemen and the Problem of Addiction: A Study in Medical Anthropology," *Culture, Medicine, and Psychiatry* 4 (1980): 311–344 (quotation on p. 312); Peter Kalix, "The Pharmacology of Khat," *General Pharmacology* 15 (1984): 179–187; and A. James Giannini et al., "Treatment of Khat Addiction," *J. of Substance Abuse Treatment* 9 (1992): 379–382. An exception to the rule of qat's failure as an export commodity is Britain, which permitted air shipments to its Somali minority. Stewart Hennessey, "More than We Can Chew," *The Independent*, 1 June 1994, LN.

5. Weston La Barre, "Old and New World Narcotics: A Statistical Question and an Ethnological Reply," *Economic Botany* 24 (1970): 73–80; Peter T. Furst, *Hallucinogens and Culture* (Novato, Calif.: Chandler and Sharp, 1976), 1–32.

6. Jan Rogoziński, *Smokeless Tobacco in the Western World, 1550–1950* (New York: Praeger, 1990), 18 (16 percent); Alexander von Gernet, "Nicotinian Dreams: The Prehistory and Early History of Tobacco in Eastern North America," in *CH*, 67–87; David Harley, "The Beginnings of the Tobacco Controversy: Puritanism, James I, and the Royal Physicians," *Bulletin of the History of Medicine* 67 (1993): 40, 44, 46; Jordan Goodman, *Tobacco in History: The Cultures of Dependence* (London: Routledge, 1993), 24, 33, 38, 49; *The Jesuit Relations and Allied Documents*, ed. Reuben Gold Thwaites, vol. 7 (Cleveland: Burrows Brothers, 1897), 137; Johannes Wilbert, "Magico-Religious Use of Tobacco among South American Indians," in *CC*, 439–461.

7. Sacks, *Island of the Colorblind*, 86.

8. Piero Camporesi, *Bread of Dreams: Food and Fantasy in Early Modern Europe*, trans. David Gentilcore (Chicago: U. of Chicago Press, 1989), quotations on pp. 123, 127.

9. Mary Kilbourne Matossian, *Poisons of the Past: Molds, Epidemics, and History* (New Haven: Yale U. Press, 1989), parts I and II.

10. David Hackett Fischer, *The Great Wave: Price Revolutions and the Rhythm of History* (New York: Oxford U. Press, 1996), 91–102.

11. Jordan Goodman, "Excitantia: Or, How Enlightenment Europe Took to Soft Drugs," in *CH*, 137.

12. "Minutes, 1969," box 20 of review board meetings, JWT.

13. Mac Marshall, "An Overview of Drugs in Oceania," in *Drugs in Western Pacific Societies*, ed. Lamont Lindstrom (Lanham, Md.: U. Press of America, 1987), 15–26; Eric Hirsch, "Efficacy and Concentration: Analogies in Betel

Use among the Fuyuge (Papua New Guinea)," in *CH*, 88–102; "Betel Quid Chewing Habit amongst a Group of Bangladeshi Adolescents in East London," *http://www.who.int/archives/tohalert/jul96/e/10.html*, 17 June 2000; Brian L. Dear, "The Taste of Money: The Kava Market Takes Off," *http://www.coconut.com/features/kava.html*, 18 Aug. 1998 (chalk, DUI, "bullish"); "Have You Heard About Kava Kava [*sic*] and Anxiety?" *http://www.ts3.com/sterling/kava.htm*, 18 Aug. 1998; "Kava Recipes," *http://www.betterlivingusa.com/kavarecipes.htm*, 17 June 2000.

14. L. Armstead, "Illicit Narcotics Cultivation and Processing: The Ignored Environmental Drama," and M. Dourojeanni, "Environmental Impact of Coca Cultivation and Cocaine Production in the Amazon Region of Peru," both in *BN* 44, no. 2 (1992): 9–19, 37–53, "Attila" on p. 43; Edward O. Wilson, *The Diversity of Life* (New York: Norton, 1993), 273–274 ("wet deserts"); Sam Dillon, "In the Hills, Marijuana Fields and a Priest's Murder," *NYT*, nat. ed., 26 May 1998, A4 (Mexico); Steven Ambrus, "Animal Subtraction," *Los Angeles Times*, 25 July 1995, n.p., in VF, "Smuggling."

15. Goodman, *Tobacco in History*, 172, 183, 243–244; Allan Kulikoff, *Tobacco and Slaves: The Development of Southern Cultures in the Chesapeake, 1680–1800* (Chapel Hill: U. of North Carolina Press, 1986), 47–48; Barry J. Ford, *Smokescreen: A Guide to the Personal Risks and Global Effects of the Cigarette Habit* (North Perth: Halcyon, 1994), 191–193; Michele Barry, "The Influence of the U.S. Tobacco Industry on the Health, Economy, and Environment of Developing Countries," *NEJM* 324 (1991): 918.

16. Charles Bergquist, *Labor in Latin America: Comparative Essays on Chile, Argentina, Venezuela, and Colombia* (Stanford: Stanford U. Press, 1986), 371; Heather Dewar, "Coffee Grown in Sun a Threat to Songbirds," *Florida Times-Union*, 30 January 1997, A1, A8; Joby Warrick, "A Growing Approach to Saving Songbirds," *Washington Post*, 4 January 1999, LN.

17. Henry N. Ridley, *The Dispersal of Plants Throughout the World* (Ashford, Kent: L. Reeve, 1930), quotation on p. 630; Todd S. Purdum, "Tiniest Terror Plaguing Los Angeles," *NYT*, nat. ed., 16 September 1997, A12.

18. Sherman Cochran, *Big Business in China: Sino-Foreign Rivalry in the Cigarette Industry, 1890–1930* (Cambridge, Mass.: Harvard U. Press, 1980), 141–142; Thomas Pinney, *A History of Wine in America: From the Beginnings to Prohibition* (Berkeley: U. of California Press, 1989), 9, 392.

19. J. W. Purseglove, "The Origins and Migrations of Crops in Tropical Africa," in *Origins of African Plant Domestication*, ed. Jack R. Harlan et al. (The Hague: Mouton, 1976), 302 (human pleasure); A. H. Grimshaw, *An Essay on*

the Physical and Moral Effects of the Use of Tobacco as a Luxury: A Prize Essay (New York: Wm. Harned, 1853), 29.

20. Wilson, *Diversity of Life*, 328.

4. The Sorcerer's Apprentices

1. James Harvey Young, *Pure Food: Securing the Federal Food and Drugs Act of 1906* (Princeton: Princeton U. Press, 1989), 28.

2. Nicolas Monardes, *Joyfull Newes Out of the Newe Founde Worlde*, trans. John Frampton, vol. 1 (New York: AMS Press, 1967 reprint ed.), 75–98, "pastyme" on p. 86, "hearbe" on p. 91.

3. Giles Everard, *Panacea; or the Universal Medicine, Being a Discovery of the Wonderful Vertues of Tobacco* . . . (London: Simon Miller, 1659; first pub. 1587), "Antidote" in John Rowland's unpaginated dedication; *The Diary of Samuel Pepys*, ed. Robert Latham and William Matthews, vol. 6 (Berkeley: U. of California Press, 1972), 120.

4. Simon Paulli, *A Treatise on Tobacco, Tea, Coffee and Chocolate*, trans. [Robert] James (London: T. Osborne, 1746; first pub. 1665), quotations on pp. 15, 18, 23, 132, 169, emphases in the original; Martha Baldwin, "Danish Medicines for the Danes and the Defense of Indigenous Medicines," *Sixteenth Century Essays and Studies* 40 (1998): 163–180. Medical interest in tobacco: Katharine T. Kell, "Tobacco in Folk Cures in Western Society," *J. of American Folklore* 78 (1965): 99–112, and Marc and Muriel Vigié, *L'Herbe à Nicot: Amateurs de Tabac, Fermiers Généraux et Contrebandiers sous l'Ancien Régime* (Paris: Fayard, 1989), ch. 2.

5. S. J. W. Tabor, "An Unprejudiced Inquiry Concerning the Effects of Tobacco on the Human System When Used as a Luxury," *Boston Medical and Surgical Journal* 32 (1845): 509–517; Charles Knowlton, "Is Tobacco a Good Thing, Otherwise than as a Medicine?" *Boston Investigator*, 9 February 1838, p. 1; Didier Nourrison, "Tabagisme et Antitabagisme en France au XIXe Siècle," *Histoire, Economie, et Société* 7 (1988): 545; [John Bell et al.], "Report in Response to a Petition from Young Men's Association of Philadelphia for Discontinuing the Use of Tobacco" (MS, 1833), 4, CPPL; Antonina Vallentin, *Picasso* (Garden City, N.Y.: Doubleday, 1963), 1.

6. Edward D. Levin, "Nicotine and Schizophrenia: Cognitive Aspects and Possible Novel Treatments," *http://www.mhsource.com/advocacy/narsad/nicotine.html*, 10 July 1998; John Schwartz, "A Cigarette Chemical Packed with Helpful Effects?" *Washington Post*, 9 November 1998, A3.

7. Tim Unwin, *Wine and the Vine: An Historical Geography of Viticulture and the Wine Trade* (London: Routledge, 1991), 179; *Talmud: Tractate Berachoth*, 35b and 58b, translated in *The Origins and Ancient History of Wine*, ed. Pat-

rick McGovern et al. (Amsterdam: Gordon and Breach, 1995), 5; John F. Nunn, *Ancient Egyptian Medicine* (Norman: U. of Oklahoma Press, 1996), 140; "Medical and Household Recipes" (MS, n.d.), CPPL; Cotton Mather, *The Angel of Bethesda*, ed. Gordon W. Jones (Barre, Mass.: American Antiquarian Society, 1972 reprint ed.), 87.

8. John J. McCusker, "Distilling and Its Implications for the Atlantic World of the Seventeenth and Eighteenth Centuries," in *PMCAB*, 7, 9; Paul Diepgen, "Der Alkohol in der Medizingeschichte" [Alcohol in Medical History], offprint from *Sonderdruck aus Jahrbuch 1937 der Gesellschaft für die Geschichte und Bibliographie des Brauwesens E. V.*, in KRF C39(g): Alcohol, "miracle" on p. 18; Mark Keller et al., *A Dictionary of Words about Alcohol*, 2nd ed. (New Brunswick: Rutgers Center of Alcohol Studies, 1982), 44, 263; R. J. Forbes, *Short History of the Art of Distillation* (Leiden: E. J. Brill, 1948), 95, 108 (spoonful), 111; Jean-Claude A. Desenclos et al., "The Protective Effect of Alcohol on the Occurrence of Epidemic Oyster-Borne Hepatitis A," *Epidemiology* 3 (1992): 371–374.

9. Sarah E. Williams, "The Use of Beverage Alcohol in Medicine, 1790–1860," *J. of Studies on Alcohol* 41 (1980): 543–566; J[ulius] Berncastle, *Australian Snake Bites: Their Treatment and Cure . . .* (Melbourne: Mason, Firth, 1868), 8; Charlie Lovett, *Olympic Marathon: A Centennial History of the Games' Most Storied Race* (Westport, Conn.: Praeger, 1997), 13.

10. B. Ann Tlusty, "Water of Life, Water of Death: The Controversy over Brandy and Gin in Early Modern Augsburg," *Central European History* 31 (1998): 1–30.

11. T[obias] Smollett, *The History of England from the Revolution in 1688, to the Death of George the Second* (Philadelphia: M'Carty and Davis, 1839), 452; Peter Clark, "The 'Mother Gin' Controversy in the Early Eighteenth Century," *Transactions of the Royal Historical Society*, 5th ser. 38 (1988): 63–84; Henry Fielding, *An Enquiry into the Causes of the Late Increase of Robbers and Related Writings*, ed. Malvin R. Zirker (Middletown, Conn.: Wesleyan U. Press, 1988), quotation on p. 90.

12. Doris Lanier, *Absinthe: The Cocaine of the Nineteenth Century* (Jefferson, N.C.: McFarland, 1995); Barnaby Conrad III, *Absinthe: History in a Bottle* (San Francisco: Chronicle Books, 1988), 91–93 (Pernod), 115 (French consumption); "Recipe Book for John H. Mundall" (MS, 1745–1785), n.p. (contagion), CPPL.

13. *DNH*, chs. 5, 8, 9; *Materia Medica Bayer* (New York: Bayer, ca. 1915), Bayer collection, MTE; Roy Porter, *The Greatest Benefit to Mankind: A Medical History of Humanity* (New York: Norton, 1997), 675 (Canadian practitioner).

14. "Compilation of New Drugs, 1941–1963," reprint from *American Professional*

Pharmacist (July 1964), KRF C39(g); Michael T. Risher, "Controlling Viagra Mania," *NYT*, nat. ed., 20 July 1998, A19.

15. Robert M. Julien, *A Primer of Drug Action*, 8th ed. (New York: W. H. Freeman, 1997), 138–142.

16. Lester Grinspoon and Peter Hedblom, *The Speed Culture: Amphetamine Use and Abuse in America* (Cambridge, Mass.: Harvard U. Press, 1975).

17. Charles O. Jackson, "The Amphetamine Democracy: Medicinal Abuse in the Popular Culture," *South Atlantic Quarterly* 74 (1975): 308–323, and Jackson, "Before the Drug Culture: Barbiturate/Amphetamine Abuse in American Society," *Clio Medica* 11 (1976): 47–58; Christopher Andersen, *Jackie after Jack: Portrait of the Lady* (New York: William Morrow, 1998), 41.

18. James Ellroy, *My Dark Places: An L.A. Crime Memoir* (New York: Knopf, 1996), 135–153, quotation on p. 135 (with spelling of "propylhexedrine" corrected).

19. *Fat People Die First* (ca. 1955), *Dexamyl Tablets and Elixir for the Management of Everyday Mental and Emotional Distress* (ca. 1951), and *Dexedrine Reference Manual*, 3rd ed. (1953), pamphlets in SKF collection, MTE.

20. Marissa Miller and Nicholas Kozel, "Amphetamine Epidemics," in *Encyclopedia of Drugs and Alcohol*, vol. 1, ed. Jerome H. Jaffe (New York: Simon and Schuster/Macmillan, 1995), 110–117; John P. Morgan, "Duplicitous Drugs: The History and Recent Status of Look-alike Drugs," *J. of Psychoactive Drugs* 19 (1987): 21–31.

21. Roger Thomas, trans., "Interview with 1966 Tour winner, Lucien Aimar," *www.cyclingnews.com/results/1998/jul98/jul31a.shtml*, 23 January 1999; Annie Cohen-Solal, *Sartre: A Life*, trans. Anna Cancogni (New York: Pantheon, 1987), 373–375; Ronald Hayman, *Sartre: A Life* (New York: Simon and Schuster, 1987), 248–249, 341–343.

22. Takemitsu Hemmi, "How We Have Handled the Problem of Drug Abuse in Japan," in *Abuse of Central Stimulants*, ed. Folke Sjöqvist and Malcolm Tottie (New York: Raven Press, 1969), 147–153; Henry Brill and Tetsuya Hirose, "The Rise and Fall of a Methamphetamine Epidemic: Japan 1945–55," *Seminars in Psychiatry* 1 (1969): 179–194; David E. Kaplan and Alec Dubro, *Yakuza: The Explosive Account of Japan's Criminal Underworld* (Reading, Mass.: Addison-Wesley, 1986), 199 ("treadmill"); Kiyoshi Morimoto, "The Problem of the Abuse of Amphetamines in Japan," *BN* 9 (July-Sept. 1957): 11 (statistics).

23. Fielding, *Enquiry*, 78; H. Richard Friman, "Awaiting the Tsunami? Japan and the International Drug Trade," *Pacific Review* 6 (1993): 41–50, and Friman, "Gaijinhanzai: Immigrants and Drugs in Contemporary Japan," *Asian Survey* 36 (1996): 964–977; "Crimes Related to Awakening Drugs a

Worry," *Mainichi Shinbun*, 11 April 1977, 5 ("whirlwind"), trans. in VF, "Addiction—Incidence; Countries, 1976–1977;" Kiyoshi Wada, "Cocaine Abuse in Japan," *Japanese J. of Alcohol and Drug Dependence* 29 (1994): 84–85; "Easy Money for Asian Gangs," *South China Morning Post*, 6 February 1994, LN.

24. *Abuse of Central Stimulants*, ed. Sjöqvist and Tottie, 187–304; Nils Bejerot with Carol Maurice-Bejerot, *Addiction and Society* (Springfield, Ill.: Charles C. Thomas, 1970), 115 (models); Richard Severo, "Mainlining Amphetamines Rising Problem in Sweden," *NYT*, 10 April 1970, 41 (quotation).

25. James M. Markham, "Quarantining of Drug Addicts Urged to Halt Epidemic," *NYT*, 8 May 1972, 74 ("controlled"); Thomas J. Hamilton, "U.N. Narcotics Group Seeking a Tighter Curb on 'Pep' Drugs," *NYT*, 25 January 1969, 1, 10; "Drug Production Grows," *Gazeta Wyborcza*, no. 45, 22 February 1995, LN; John-Thor Dahlburg, "Tracking the Russian Connection," *Los Angeles Times*, 6 June 1993, LN ("Narcostan").

26. "Swedish Premier's Convicted Killer Confesses to 600 Robberies," *Reuter Library Report*, 14 Sept. 1989, LN.

27. J[ohn] C. Ball et al., "Changing World Patterns of Drug Abuse, 1945–1974," *International J. of Clinical Pharmacology* 12 (1975): 109–113, quotation on pp. 110–111; "Amphetamine Abuse a World Epidemic," *Chicago Tribune*, 17 November 1996, LN; United Nations, *Special Session on the World Drug Problem, New York, 8–10 June 1998*, information sheet no. 2 (1998), 3 (sixfold), and United Nations, *Report of the International Narcotics Control Board for 1997* (New York: 1998), 5 (Internet).

28. Michael Bliss, *William Osler: A Life in Medicine* (New York: Oxford U. Press, 1999), 276.

29. Charles B. Shuey to Lawrence Kolb, 2 May 1961, KP. Representative articles about the misuse or overuse of different drugs in different cultural settings are "Wyma.," "Opium-Eating Teetotallers," *J. of Psychological Medicine and Mental Pathology*, n.s. 7 (1881): 74–77; Ovide Bouret, "Un Nouveau Cas de Caféisme Chronique," *L'Écho Médical du Nord* 6 (1902): 171–173; and Samuel W. Goldstein, "Barbiturates: A Blessing and a Menace," *J. of the American Pharmaceutical Association* 36 (January 1947): 5–14.

30. Joseph F. Spillane, *Cocaine: From Medical Marvel to Modern Menace in the United States, 1884–1920* (Baltimore: Johns Hopkins U. Press, 2000), ch. 4, quotation on p. 70; Sharon Bernstein, "Drug Maker to Pitch Prozac in Television Infomercial," *Los Angeles Times*, 14 May 1999, LN; Stephen J. W. Tabor, "Early Names and History of Tobacco," *Boston Medical and Surgical Journal* 32 (1844): 15.

31. "We Want to Know," *Pharmaceutical Era* 29 (1903): 445; J. Stanford Stowell,

"Experiences of a Dispensing Pharmacist with Opium Fiends," *Merck's Report* 6 (1897): 629.

32. William B. McAllister, *Drug Diplomacy in the Twentieth Century: An International History* (London: Routledge, 2000), 3 ("bottleneck thinking").

33. Charles F. Levinthal, "Milk of Paradise/Milk of Hell—The History of Ideas about Opium," *Perspectives in Biology and Medicine* 28 (1985): 572 (etorphine and other synthetic opiates).

34. *Psychotropic Drugs in the Year 2000: Use by Normal Humans*, ed. Wayne O. Evans and Nathan S. Kline (Springfield, Ill.: Charles C. Thomas, 1971), xx, 77.

35. Peter Stafford, *Psychedelics Encyclopedia*, 3rd ed. (Berkeley: Ronin, 1992), 51 ("Harvard"); Albert Hofmann, *LSD: My Problem Child* (New York: McGraw-Hill, 1980), xii (quotation), 73–80.

36. Nils Bejerot, *Addiction: An Artificially Induced Drive* (Springfield, Ill.: Charles C. Thomas, 1972), 13; "Intoxication: Historical Perspectives on Alcohol and Other Drugs," 3–4, unpublished paper kindly furnished by Joel Bernard.

5. A Trap Baited with Pleasure

1. Andrew Weil, *The Natural Mind: An Investigation of Drugs and the Higher Consciousness*, rev. ed. (Boston: Houghton Mifflin, 1986), ch. 2.

2. Ronald K. Siegel, *Intoxication: Life in Pursuit of Artificial Paradise* (New York: E. P. Dutton, 1989); Mark Nathan Cohen, *Health and the Rise of Civilization* (New Haven: Yale U. Press, 1989); Jared Diamond, *Guns, Germs, and Steel: The Fates of Human Societies* (New York: Norton, 1997), ch. 11; Nathan S. Kline, foreword to Robert S. de Ropp, *Drugs and the Mind* (New York: St. Martin's Press, 1957), viii.

3. Stephen Braun, *Buzz: The Science and Lore of Alcohol and Caffeine* (New York: Oxford U. Press, 1996); Ichiro Kawachi et al., "A Prospective Study of Coffee Drinking and Suicide in Women," *Archives of Internal Medicine* 156 (1996): 521–525. Robert M. Julien, *A Primer of Drug Action*, 8th ed. (New York: W. H. Freeman, 1997), is a concise guide to the neurochemical effects of drugs.

4. David Irving, *Göring: A Biography* (New York: William Morrow, 1989), ch. 5, quotation on pp. 86–87; *The Letters of William S. Burroughs, 1945–1959*, ed. Oliver Harris (New York: Viking, 1993), 215.

5. D. C. Galletly et al., "Does Caffeine Withdrawal Contribute to Postanaesthetic Morbidity?" *Lancet* 1 (10 June 1989): 1335; Eric C. Strain et al., "Caffeine Dependence Syndrome: Evidence from Case Histories and Experimental Evaluations," *JAMA* 272 (1994): 1043–1048; [Jean-Baptiste]

Nacquart, "Notes sur les Derniers Moments de M. de Balzac," in Armand Baschet, *Honoré de Balzac: Essai sur l'Homme et sur l'Oeuvre* (Paris: D. Giraud et Dagneau, 1852), 158.

6. Nils Bejerot, *Addiction: An Artificially Induced Drive* (Springfield, Ill.: Charles C. Thomas, 1972), 4; Kurt Pohlisch, "Die Verbreitung des chronischen Opiatmißbrauchs in Deutschland" [The Extent of the Chronic Misuse of Opiates in Germany], *Deutsche Medizinische Wochenschrift*, no. 47 (1931): 1984–1986; Anslinger in Albert Q. Maisel, "Getting the Drop on Dope," *Liberty*, 24 November 1945, unpaginated reprint in VF, "U.S. Bureau of Narcotics—History."

7. Stanton Peele's views are summarized in "Values and Beliefs: Existential Models of Addiction," in *Encyclopedia of Drugs and Alcohol*, vol. 3, ed. Jerome H. Jaffe (New York: Simon and Schuster/Macmillan, 1995), 1241–1242, and in several articles available at his Web site, *http://www.peele.net*. The quotation is from "The Addiction Experience."

8. John Watkins, "Karl Popper: A Memoir," *American Scholar* 66 (Spring 1997): 210; David Maraniss, *First in His Class: A Biography of Bill Clinton* (New York: Simon and Schuster, 1995), 153–154; "Gene Keeps Some from Nicotine Addiction," *NYT*, nat. ed., 25 June 1998, A18; John Uri Lloyd, "Opium," *Pharmaceutical Era* 39 (1908): 80 (Turkish taboo); Yuet W. Cheung and James M. N. Ch'ien, "Drug Use and Drug Policy in Hong Kong: Changing Patterns and New Challenges," *SUM* 31 (1996): 1589 (Chinese); Joji Sakurai, "Japanese Drinking Habits Increasing," *AP Online*, 13 July 1998, LN.

9. Peter Avery, *Modern Iran* (New York: Praeger, 1965), 238; Donald N. Wilber, *Iran: Past and Present*, 8th ed. (Princeton: Princeton U. Press, 1976), 286–287; "Iran's Opium Use Down, Heroin Addicts Rise," unpaginated 1968 clipping from *Medical Tribune* in VF, "Iran;" John Simpson, *Inside Iran: Life Under Khomeini's Regime* (New York: St. Martin's, 1988), 123–124.

10. W. A. Penn, *The Soverane Herb: A History of Tobacco* (London: Grant Richards, 1902), 48–49 (Cuba); Joseph Westermeyer, "Influence of Opium Availability on Addiction Rates in Laos," *American J. of Epidemiology* 109 (1979): 550–562, and Westermeyer, "Opium Availability and the Prevalence of Addiction in Asia," *BJA* 76 (1981): 85–90; Yahya H. Affinnih, "Drug Use in Greater Accra, Ghana: Pilot Study," and "A Review of Literature on Drug Use in Sub-Saharan Africa . . .," *SUM* 34 (1999): 157–169, 443–454; Roger Doyle, "Lung Cancer in U.S. Males," *Scientific American* 216 (June 1997): 28 (Kentuckians); Philip Baridon, "A Comparative Analysis of Drug Addiction in 33 Countries," *Drug Forum* 2 (1973): 335–355, quotation on p. 342.

11. Lionel Tiger, *The Pursuit of Pleasure* (Boston: Little, Brown, 1992), 100 (coffee to Japan); Madelon Powers, *Faces along the Bar: Lore and Order in the*

Workingman's Saloon, 1870–1920 (Chicago: U. of Chicago Press, 1998), 223–224 (salesman); John A. O'Donnell et al., *Young Men and Drugs—A Nationwide Survey* (Rockville, Md.: National Institute on Drug Abuse, 1976); U.S. Public Health Service press release, 22 June 1955, box 109, folder 13, HP (statistics).

12. Gary S. Becker, *Accounting for Tastes* (Cambridge, Mass.: Harvard U. Press, 1996), ch. 4, and Michael Grossman, "The Economic Approach to Addictive Behavior," in *The New Economics of Human Behavior,* ed. Mariano Tommasi and Kathryn Ierulli (Cambridge: Cambridge U. Press, 1995), 157–171.

13. M. V. O'Shea, *Tobacco and Mental Efficiency* (New York: Macmillan, 1923), 28.

14. Alfred Rive, "The Consumption of Tobacco since 1600," *Economic History* 1 (1926–1929): 65; "British-American Tobacco," reprint from London *Times,* 11 January 1936, in James Augustus Thomas Papers, SCL; Jack J. Gottsegen, *Tobacco: A Study of Its Consumption in the United States* (New York: Pitman, 1940), 56 (sales measured in constant 1913 dollars); Bruce Barton to Paul Hahn, 28 December 1953, BP (Barron).

15. "Fashion," *International Quarterly* 10 (1904): 130–155, quotation on pp. 138–139. Whether Simmel's theory applies to a world in which mass media simultaneously expose all social classes to new trends is debatable. There is, nevertheless, broad agreement that fashion worked in top-down cycles in the West prior to the twentieth century.

16. "Opium Smoking in the East End of London," 1864 article reprinted in *All About Opium,* ed. Hartmann Henry Sultzberger (London: Wertheimer, Lea, 1884), 176.

17. Robert L. DuPont, *The Selfish Brain: Learning from Addiction* (Washington, D.C.: American Psychiatric Press, 1997), 99 (plateau); Siegel, *Intoxication,* 274 (FDR); David Thomson, *Showman: The Life of David O. Selznick* (New York: Knopf, 1992), 231, 610; Randy Roberts and James S. Olson, *John Wayne: American* (New York: Free Press, 1995), 510.

18. Quoted in Philip J. Hilts, *Smokescreen: The Truth Behind the Tobacco Industry Cover-Up* (Reading, Mass.: Addison-Wesley, 1996), 1.

19. Francis Bacon, *The Historie of Life and Death* (London: I. Okes for Humphrey Mosley, 1638 translation), 151; "Letter of Tomé Pires to King Manuel," trans. Amando Cortesão, *Works Issued by the Hakluyt Society,* 2nd ser., no. 90 (1944): 513; Jessica Warner, "'Resolv'd to Drink No More': Addiction as a Preindustrial Construct," *J. of Studies on Alcohol* 55 (1994): 685–691, "turne" on p. 687.

20. Ralph S. Hattox, *Coffee and Coffeehouses: The Origins of a Social Beverage in the Medieval Near East* (Seattle: U. of Washington Press, 1985), 60, 89–91.

21. Jürgen Schneider, "'. . . Macht munter und vertreibt den Schlaf . . .': Produktion, Handel und Konsum von Kaffee" [freely translated: "'It Makes You Rise and Shine': Production, Trade, and Consumption of Coffee"], *Kultur und Technik* 4 (1988): 237; Peter Albrecht, "Coffee-Drinking as a Symbol of Social Change in Continental Europe in the Seventeenth and Eighteenth Centuries," *Studies in Eighteenth-Century Culture* 18 (1988): 91–103.

22. Elisabeth Rosenthal with Larry Altman, "China, a Land of Heavy Smokers, Looks Into Abyss of Fatal Illness," *NYT*, nat. ed., 20 November 1998, A10; John Uri Lloyd, *Coffee* (reprint of 1929 *Eclectic Medical Journal* series), 8, KRF C39(g): Coffee.

23. Richard Kluger, *Ashes to Ashes: America's Hundred-Year Cigarette War, the Public Health, and the Unabashed Triumph of Philip Morris* (New York: Knopf, 1996), 65; quotations from cigarette smoking study in "Minutes, 1969," box 20 of review board meetings, JWT.

24. Caroline Knapp, *Drinking: A Love Story* (New York: Dial Press, 1996), 74; *Macbeth*, act 2, scene 1.

25. Francisco Guerra, "Sex and Drugs in the 16th Century," *BJA* 69 (1974): 269–273, quotations on p. 273.

26. Gösta Rylander, "Clinical and Medico-Criminological Aspects of Addiction to Central Stimulating Drugs," in *Abuse of Central Stimulants*, ed. Folke Sjöqvist and Malcolm Tottie (New York: Raven Press, 1969), 256 ("pump"); David Healy, *The Antidepressant Era* (Cambridge, Mass.: Harvard U. Press, 1997), 209 ("film star"); P. V. Taberner, *Aphrodisiacs: The Science and the Myth* (Philadelphia: U. of Pennsylvania Press, 1985).

27. Timothy Leary, *The Politics of Ecstasy* (Berkeley: Ronin, 1990), 127, 129; CC, 46, 98, 164, 196, 202, 210–213, 367; Edward R. Bloomquist, "Marijuana: Social Benefit or Social Detriment?" *California Medicine* 106 (1967): 348; George R. Gay et al., "Love and Haight: The Sensuous Hippie Revisited. Drug/Sex Practices in San Francisco, 1980–1981," *J. of Psychoactive Drugs* 14 (1982): 111–123.

28. Erich Goode, "Marijuana and Sex," *Evergreen Review* 13 (May 1969): 21 (student); Joseph McIver and George E. Price, "Drug Addiction: Analysis of One Hundred and Forty-seven Cases at the Philadelphia General Hospital," *JAMA* 66 (1916): 478.

29. *Basketball Diaries* (New York: Penguin, 1995), 30; Count [Egon Caesar] Corti, *A History of Smoking*, trans. Paul England (New York: Harcourt, Brace, 1932), 72 (Elizabeth); Laura L. Phillips, "In Defense of Their Fam-

ilies: Working-Class Women, Alcohol, and Politics in Revolutionary Russia," *J. of Women's History* 11 (1999): 99–100; Frank McCourt, *Angela's Ashes: A Memoir* (New York: Scribner, 1996), 345; John Updike, "My Father on the Verge of Disgrace," *New Yorker* 73 (10 March 1997): 84.

30. Erik Aerts and Richard Unger, "Brewing in the Low Countries," in *PMCAB*, 99–100; *CC*, 339–340; E. A. Ayandele, *The Missionary Impact on Modern Nigeria, 1842–1914: A Political and Social Analysis* (London: Longmans, 1966), 308; "Confidential Case History of the General Cigar Company" (TS, 1961), 31, box 6 of account files, JWT; Jan R. McTavish, "Aspirin in Germany: The Pharmaceutical Industry and the Pharmaceutical Profession," *Pharmacy in History* 29 (1987): 104.

31. On tobacco and alcohol as gateway drugs see, e.g., Dean I. Manheimer and Glen D. Mellinger, "Marijuana Use Among Urban Adults," *Science* 166 (1969): 1545.

32. The examples of externalities were culled from several dozen sources, too numerous to cite in their entirety. Representative sources are Anon., *The Smoker's Guide, Philosopher, and Friend* (London: Hardwicke and Bogue, 1876), 97 (Meerschaum) and *Maltine with Coca Wine* (pamphlet, ca. 1895), 16, MTE (withdrawal). "Got a hangover?" is from "The Sun Never Sets on Cacoola," *Time* 55 (15 February 1950): 29; "day most Bromo-Seltzer" from Philip Richardson, "Emerson Drug Company" (TS), 6, forum series, 12 January 1937, JWT; and "Soothes" from the author's collection. Cigarette-paper extrapolation: "Marijuana Consumption Estimates" (TS, 1979), VF "Addiction—Incidence, 1976–1979."

33. The 1992 data are from National Institute on Drug Abuse, "The Economic Costs of Alcohol and Drug Abuse in the United States—1992," *http:// www.nida.nih.gov/EconomicCosts/Table4_1.html*, 22 June 2000. William White (whence "dip shops") assisted me in tracking down information on treatment expenditures.

34. Thomas L. Friedman, "Big Mac II," *NYT*, nat. ed., 11 December 1996, A21; Trip Gabriel, "Will 55¢ Hamburgers Cheapen the Diet?" *NYT*, nat. ed., 5 March 1997, B1; Jolie Solomon and John McCormick, "A Really Big Mac," *Newsweek* 130 (17 November 1997): 56; Alexander Stille, "Perils of the Sphinx," *New Yorker* 72 (10 February 1997): 54; Orville Schell, *Discos and Democracy: China in the Throes of Reform* (New York: Pantheon, 1988), 380; and AP wire stories.

35. Susan L. Speaker, personal communication, 23 September 1999; Randolph M. Nesse and George C. Williams, "Evolution and the Origins of Disease," *Scientific American* 279 (November 1998): 91.

36. Richard Klein, *Eat Fat* (New York: Pantheon, 1996), 194.

37. Jean Dawnay, *Model Girl* (London: Weidenfeld and Nicolson, 1956), 143; Neil E. Grunberg, "Nicotine as a Psychoactive Drug: Appetite Regulation," *Psychopharmacology Bulletin* 22 (1986): 875–881; Andie MacDowell in Anita Chaudhuri, "The Mane Event," *The Guardian* (London), 19 September 1996, LN; Michael Fleming, "Playboy Interview: Robert Downey Jr.," *Playboy* 44 (December 1997), LN.

38. Thomas Merton, *The Seven Storey Mountain* (San Diego: Harcourt Brace Jovanovich, 1976 reprint ed.), 133.

6. Escape from Commodity Hell

1. "The Challenge of Reducing Drug Abuse and Its Consequences: A Historical Perspective," speech before the Commonwealth Club, San Francisco, 2 July 1997 (Washington, D.C.: Office of National Drug Control Policy, 1997), 4.

2. FTC field report, 5 February 1943, box 7, Paris Cleveland Gardner Papers, SCL.

3. James Surowiecki, "The Billion-Dollar Blade," *New Yorker* 74 (15 June 1998): 46 ("commodity hell"); Li-Tzy Wu and James C. Anthony, "Tobacco Smoking and Other Suspected Antecedents of Nonmedical Psychostimulant Use in the United States, 1995," *SUM* 34 (1999): 1243–1259; A. D. Lê et al., "Involvement of Nicotinic Receptors in Alcohol Self-Administration," *Alcoholism: Clinical and Experimental Research* 24 (2000): 155–163; Charles B. Towns, *Habits That Handicap: The Menace of Opium, Alcohol, and Tobacco, and the Remedy* (New York: Century, 1916), 152–153, 172 (quotation). Work on tobacco as a gateway drug is reviewed in Gordon B. Lindsay and Jacquie Rainey, "Psychological and Pharmacologic Explanations of Nicotine's 'Gateway Drug' Function," *J. of School Health* 67 (1997): 123–126.

4. Archer quoted in *Contemporary Authors*, new rev. series, vol. 52 (Detroit: Gale, 1996), 15. Duke: "Death of Mr. James Buchanan Duke," *B.A.T. Bulletin* 16 (October 1925): 154 ("loved").

5. Wolfgang Schivelbusch, *Tastes of Paradise: A Social History of Spices, Stimulants, and Intoxicants*, trans. David Jacobson (New York: Pantheon, 1992), 111–116; "Going Up in Smoke," *NYT*, 24 September 1925, p. 24 (quotation).

6. This account of Duke's career draws on John K. Winkler, *Tobacco Tycoon: The Story of James Buchanan Duke* (New York: Random House, 1942); Richard Kluger, *Ashes to Ashes: America's Hundred-Year Cigarette War, the Public Health, and the Unabashed Triumph of Philip Morris* (New York: Knopf, 1996), ch. 1; and Cassandra Tate, *Cigarette Wars: The Triumph of "the Little White Slaver"* (New York: Oxford U. Press, 1999), ch. 1, "dope sticks" on pp. 26–27. The hypodermic analogy is from Henner Hess, *Rauchen:*

Geschichte, Geschäfte, Gefahren [Smoking: History, Business, Dangers] (Frankfurt: Campus Verlag, 1987), 49.

7. Emma Goldman, *Living My Life* (New York: AMS Press, 1970 reprint ed.), 141, italics added.

8. Stevenson: *From Scotland to Silverado*, ed. James D. Hart (Cambridge, Mass.: Harvard U. Press, 1966), 109; Winkler, *Tobacco Tycoon*, 66 ("whopping").

9. Winkler, *Tobacco Tycoon*, 111–112, 206.

10. Jacob Riis, "What Ails Our Boys?" *Craftsman* 21 (October 1911): 5–6.

11. Maurice Corina, *Trust in Tobacco: The Anglo-American Struggle for Power* (New York: St. Martin's Press, 1975), chs. 4–6; Winkler, *Tobacco Tycoon*, world trust on p. 147; Sherman Cochran, *Big Business in China: Sino-Foreign Rivalry in the Cigarette Industry, 1890–1930* (Cambridge, Mass.: Harvard U. Press, 1980), "we are going to sell" on pp. 10–11.

12. Cochran, *Big Business in China*, "missionary" on p. 15, fools enough on p. 17; Wu Sing Pang, "Mr. Wu Recalls His Family's BAT Links of Pre-War Years," *BAT News*, no vol. (Spring 1988): 10; James A. Thomas, *A Pioneer Tobacco Merchant in the Orient* (Durham, N.C.: Duke U. Press, 1928), quotations on pp. 58, 237; "China," *B.A.T. Bulletin* 20 (March 1930): 166 (clock); "Head Office," *B.A.T. Bulletin* 16 (December 1925): 221 (dividends).

13. Cochran, *Big Business in China*, "weaning" on p. 246 n. 67. Cochran, 11, 225, estimates sales of 12 billion in 1916; Howard Cox, *The Global Cigarette: Origins and Evolution of British American Tobacco, 1880–1945* (Oxford: Oxford U. Press, 2000), 157, estimates a more conservative 9.6 billion.

14. Robert F. Durden, "Tar Heel Tobacconist in Tokyo, 1899–1904," *North Carolina Historical Review* 53 (1976): 347–363; Tengu ad in box 7, Edward James Parrish Papers, SCL.

15. Myron Levin, "World's Two Top Cigarette Manufacturers Conspired to Fix Latin American Prices," *Philadelphia Inquirer*, 18 September 1998, A10; Glenn Collins, "U.S. Tobacco Industry Looks Longingly at Chinese Market, but in Vain," *NYT*, nat. ed., 20 November 1998, A10.

16. Charles A. Lindbergh, *Autobiography of Values*, ed. William Jovanovich and Judith A. Schiff (New York: Harcourt Brace Jovanovich, 1976), 14; Staff meetings, representatives' meeting minutes, 9 January 1929, JWT (Tareyton); Cox, *Global Cigarette*, plate 46 (Chile); Roger E. Bilstein, *Flight in America: From the Wrights to the Astronauts*, rev. ed. (Baltimore: Johns Hopkins U. Press, 1994), 62.

17. Barton memoranda, with one minor change in punctuation, 3 May 1948, 23 July 1948, 24 August 1948, 23 February 1949, 14 November 1949, and 25 September 1950, in American Tobacco folder, box 75, BP; Michael Bloch, *The*

Secret File of the Duke of Windsor (New York: Harper and Row, 1988), 229–235.

18. JJD to John W. Hill, 14 December 1953, box 110, folder 10, HP.

19. Steve Karnowski, "Ammonia Called Marlboro's Secret," *AP Online*, 8 February 1998, LN.

20. "Minutes, 1969," box 20 of review board meetings, JWT.

21. David A. Kessler et al., "The Food and Drug Administration's Regulation of Tobacco Products," *NEJM* 335 (1996): 989.

22. Paul M. Hahn to John W. Hill, 5 February 1958, in box 108, folder 10, HP, is representative of industry rationalization. Canaries: Donald L. Maggin, *Stan Getz: A Life in Jazz* (New York: William Morrow, 1996), 99. Medical turn: John C. Burnham, "American Physicians and Tobacco Use: Two Surgeons General, 1929 and 1964," *Bulletin of the History of Medicine* 63 (1989): 1–31.

23. Godfrey quote in *Advertising Age* reprint, 6 November 1961, account files (Liggett and Meyers), box 12, JWT, with minor change in spelling.

24. Boxes 108–111 of HP; Philip J. Hilts, *Smokescreen: The Truth Behind the Tobacco Industry Cover-Up* (Reading, Mass.: Addison-Wesley, 1996), chs. 1–3.

25. Paris: "Report from France on Cigarette Controversy" (TS, 1954), box 109, folder 6, HP. TMSC: box 109, folder 5, HP, quotations from Campbell-Johnson to John Hill, 12 June 1956, "Survey of Opinion on Smoking and Lung Cancer" (TS, 1958), 2, and Campbell-Johnson to Hill, 23 April 1958.

26. National Clearinghouse on Tobacco and Health, "Daily Consumption of Cigarettes (per capita 15+)," *http://www.cctc.ca/ncth/stats/sales/sales-caus-6191.pdf*, 11 February 2000; Kluger, *Ashes to Ashes*, 703.

27. Barry Meier, "Files of R. J. Reynolds . . .," *NYT*, nat. ed., 15 January 1998, A10 ("ensure"); Kluger, *Ashes to Ashes*, 445 ("pot"), 570; "Minutes, 1961: L&M 3 Brands," in box 19 of review board meetings, JWT ("dangerously").

28. Stan Sesser, "Opium War Redux," *New Yorker* 59 (13 September 1993): 81 ("Dean"); Hilts, *Smokescreen*, ch. 6, "kids" on pp. 96–97.

29. Kluger, *Ashes to Ashes*, 443, 710 (Japanese label); Mac Marshall, "An Overview of Drugs in Oceania," in *Drugs in Western Pacific Societies*, ed. Lamont Lindstrom (Lanham, Md.: U. Press of America, 1987), 35–36; Anna White, "Joe Camel's World Tour," *NYT*, nat. ed., 23 April 1997, A21; Kjell Bjartveit, "The History of the Norwegian Ban on Tobacco Advertising," in *AA*, 216–220; Simon Chapman, "Cigarette Advertising and Smoking: A Review of the Evidence," in *Smoking Out the Barons: The Campaign Against the Tobacco Industry* (Chichester: Wiley, 1986), 90–92.

30. World Health Organization, "The Tobacco Epidemic: A Global Public Health Emergency," *http://www.who/int/inf-fs/en/fact118.html*, 29 June 2000; Shankar Vedantam, "Cancer and Heart Death Rise Predicted," *Philadelphia*

Inquirer, 5 May 1997, A8 (1 percent); Tom Stevenson, "BAT Draws on Massive Third World Craving," *The Independent*, 7 March 1996, LN; "BAT Companies Take Strong Eastern Bloc Position," *Tobacco International* 193 (15 June 1991): 52 (Sheehy); Kluger, *Ashes to Ashes*, 709–711 (Japanese market); Jonathan D. Canter et al., *Harvard/Radcliffe Class of 1970 25th Reunion: Answers to the Anonymous Questionnaire* (1995), kindly furnished by the Harvard Alumni Office.

31. David M. Halbfinger, "Icy, Fruity Malt Liquor Lures Minors, Critics Say," *NYT*, 24 July 1997, LN; David H. Jernigan, *Thirsting for Markets: The Global Impact of Corporate Alcohol* (San Rafael, Calif.: Marin Institute, 1997); *Life with Heroin: Voices from the Inner City*, ed. Bill Hanson et al.(Lexington, Mass.: Lexington Books, 1985), 117.

32. Jordan Goodman, *Tobacco in History: The Cultures of Dependence* (London: Routledge, 1993), 228.

33. R. N. Chopra and Gurbaksh Singh Chopra, "Cocaine Habit in India," *Indian J. of Medical Sciences* 18 (1931): 1018–1022; Ernest K. Gann, *Ernest K. Gann's Flying Circus* (New York: Macmillan, 1974), 39 (Alaska); Lindbergh, *Autobiography of Values*, 31, 41; Benjamin R. Barber, *Jihad vs. McWorld* (New York: Times Books, 1995).

34. Albert Stridsberg to Dan Seymour, 9 August 1965, box 25, Edward G. Wilson Papers, JWT; Stridsberg's late 1960s writings in box 33, Writings and Speeches collection, JWT, quotation from *Advertising Age* offprint, 31 March 1969, p. 3; Arne H. Eide and S. W. Acuda, "Cultural Orientation and Use of Cannabis and Inhalants among Secondary School Children in Zimbabwe," *Social Science and Medicine* 45 (1997): 1241–1249.

35. Richard Rhodes, *The Making of the Atomic Bomb* (New York: Simon and Schuster, 1986), 778–788.

36. 80 million: R. T. Ravenholt, "Tobaccosis," in *The Cambridge World History of Human Disease*, ed. Kenneth F. Kiple (Cambridge: Cambridge U. Press, 1993), 185, plus estimated toll for 1990s from the World Health Organization's "Tobacco Epidemic." The WHO also estimates that in one year, 1990, alcohol caused 750,000 more deaths than it averted, with most of the excess deaths in developing regions. (*The Global Burden of Disease: Summary*, ed. Christopher J. L. Murray and Alan D. Lopez [Cambridge, Mass.: Harvard U. Press, 1996], 29–30.) Factoring in population and technological change (i.e., fewer people, machines, and cars earlier in the century than in 1990), a rough minimum estimate of the net number of premature, alcohol-related deaths would be 25 million. The century's toll of premature deaths attributable to drugs other than tobacco and alcohol is unknown, but must also run into the millions.

7. Opiates of the People

1. Frank Browne, "Opium: Its Nature, Composition, Preparations, and Methods of Consumption," *Pharmaceutical J. and Pharmacist* 84 (1910): 453 ("reliable"); Gunther Barth, *Bitter Strength: A History of the Chinese in the United States, 1850–1870* (Cambridge, Mass.: Harvard U. Press, 1964); Walton Look Lai, *Indentured Labor, Caribbean Sugar: Chinese and Indian Migrants to the British West Indies, 1838–1918* (Baltimore: Johns Hopkins University Press, 1993), 100 (overdose).

2. Lynn Pan, *Sons of the Yellow Emperor* (Boston: Little, Brown, 1990), 118–120; William G. Skinner, *Chinese Society in Thailand: An Analytical History* (Ithaca: Cornell U. Press, 1957), 119–125; Carl A. Trocki, *Opium and Empire: Chinese Society in Colonial Singapore, 1800–1910* (Ithaca: Cornell U. Press, 1990), 2, 67, 69.

3. Baron Harry D'Erlanger, *The Last Plague of Egypt* (London: Lovat Dickson and Thompson, 1936), 15–16; Peter Loverde, "Heroin in the Hills . . .: Drug Abuse Patterns among Three Groups in Thailand," *Community Epidemiology Work Group, June 1995, Proceedings*, vol. 2 (Rockville, Md · National Institutes of Health, 1995), 362.

4. Vera Rubin and Lambros Comitas, *Ganja in Jamaica: A Medical Anthropological Study of Chronic Marijuana Use* (The Hague: Mouton, 1975), 43, 150, 165–167; I. C. Chopra and R. N. Chopra, "The Use of Cannabis Drugs in India," *BN* 9 (Jan.–March 1957): 18, 27; William L. Partridge, "Cannabis and Cultural Groups in a Colombian *Municipio*," in *CC*, 163.

5. Stephen White, *Russia Goes Dry: Alcohol, State and Society* (Cambridge: Cambridge U. Press, 1996), ch. 1; Elizbieta Kaczyńska and Barbara Petz, "Alcoholic Beverages: Economic Gain and Social Pathology in Poland and Russia," in *PMCAB*, 49 (paid in vodka); Ernest Poole, *The Village: Russian Impressions* (New York: Macmillan, 1918), 152–154 (Tarasov); Émile Zola, *Les Rougon-Macquart: Histoire Naturelle et Sociale d'une Famille sous le Second Empire*, vol. 2 (Paris: Gallimard, 1961), 1540.

6. Letter from Frithjof Meidell to his mother, 7 August 1855, trans. in *Land of Their Choice: The Immigrants Write Home*, ed. Theodore Blegen (Minneapolis: U. of Minnesota Press, 1955), 312.

7. *The Autobiography of Benjamin Franklin*, ed. Leonard W. Labaree et al. (New Haven: Yale U. Press, 1964), 100.

8. P. K. Gode, "References to Tobacco in Some Sanskrit Works between A.D. 1600 and 1900," in *Studies in Indian Cultural History*, vol. 1 (Hoshiarpur: Vishveshvaranand Vedic Research Institute, 1960), 412; Rowland, unpaginated dedication to Giles Everard, *Panacea; or the Universal Medicine, Being*

a Discovery of the Wonderful Vertues of Tobacco . . . (London: Simon Miller, 1659; first pub. 1587); Thomas Short, *Discourses on Tea, Sugar, Milk, Made-wines, Spirits, Punch, Tobacco, &c: With Plain and Useful Rules for Gouty People* (London: T. Longman and A. Millar, 1750), 250 ("Scantling"); V. G. Kiernan, *Tobacco: A History* (London: Hutchinson Radius, 1991), 160 (Petty); T. J. Woofter, Jr., *The Plight of Cigarette Tobacco* (Chapel Hill: U. of North Carolina Press, 1931), 63–64; Jack J. Gottsegen, *Tobacco: A Study of Its Consumption in the United States* (New York: Pitman, 1940), 64.

9. Representative discussions of infant drugging are Sami Hamarneh, "Pharmacy in Medieval Islam and the History of Drug Addiction," *Medical History* 16 (1972): 230, 234; Jean-Jacques Yvorel, *Les Poisons de l'Espirit: Drogues et Drogués au XIXᵉ Siècle* (Paris: Quai Voltaire, 1992), 49–54; and James Fisher, "Cannabis in Nepal: An Overview," in CC, 251.

10. Personal communications from Deborah Maloy (zoos) and Farol Tomson (labs), March 1999; "'Four-legged Person'; Animal Behaviorist Defends Giving Bear Prescription for Anti-depressant," *Calgary Herald*, 8 January 1995, LN; Alex Lo, "Hong Kong's Dogs . . .," *South China Morning Post*, 31 January 1999, LN.

11. Stephen Braun, *Buzz: The Science and Lore of Alcohol and Caffeine* (New York: Oxford U. Press, 1996), 143 (Tibet); Lester Grinspoon and Peter Hedblom, *The Speed Culture: Amphetamine Use and Abuse in America* (Cambridge, Mass.: Harvard U. Press, 1975), 24 (hens); Jean Benoist, "Réunion: Cannabis in a Pluricultural and Polyethnic Society," in CC, 231 (cocks); Ronald K. Siegel, *Intoxication: Life in Pursuit of Artificial Paradise* (New York: E. P. Dutton, 1989), 135–137 (elephants).

12. Siegel, *Intoxication*, 135 (Turkey); Samuel Morewood, *A Philosophical and Statistical History of . . . Inebriating Liquors* (Dublin: William Curry, 1838), 2nd ed., 117 (race horses); Donald MacLaren [and William Moore], "Opium Eating and Smoking," *Medical Brief* 35 (1907): 594 (Rajputs).

13. J. F. Siler et al., "Mariajuana [*sic*] Smoking in Panama," *Military Surgeon* 73 (1933): 273; Roger Joseph, "The Economic Significance of *Cannabis sativa* in the Moroccan Rif," in CC, 191.

14. John Maxwell O'Brien, *Alexander the Great: The Invisible Enemy* (London: Routledge, 1992), 196; Anthony A. Braccia, "Wine and Grog in Naval History," *Bulletin of the Society of Medical Friends of Wine* 16 (September 1974): n.p.; Joseph Plumb Martin, *Private Yankee Doodle: Being a Narrative of Some of the Adventures, Dangers and Sufferings of a Revolutionary Soldier*, ed. George F. Scheer (Boston: Little, Brown, 1962), 89–90.

15. Paul E. Kopperman, "'The Cheapest Pay': Alcohol Abuse in the Eighteenth-

Century British Army," *J. of Military History* 60 (1996): 445–470, quotations on pp. 455, 468.

16. Stephen E. Ambrose, *Undaunted Courage: Meriwether Lewis, Thomas Jefferson, and the Opening of the American West* (New York: Simon and Schuster, 1996), 108; James M. McPherson, *For Cause and Comrades: Why Men Fought in the Civil War* (New York: Oxford U. Press, 1997), 52–53; William E. Unrau, *White Man's Wicked Water: The Alcohol Trade and Prohibition in Indian Country, 1802–1892* (Lawrence: U. Press of Kansas, 1996), 7.

17. Benjamin Rush, *Essays, Literary, Moral and Philosophical* (Philadelphia: Thomas and Samuel F. Branford, 1798), 264; Anon., *The Smoker's Guide, Philosopher and Friend* (London: Hardwicke and Bogue, 1876), 64 (Solferino).

18. Cassandra Tate, *Cigarette Wars: The Triumph of "the Little White Slaver"* (New York: Oxford U. Press, 1999), ch. 3, quotation on p. 88; James R. Mellow, *Hemingway: A Life Without Consequences* (Boston: Houghton Mifflin, 1992), 60.

19. Meyers to her parents, 4 November 1918, MS collection 70A, KSHS; von Kennell diary, miscellaneous MS, box 7, KSHS (with minor changes in spelling); Denis Winter, *The First of the Few: Fighter Pilots of the First World War* (Athens: U. of Georgia Press, 1983), 152 and passim; George Coppard, *With a Machine Gun to Cambrai: The Tale of a Young Tommy in Kitchener's Army, 1914–1918* (London: His Majesty's Stationery Office, 1969), 44, 120; Virginia Berridge, *Opium and the People: Opiate Use and Drug Control Policy in Nineteenth and Early Twentieth Century England* (London: Free Association Books, 1999), 249 (packets).

20. Mikuláš Teich, "The Industrialization of Brewing in Germany (1800–1914)," in *PMCAB*, 102; *International Smoking Statistics: A Collection of Historical Data from 22 Economically Developed Countries*, ed. Ans Nicolaides-Bouman et al. (London: Wolfson Institute of Preventive Medicine, 1993), 255 (Japan); Richard Kluger, *Ashes to Ashes: America's Hundred-Year Cigarette War, the Public Health, and the Unabashed Triumph of Philip Morris* (New York: Knopf, 1996), 112–123; Stephen E. Ambrose, *The Victors: Eisenhower and His Boys: The Men of World War II* (New York: Simon and Schuster, 1998), 75 (airborne).

21. Robert N. Proctor, "The Nazi War on Tobacco: Ideology, Evidence, and Possible Cancer Consequences," *Bulletin of the History of Medicine* 71 (1997): 480; Larry Collins and Dominique Lapierre, *Is Paris Burning?* (New York: Simon and Schuster, 1965), 278; Thomas Keneally, *Schindler's List* (New York: Touchstone, 1993), 214; Daniel Jonah Goldhagen, *Hitler's Willing Execu-*

tioners: Ordinary Germans and the Holocaust (New York: Knopf, 1996), 221,
224–230; *"The Good Old Days": The Holocaust as Seen by Its Perpetrators and Bystanders*, ed. Ernst Klee et al., trans. Deborah Burnstone (New York: Free Press, 1991), xiii, 62, 67, 259 (Kremer quotation).

22. Josie Washburn, *The Underworld Sewer: A Prostitute Reflects on Life in the Trade, 1871–1909* (Lincoln: U. of Nebraska Press, 1997 reprint ed.), quotations on pp. 170, 211–212, 328.

23. Kathryn Meyer, "Garden of Grand Vision: Economic Life in a Flophouse Complex, China—1941" (unpublished paper, 1999), and personal communication, 20 December 1999; James A. Inciardi et al., "Male Transvestite Prostitution and Drug Use in Rio de Janeiro," paper presented at the American Society of Criminology meeting, Washington, D.C., 14 November 1998.

24. Yahya H. Affinnih, "A Review of Literature on Drug Use in Sub-Saharan Africa . . .," *SUM* 34 (1999): 448; Donald R. Wesson, "Cocaine Use by Masseuses," *J. of Psychoactive Drugs* 14 (1982): 75; George R. Gay et al., "Love and Haight: The Sensuous Hippie Revisited. Drug/Sex Practices in San Francisco, 1980–1981," *J. of Psychoactive Drugs* 14 (1982): 115–118 (informants); James A. Inciardi and Hilary L. Surratt, "Children in the Streets of Brazil: Drug Use, Crime, Violence, and HIV Risks," *SUM* 33 (1998): 1470 (quotation).

25. Paul E. Lovejoy, "Kola Nuts: The 'Coffee' of the Central Sudan," in *CH*, 114; William E. Wormsley, "Beer and Power in Enga," in *Drugs in Western Pacific Societies*, ed. Lamont Lindstrom (Lanham, Md.: U. Press of America, 1987), 205. Germany: Frank McCourt, *'Tis: A Memoir* (New York: Scribner, 1999), 95–96, and Mark Pendergrast, *For God, Country and Coca-Cola* (New York: Charles Scribner's Sons, 1993), 215–216. Staircase: Bruce D. Johnson et al., "Nurturing for Careers in Drug Use and Crime: Conduct Norms for Children and Juveniles in Crack-Using Households," *SUM* 33 (1998): 1529. Delawares: *Journals of Charles Beatty, 1762–1769*, ed. Guy Soulliard Klett (University Park: Pennsylvania U. Press, 1962), 67.

26. Philip D. Curtin, *The Rise and Fall of the Plantation Complex: Essays in Atlantic History* (Cambridge: Cambridge U. Press, 1990), 14–15.

27. Andrew Weil, "The New Politics of Coca," *New Yorker* 71 (15 May 1995): 74.

28. Peter Mancall, *Deadly Medicine: Indians and Alcohol in Early America* (Ithaca: Cornell U. Press, 1995); *Documents Relative to the Colonial History of the State of New-York . . .*, vol. 7, ed. E. B. O'Callaghan (Albany: Weed, Parsons, 1856), 613 ("spurs them on"); John Heckewelder, *History, Manners, and Customs of the Indian Nations Who Once Inhabited Pennsylvania and the Neighbouring States*, rev. ed. (Philadelphia: Historical Society of Penn-

sylvania, 1876), 267 ("drunken dog"); Anthony F. C. Wallace, *Jefferson and the Indians: The Tragic Fate of the First Americans* (Cambridge, Mass.: Harvard U. Press, 1999), 297 (two dollars).

29. John Lawson, *A New Voyage to Carolina* (Ann Arbor: University Microfilms, 1966 facsimile of 1709 London ed.), 200–203, 231; *The Documentary History of the State of New-York*, ed. E. B. O'Callaghan, vol. 2 (Albany: Weed, Parsons, 1849), 92.

30. Mancall, *Deadly Medicine*; Louvigny, memorial of 15 October 1720, in *Wisconsin Historical Collections*, vol. 16 (Madison: Wisconsin Historical Society, 1902), 388–389.

31. *The World Turned Upside Down: Indian Voices from Early America*, ed. Colin G. Calloway (Boston: Bedford, 1994), 108 (Nopkehe); David T. Courtwright, *Violent Land: Single Men and Social Disorder from the Frontier to the Inner City* (Cambridge, Mass.: Harvard U. Press, 1996), ch. 6 (nineteenth century).

32. Proctor, "Nazi War on Tobacco," 471 ("wrath"); Alexander von Gernet, "Nicotinian Dreams: The Prehistory and Early History of Tobacco in Eastern North America," in *CH*, 72, 77–80; and Arthur Woodward, *The Denominators of the Fur Trade* (Pasadena: Socio-Technical Publications, 1970), 45.

33. Curtin, *Plantation Complex*, 38–39, 211, and José Carlos Curto, "Alcohol and Slaves: The Luso-Brazilian Alcohol Commerce at Mpinda, Luanda, and Benguela during the Atlantic Slave Trade c. 1480–1830 and its Impact on the Societies of West Central Africa" (Ph.D. diss., U. of California at Los Angeles, 1996), Vasconcelos on p. 442.

34. Jordan Goodman, *Tobacco in History: The Cultures of Dependence* (London: Routledge, 1993), 163; Ernst Pijning, "Conflicts in the Portuguese Colonial Administration . . .," *Colonial Latin American Review* 2 (1993): 412; George Metcalf, "A Microcosm of Why Africans Sold Slaves: Akan Consumption Patterns in the 1770s," *J. of African History* 28 (1987): 377–394, Miles on p. 382; Jay Coughtry, *The Notorious Triangle: Rhode Island and the African Slave Trade, 1700–1807* (Philadelphia: Temple University Press, 1981), 84; Russell R. Menard and John J. McCusker, *The Economy of British North America, 1607–1789* (Chapel Hill: U. of North Carolina Press, 1985), 108.

35. Sidney W. Mintz, *Sweetness and Power: The Place of Sugar in Modern History* (New York: Viking, 1985), 72; Curto, "Alcohol and Slaves," 354 (church).

36. W. G. L. Randles, *L'Ancien Royaume du Congo: Des Origines à la Fin du XIXe Siècle* (Paris: Mouton, 1968), 188; E. A. Ayandele, *The Missionary Impact on Modern Nigeria, 1842–1914: A Political and Social Analysis* (London: Longmans, 1966), 308–309, 317; Charles Ambler, "The Alcohol Question in

British West Africa," paper presented at the American Historical Association meeting, January 1997; *Fillmore's Prohibition Songs*, ed. Charles M. Fillmore and J. H. Fillmore (Cincinnati: Fillmore and Brothers, 1903), no. 176.

37. A. Olorunfemi, "The Liquor Traffic Dilemma in British West Africa: The Southern Nigeria Example, 1895–1918," *International J. of African Historical Studies* 17 (1984): 237 (Lagos); Jean Cuvelier, *L'Ancien Royaume de Congo* (Bruges: Desclée de Brouwer, 1946), 227–228 (trading partners).

38. Brian Roberts, *Cecil Rhodes: Flawed Colossus* (New York: Norton, 1987), 106, 124–133.

8. Taxes and Smuggling

1. Jacob M. Price, "The Tobacco Adventure to Russia: Enterprise, Politics, and Diplomacy in the Quest for a Northern Market for English Colonial Tobacco," *Transactions of the American Philosophical Society*, n.s. 51 (1961): 20 (Peter the Great); Joel Best, "Economic Interests and the Vindication of Deviance: Tobacco in Seventeenth Century Europe," *Sociological Quarterly* 20 (Spring 1979): 171–182; Edmund S. Morgan, *American Slavery, American Freedom: The Ordeal of Colonial Virginia* (New York: Norton, 1975), 193, 197.

2. C. van Arendonk and K. N. Chaudhuri, "Kahwa," *Encyclopedia of Islam*, new ed., vol. 4 (Leiden: E. J. Brill, 1978), 452; S. W. F. Holloway, "The Regulation of the Supply of Drugs in Britain before 1868," in *DNH*, 82.

3. Jan Rogoziński, *Smokeless Tobacco in the Western World, 1550–1950* (New York: Praeger, 1990), ch. 4; James R. Rush, *Opium to Java: Revenue Farming and Chinese Enterprise in Colonial Indonesia, 1860–1910* (Ithaca: Cornell U. Press, 1990).

4. Benjamin Woods Labaree, *The Boston Tea Party* (New York: Oxford U. Press, 1964).

5. Firuz Kazemzadeh, *Russia and Britain in Persia, 1864–1914: A Study in Imperialism* (New Haven: Yale U. Press, 1968), ch. 4; Peter Avery, *Modern Iran* (New York: Praeger, 1965), ch. 7; Sandra Mackey with W. Scott Harrop, *The Iranians: Persia, Islam and the Soul of a Nation* (New York: Dutton, 1996), 136–143.

6. Lynn Pan, *Sons of the Yellow Emperor* (Boston: Little, Brown, 1990), 120 (Singapore); Kathryn Meyer and Terry Parssinen, *Webs of Smoke: Smugglers, Warlords, Spies, and the History of the International Drug Trade* (Lanham, Md.: Rowman and Littlefield, 1998), ch. 3; Carl A. Trocki, *Opium and Empire: Chinese Society in Colonial Singapore, 1800–1910* (Ithaca: Cornell U. Press, 1990), chs. 7–8; Harold Traver, "Opium to Heroin: Restrictive Opium

Legislation and the Rise of Heroin Consumption in Hong Kong," *J. of Policy History* 4 (1992): 307–324.

7. *The Diary of John Evelyn* (Oxford: Clarendon Press, 1955), vol. 1, 15 (*De Vita Propria*); David Christian, *Living Water: Vodka and Russian Society on the Eve of Emancipation* (Oxford: Clarendon Press, 1990), 47.

8. Rogoziński, *Smokeless Tobacco*, 64 (France); T. J. Woofter, Jr., *The Plight of Cigarette Tobacco* (Chapel Hill: U. of North Carolina Press, 1931), 57; John C. Burnham, *Bad Habits: Drinking, Smoking, Taking Drugs, Gambling, Sexual Misbehavior, and Swearing in American History* (New York: New York U. Press, 1993), 46 (du Pont); Esther Kellner, *Moonshine: Its History and Folklore* (Indianapolis: Bobbs-Merrill, 1971), 139.

9. Ian Tyrrell, *Woman's World/Woman's Empire: The Woman's Christian Temperance Union in International Perspective, 1880–1930* (Chapel Hill: U. of North Carolina Press, 1991), 162–166, running ahead on p. 162; Jivraj N. Mehta, *Alcohol and State Revenue* (New Delhi: All India Prohibition Council, n.d.).

10. *The Collected Works of Mahatma Gandhi* (New Delhi: Ministry of Information and Broadcasting, 1966), vol. 19, pp. 285–286; vol. 20, pp. 120, 190–191, 399 (quotation); vol. 21, p. 20.

11. Sushila Nayar, *History of Prohibition in India*, rev. ed. (New Delhi: All India Prohibition Council, 1977).

12. This account draws on the following LN news sources: "The Fashion for Going Dry," *Economist*, 22 June 1996; John F. Burns, "Indian State's Alcohol Ban Pleases Women, Annoys Men," *NYT*, 18 Aug. 1996, LN; Molly Moore, "Indian Village Women Fight State, Husbands to Ban Liquor," *Washington Post*, 19 December 1993; Christopher Thomas, "Indian Wives Turn the Land Dry," *The Times*, 3 September 1996 ("maidservants"), and Thomas, "State Prepares for Drunken April Fools as Prohibition is Abandoned," *The Times*, 19 March 1998; Priya Ramani, "Indian State Fulfills Poll Promise, Bans Booze," *Reuters World Service*, 17 January 1995; Rohit Parihar, "Haryana: Tipsy-Turvy World," *India Today*, 22 September 1997; Ramesh Vinayak, "Haryana: Hic Hic Hurray," *India Today*, 30 March 1998; "Quiet Flows Liquor in Dry Haryana," *The Statesman* (India), 7 February 1998 ("don't change"); and Ian Mackinnon, "Men Sobered as India's Women Seek New Order," *The Scotsman*, 13 August 1997.

13. Paul Iredale, "Indian Matinee Idol Turned Political Leader Dies," *Reuters World Service*, 18 January 1996; R. J. Rajendra Prasad, "India: Surprise Over World Bank . . .," *The Hindu*, 27 October 1997; and three articles by D. Ravi Kanth, "U.S. $3.5 Billion Windfall—With Strings Attached," "Indian State

Driven Back to the Bottle," and "Outrage Spills Over Liquor Sale" ("bowing down to pressure"), in *Asia Times*, 4 February 1997, 25 February 1997, and 2 April 1997, all LN. "State-sponsored liquor addiction" is from Svati Bhatkal, "We do not want liquor in our village," India Network Archives, *http://www.indnet.org/art/0001.html*, 29 June 2000.

14. H. B. French, "The Price of Crude Drugs," *Pharmaceutical Era* 29 (1912): 80 (cannabis tax); Licensed Beverage Industry, "A Survey of Illegal Distilling in the U.S. Today" (TS, 1951), 23–24, folder 11, box 96, HP.

15. Morgan, *American Slavery, American Freedom*, 204, 291; Alfred Rive, "A Short History of Tobacco Smuggling," *Economic History* 1 (1926–1929): 554–569. My description of British smuggling here and in subsequent paragraphs draws on David Phillipson, *Smuggling: A History* (Newton Abbot: David and Charles, 1973), chs. 1, 4, and 5, and Geoffrey Morley, *The Smuggling War: The Government's Fight Against Smuggling in the 18th and 19th Centuries* (Stroud, Gloucestershire: Alan Sutton, 1994).

16. James Woodforde, *The Diary of a Country Parson, 1758–1802*, ed. John Beresford (London: Oxford U. Press, 1967 reprint ed.), 131. As an aside, Woodforde mentions someone drinking a glass of water—a woman who wished to express her displeasure—only once in 44 years. Its absence from the most famous diary of eighteenth-century English dietary habits underlines both the prejudice against water and the array of alternatives offered by the beverage revolution. R. G. Wilson and T. R. Gourvish, "Introduction," in *The Dynamics of the International Brewing Industry since 1800*, ed. Wilson and Gourvish (London: Routledge, 1998).

17. Henry Hobhouse, *Seeds of Change: Five Plants That Transformed Mankind* (New York: Harper and Row, 1986), 105–106; Hoh-Cheung and Lorna H. Mui, "Smuggling and the British Tea Trade before 1784," *American Historical Review* 74 (1968): 44–73; *Eighteenth Century Documents Relating to the Royal Forests, the Sheriffs, and Smuggling*, ed. Arthur Lyon Cross (New York: Macmillan, 1928), 27 (Pitt).

18. Adam Smith, *An Inquiry into the Nature and Causes of the Wealth of Nations* (New York: Modern Library, 1937), 849.

19. *Eighteenth Century Documents*, ed. Cross, ch. 3, "gainful" on p. 27; Edward Carson, *The Ancient and Rightful Customs: A History of the English Customs Service* (Hamden, Conn.: Archon, 1972), ch. 8.

20. Thomas Brennan, *Public Drinking and Popular Culture in Eighteenth-Century Paris* (Princeton: Princeton U. Press, 1988), 82–84.

21. R. Morris Coats, "A Note on Estimating Cross-Border Effects of Cigarette Taxes," *National Tax Journal* 48 (1995), LN (Virginia).

22. Graham A. MacGregor and Hugh E. de Wardener, *Salt, Diet and Health*

(Cambridge: Cambridge U. Press, 1998), 2–13, 33–50; Simon Schama, *Citizens: A Chronicle of the French Revolution* (New York: Knopf, 1989), 74–75.

23. David T. Courtwright, "Drug Legalization, the Drug War, and Drug Treatment in Historical Perspective," *J. of Policy History* 3 (1991): 393–414.

24. Jacob Sullum, *For Your Own Good: The Anti-Smoking Crusade and the Tyranny of Public Health* (New York: Free Press, 1998), 136–137; Ian Harvey, "Run for the Money," *Toronto Sun*, 12 November 1995, LN; William Marsden, "Tobacco Giant Targeted: RJR-Macdonald Hit with $1-Billion Suit by Ottawa," *Montreal Gazette*, 22 December 1999, LN.

25. World Health Organization, "The Tobacco Epidemic: A Global Public Health Emergency," *http://www.who/int/inf-fs/en/fact118.html*, 29 June 2000, p. 5; "In Colombia, Smuggling Is an Old, Old Custom," *NYT*, nat. ed., 21 November 1996, A6; Raymond Bonner, "2 Cases Shed Light on Cigarette Smuggling in Italy," *NYT*, nat. ed., 2 September 1997, C13.

9. *About-Face: Restriction and Prohibition*

1. Alan A. Block, "European Drug Traffic and Traffickers Between the Wars: The Policy of Suppression and Its Consequences," *J. of Social History* 23 (1989): 320.

2. Elizabeth Marshall Thomas, *The Tribe of Tiger* (New York: Simon and Schuster, 1994), 125 (lions); Erich Hesse, *Narcotics and Drug Addiction*, trans. Frank Gaynor (New York: Philosophical Library, 1946, first pub. 1938), 47.

3. Virginia Berridge, "Science and Policy: The Case of Postwar British Smoking Policy," and Allan M. Brandt, "Blow Some My Way: Passive Smoking, Risk and American Culture," both in *AA*, 153–154, 166–171.

4. "Los Crímenes y la Toxicomanía," 21 May 1936, trans. William O. Walker III, in *Drugs in the Western Hemisphere: An Odyssey of Cultures in Conflict*, ed. Walker (Wilmington, Del.: Scholarly Resources, 1996), 63; Gary M. Lavergne, *A Sniper in the Tower: The Charles Whitman Murders* (Denton: U. of North Texas Press, 1997), 73–75; Robert Stokes to Lawrence Kolb, 15 December 1966, KP (amphetamines found on Whitman's body).

5. Robin Room, "Alcohol Consumption and Social Harm—Conceptual Issues and Historical Perspectives," *Contemporary Drug Problems* 23 (1996): 373–388; Jacob Sullum, *For Your Own Good: The Anti-Smoking Crusade and the Tyranny of Public Health* (New York: Free Press, 1998), 128–134.

6. Jayashree Nimmagadda, "A Pilot Study of the Social Construction of the Meanings Attached to Alcohol Use: Perceptions from India," *SUM* 34 (1999): 251–267; P. K. Gode, "References to Tobacco in Marathi Literature and Records between A.D. 1600 and 1900," *Studies in Indian Cultural His-*

tory, vol. 1 (Hoshiarpur: Vishveshvaranand Vedic Research Institute, 1960), 418–426; Ahmad K. Khalifa, "Traditional Patterns of Hashish Use in Egypt," and Khwaja A. Hasan, "Social Aspects of the Use of Cannabis in India," both in *CC*, 203, 235–246; Gabriel G. Nahas, "Hashish in Islam, 9th to 18th Century," *Bulletin of the New York Academy of Medicine* 58 (1982): 814–831; and Franz Rosenthal, *The Herb: Hashish versus Medieval Muslim Society* (Leiden: E. J. Brill, 1971).

7. Gerald L. Klerman, "Psychotropic Hedonism vs. Pharmacological Calvinism," *Hastings Center Report* 2 (September 1972): 3; David T. Courtwright, "Morality, Religion, and Drug Use," in *Morality and Health*, ed. Allan M. Brandt and Paul Rozin (New York: Routledge, 1997), 231–250; Joseph Westermeyer, *Poppies, Pipes, and People: Opium and Its Use in Laos* (Berkeley: U. of California Press, 1982), 278. Representative of the empirical studies which show higher rates of abstention and anti-drug militancy among the religious is Michael E. Hilton, "Abstention in the General Population of the U.S.A.," *British Journal of Addiction* 81 (1986): 95–112.

8. Michael Pollan, "A Very Fine Line," *NYT Magazine*, 12 September 1999, 27–28 ("Hardy Boy"); Patricia G. Erickson, "The Law, Social Control, and Drug Policy: Models, Factors, and Processes," *IJA* 28 (1993): 1164.

9. Ernest M. Satow, "The Introduction of Tobacco into Japan," *Transactions of the Asiatic Society of Japan* 6 (1878): 72, 79; Anslinger speech (TS, February 1942), 1, VF "Anslinger, 1941–1950"; David F. Musto, "The Rise and Fall of Epidemics: Learning from History," in *Drugs, Alcohol, and Tobacco: Making the Policy Connections*, ed. Griffith Edwards et al. (New York: Oxford U. Press, 1993), 282 (*Pravda*); "Statistics of Narcotics Cases in Taiwan Issued," *Chung-yang Jih-pao*, 6 December 1972, p. 3, trans. in VF "China"; Peter T. White, "The Poppy," *National Geographic* 167 (February 1985): 160–161 (Iran).

10. Box 56, Richmond P. Hobson Papers, LC; "Drug Problem Becoming More Acute," *L'Unita*, 12 November 1976, p. 4, trans. in VF "Addiction—Incidence; Countries, 1976–1977"; Urban Weber and Werner Schneider, "Syringe Exchange in Germany," *SUM* 33 (1998): 1098–1099; L. Sanchez, "The Drug Problem in Venezuela" (TS, 1971), VF "Addiction—Incidence; Countries [to] 1973"; Walter C. Bailey and Mary Koval, "Drug Use among White and Nonwhite College Activists" (TS, 1970), 21 (quotation), VF "Addiction—Incidence, 1970–1972."

11. Carl A. Trocki, *Opium and Empire: Chinese Society in Colonial Singapore, 1800–1910* (Ithaca: Cornell U. Press, 1990), 203.

12. W. J. Rorabaugh, *The Alcoholic Republic: An American Tradition* (New York: Oxford U. Press, 1979), 61–92, 232–233; Esther Kellner, *Moonshine: Its His-*

tory and Folklore (Indianapolis: Bobbs-Merrill, 1971), 64; Patricia E. Prestwich, *Drink and the Politics of Social Reform: Antialcoholism in France Since 1870* (Palo Alto: Society for the Promotion of Science and Scholarship, 1988), 5.

13. Benjamin Rush, *Essays, Literary, Moral and Philosophical* (Philadelphia: Thomas and Samuel F. Branford, 1798), 272; Stephen R. Smith, "Alcohol in Japanese Society," *Social History of Alcohol Review*, nos. 34–35 (Spring/Fall 1997): 38; James H. Timberlake, *Prohibition and the Progressive Movement* (Cambridge, Mass.: Harvard U. Press, 1966), ch. 3.

14. Ian R. Tyrrell, "Temperance and Economic Change in the Antebellum North," in *Alcohol, Reform and Society: The Liquor Issue in Social Context*, ed. Jack S. Blocker, Jr. (Westport, Conn.: Greenwood Press, 1979), 45–67.

15. Lilian Lewis Shiman, *Crusade against Drink in Victorian England* (New York: St. Martin's Press, 1988), 2, 47 (Norwich); Ron Chernow, *Titan: The Life of John D. Rockefeller, Sr.* (New York: Random House, 1998), quotation on p. 190.

16. Charles Ambler and Jonathan Crush, "Alcohol in Southern African History," and Pamela Scully, "Liquor and Labor in the Western Cape," in *Liquor and Labor in Southern Africa*, ed. Crush and Ambler (Athens, Ohio: Ohio University Press, 1992), 1–55, 56–77; Leslie London, "The 'Dop' System . . . in South Africa," *Social Science and Medicine* 48 (1999): 1407–1414.

17. Jack S. Blocker, *American Temperance Movements: Cycles of Reform* (Boston: Twayne, 1989), 68–69, quotation on p. 69.

18. Madelon Powers, *Faces along the Bar: Lore and Order in the Workingman's Saloon, 1870–1920* (Chicago: U. of Chicago Press, 1998), 234–235 (decline of saloon); Ivor Montagu, *Film World: A Guide to the Cinema* (Harmondsworth: Penguin, 1964), 221 (go to the local); John Burnett, *Liquid Pleasures: A Social History of Drinks in Modern Britain* (London: Routledge, 1999), 172–173 (1920s and 1930s); Peter Miskell, "Seduced by the Silver Screen: Attitudes to Addictive Cinema Attendance in Britain, 1918–1951," paper presented at the Business of Addiction Workshop, University of Reading, 11 December 1999 (avid).

19. Susanna Barrows and Robin Room, "Introduction," in *Drinking: Behavior and Belief in Modern History*, ed. Barrows and Room (Berkeley: U. of California Press, 1991), 13–14; Ronny Ambjörnsson, "The Honest and Diligent Worker," *http://www.skeptron.ilu.uu.se/broady/sec/ske-5.htm*, 26 June 1998.

20. Tek Chand, *History's Verdict on Bachhus [sic]* (Amritsar: Guru Nanak University, 1974), 21.

21. "A Pestilential Drug," article from *San Francisco Chronicle* reprinted in *The Pharmacist* 10 (1877): 115; Desmond Manderson, *From Mr. Sin to Mr. Big: A*

History of Australian Drug Laws (Melbourne: Oxford U. Press, 1993), chs. 1–2; Teishiro Kawamura, "Concerning the Opium Law of Japan," *Pharmaceutical Era* 53 (1920): 37–38; Terry M. Parssinen, *Secret Passions, Secret Remedies: Narcotic Drugs in British Society, 1820–1930* (Philadelphia: Institute for the Study of Human Issues, 1983), ch. 9; Virginia Berridge, *Opium and the People: Opiate Use and Drug Control Policy in Nineteenth and Early Twentieth Century England* (London: Free Association Books, 1999), ch. 18.

22. Thomas R. Pegram, *Battling Demon Rum: The Struggle for a Dry America, 1800–1933* (Chicago: Ivan R. Dee, 1998), 144–147; Bentley Brinkerhoff Gilbert, *David Lloyd George, a Political Life: Organizer of Victory, 1912–1916* (Columbus: Ohio State U. Press, 1992), 162; Burnett, *Liquid Pleasures*, 172–173 (consumption decline); David M. Fahey, "The Decline of Prohibition in English Politics, 1895–1921," paper presented at the American Historical Association meeting, January 1997 (George V).

23. Samuel Hopkins Adams, "On Sale Everywhere," *Colliers* 68 (16 July 1921): 7.

24. John J. Rumbarger, *Profits, Power, and Prohibition: Alcohol Reform and the Industrializing of America, 1800–1930* (Albany: State University of New York Press, 1989); Selden D. Bacon, "Alcohol and Complex Society," in *Society, Culture, and Drinking Patterns*, ed. David J. Pittman and Charles R. Snyder (Carbondale: Southern Illinois U. Press, 1962), 78–93.

25. C. M. Ford, "Cocaine Not an Essential," *Pharmaceutical Era* 45 (February 1912): 146; A. E. Gundry to A. D. Wilcox, 22 May 1901, correspondence folder Jan.–June 1901, History of Temperance collection, MS 645, KSHS; "The Treatment of Coughs without Diagnosis" (TS, 1909), 3, box 6, folder 1, Francis Edward Stewart Papers, State Historical Society of Wisconsin.

26. Roy Porter, *The Greatest Benefit to Mankind: A Medical History of Humanity* (New York: Norton, 1997), 427 (TB decline).

27. James H. Cassedy, *American Medicine and Statistical Thinking, 1800–1860* (Cambridge, Mass.: Harvard U. Press, 1984), 50 (Cartwright); Norman Kerr, *Inebriety or Narcomania: Its Etiology, Pathology, Treatment, and Jurisprudence*, 3rd ed. (London: H. K. Lewis, 1894), 576 (Madras); Kellner, *Moonshine*, 75.

28. New Zealand Alliance for the Abolition of the Liquor Traffic, *Three Reasons Why a Young Man Should Abstain* (n.c., pamphlet, ca. 1930); Sir Richard Doll, "The First Reports on Smoking and Lung Cancer," in *AA*, 135; Spencer Rich, "Substance Abuse Costly, Study of Medicaid Finds," *Washington Post*, 16 July 1993, A2; Allan M. Brandt, "Behavior, Disease, and Health in the Twentieth-Century United States," in *Morality and Health*, ed. Brandt and Rozin, 53–77.

29. H. H. Kane, "The Rapid Spread of the Morphia Habit . . . in Germany," *Maryland Medical J.* 8 (1881): 339.

30. Lawson Crowe, "Alcohol and Heredity: Theories About the Effects of Alcohol Use on Offspring," *Social Biology* 32 (1985): 146–161; David F. Musto, "Cocaine's History, Especially the American Experience," in *Cocaine: Scientific and Social Dimensions* (Chichester, England: Wiley, 1992), 9; Joanne Woiak, "Drunkenness, Degeneration, and Eugenics in Britain," paper presented at the American Association for the History of Medicine meeting, Toronto, 8 May 1998 (Saleeby).

31. T. D. Crothers, "A Review of the History and Literature of Inebriety," *J. of Inebriety* 33 (1912): 143 (infidel); Harry Gene Levine, "The Discovery of Addiction: Changing Conceptions of Habitual Drunkenness in America," *J. of Studies on Alcohol* 3 (1978): 143–174, Gough on p. 49; Didier Nourrison, "Tabagisme et Antitabagisme en France au XIXe Siècle," *Histoire, Economie, et Société* 7 (1988): 541.

32. Norman Kerr, *Wines: Scriptural and Ecclesiastical,* 2nd ed. (London: National Temperance Publication Depot, 1887), 2; A[lexander] MacAlister, "Food," *A Dictionary of the Bible,* vol. 2 (New York: Charles Scribner's Sons, 1902), 34 ("pleading").

33. A. E. Moule, "The Use of Opium and Its Bearing on the Spread of Christianity in China," *Records of the General Conference of the Protestant Missionaries in China Held at Shanghai, May 10–24, 1877* (Shanghai: Presbyterian Mission Press, 1878), 362 ("Christian sin"); Roger V. Des Forges, *Hsi-Liang and the Chinese National Revolution* (New Haven: Yale U. Press, 1973), 94 (Chang); Kathleen L. Lodwick, *Crusaders Against Opium: Protestant Missionaries in China, 1874–1917* (Lexington: U. of Kentucky Press, 1996); William O. Walker III, *Opium and Foreign Policy: The Anglo American Search for Order in Asia, 1912 1954* (Chapel Hill: U. of North Carolina Press, 1991), 14 (students).

34. J. F. Richards, "The Indian Empire and Peasant Production of Opium in the Nineteenth Century," *Modern Asian Studies* 15 (1981): 69.

35. John M. Jennings, *The Opium Empire: Japanese Imperialism and Drug Trafficking in Asia, 1895–1945* (Westport, Conn.: Praeger, 1997), 45 (Nitan'osa); Kathryn Meyer and Terry Parssinen, *Webs of Smoke: Smugglers, Warlords, Spies, and the History of the International Drug Trade* (Lanham, Md.: Rowman and Littlefield, 1998); Alfred W. McCoy, *The Politics of Heroin: CIA Complicity in the Global Drug Trade* (New York: Lawrence Hill, 1991); Paul Lowinger, "How the People's Republic of China Solved the Drug Abuse Problem," *American J. of Chinese Medicine* 1 (1973): 275–282; BBC

transcription of address by Yui Lei, 22 March 1992, VF "China" (cross-border traffic).

36. William B. McAllister, *Drug Diplomacy in the Twentieth Century: An International History* (London: Routledge, 2000), esp. part I. My summary of the Chinese situation and its diplomatic consequences derives from McAllister; Walker, *Opium and Foreign Policy*, chs. 1–2; and Meyer and Parssinen, *Webs of Smoke*.

10. Licit and Illicit Drugs

1. Jasper Becker, "Final Reckoning for Big Spender," *South China Morning Post*, 6 Dec. 1998, and Calum Macleod, "Executions Hit New High in China's Drugs [sic] Wars," *The Independent*, 28 June 2000, both LN. The regulatory categories are adapted from Robert MacCoun et al., "Assessing Alternative Drug Control Regimes," *J. of Policy Analysis and Management* 15 (1996): 331–335.

2. "40,000 Barrels of Whiskey," *Baltimore Sun*, 3 September 1925, unpaginated reprint, MTE, and George Griffenhagen, "Medicinal Liquor in the United States," *Pharmacy in History* 29 (1987): 31.

3. John Uri Lloyd, *Coffee* (reprint of 1929 *Eclectic Medical Journal* series), 7, KRF C39(g): Coffee ("nerve-wrecked"); Mary B. Ballou to Selden Ballou, 30 October 1852, Western Americana Collection, Beinecke Library, Yale University ("strong enough"); Wolfgang Schivelbusch, *Tastes of Paradise: A Social History of Spices, Stimulants, and Intoxicants*, trans. David Jacobson (New York: Pantheon, 1992), ch. 2; McCann quoted in Stephen Braun, *Buzz: The Science and Lore of Alcohol and Caffeine* (New York: Oxford U. Press, 1996), 137.

4. Joel Greenberg, "Who in Israel Loves the Orthodox? Their Grocers," *NYT*, nat. ed., 17 October 1997, A4; Sen Sōshitsu XV, *The Japanese Way of Tea: From Its Origins in China to Sen Rikyū*, trans. V. Dixon Morris (Honolulu: U. of Hawaii Press, 1998), 75 ("devil of sleep"); Simon Paulli, *A Treatise on Tobacco, Tea, Coffee and Chocolate*, trans. [Robert] James (London: T. Osborne, 1746; first pub. 1665), 48 (confessional); Vincent M. Hendriks et al., "A 'Parliamentary Inquiry' into Alcohol and Drugs: A Survey of Psychoactive Substance Use and Gambling among Members of the Dutch Parliament," *SUM* 32 (1997): 684.

5. Maurice Seevers, "Drug Addiction," in *Pharmacology in Medicine*, 2nd ed., ed. Victor A. Drill (New York: McGraw-Hill, 1958), ch. 19; Lawrence Kolb to John Presmont, 1 November 1957, KP.

6. Edward M. Brecher, *Licit and Illicit Drugs* (Boston: Little, Brown, 1972).

7. Patricia E. Prestwich, *Drink and the Politics of Social Reform: Antialcoholism in France Since 1870* (Palo Alto: Society for the Promotion of Science and Scholarship, 1988), 18; David Christian, *Living Water: Vodka and Russian Society on the Eve of Emancipation* (Oxford: Clarendon Press, 1990), 6 (military budget). The core/periphery distinction is from Immanuel Wallerstein, *The Modern World-System*, vol. 1: *Capitalist Agriculture and the Origins of the European World-Economy in the Sixteenth Century* (New York: Academic Press, 1974).

8. Sidsel Eriksen, "The Making of the Danish Liberal Drinking Style: The Construction of 'Wet' Alcohol Discourse in Denmark," *Contemporary Drug Problems* 20 (1993): 1–31.

9. William B. McAllister, *Drug Diplomacy in the Twentieth Century: An International History* (London: Routledge, 2000), 36–37, 128.

10. Richard Kluger, *Ashes to Ashes: America's Hundred-Year Cigarette War, the Public Health, and the Unabashed Triumph of Philip Morris* (New York: Knopf, 1996), 263; Jordan Goodman, *Tobacco in History: The Cultures of Dependence* (London: Routledge, 1993), 9 (100 million).

   Kluger thinks there were "close to 70 million" smokers in 1964. This apparently includes an estimate, by unspecified means, of under-18 smokers. The official prevalence figure for the 18-and-over population (42.4 percent in 1965) yields 52 million adult smokers—still a hefty number.

11. "ACLU Linked to Tobacco," *National Law J.*, 25 November 1996, LN.

12. Lester Grinspoon and James B. Bakalar, *Marijuana, the Forbidden Medicine* (New Haven: Yale U. Press, 1993), 14.

13. Goodman, *Tobacco in History*, 78; Kathleen L. Lodwick, *Crusaders Against Opium: Protestant Missionaries in China, 1874–1917* (Lexington: University of Kentucky Press, 1996), 164–165.

14. Michael Kernan, "Turning the World Off," *Washington Post*, 5 October 1971, B1, B5 (Anslinger quotation); Harvey W. Wiley, "The Alcohol and Drug Habit and Its Prophylaxis," *Proceedings of the Second Pan American Scientific Congress*, vol. 9 (Washington, D.C.: G. P. O., 1917), 150.

15. Sir Richard Doll, "The First Reports on Smoking and Lung Cancer," in *AA*, 131, 141 (quotation); John C. Burnham, "American Physicians and Tobacco Use: Two Surgeons General, 1929 and 1964," *Bulletin of the History of Medicine* 63 (1989): 13, and Burnham, *Bad Habits: Drinking, Smoking, Taking Drugs, Gambling, Sexual Misbehavior, and Swearing in American History* (New York: New York U. Press, 1993), chs. 1, 9, Brown/movies on p. 37.

16. Stephen White, *Russia Goes Dry: Alcohol, State and Society* (Cambridge: Cambridge U. Press, 1996), ch. 1, Semashko on p. 17, Trotsky on p. 18, Stalin on p. 27.

17. White, *Russia Goes Dry*, ch. 2; Vladimir G. Treml, *Alcohol in the USSR: A Statistical Study* (Durham, N.C.: Duke U. Press, 1982), 56 (sugar); Mikhail Gorbachev, *Memoirs* (New York: Doubleday, 1995), 219–222.

18. Steve Lohr, "Vladimir A. Yamnikov, 56, Premium Russian Vodka Maker," *NYT*, nat. ed., 3 February 1997, A15.

19. White, *Russia Goes Dry*, chs. 3–7, "without beer" on p. 119, "Chernobyl" on p. 139; Yegor Ligachev, *Inside Gorbachev's Kremlin* (New York: Pantheon, 1993), 335–339. Note that Ligachev disputes the destruction of vineyards, but both Gorbachev and White affirm it. For policy under Nicholas II, see J. F. Hutchinson, "Science, Politics and the Alcohol Problem in post-1905 Russia," *Slavonic and East European Review* 58 (1980): 232–254.

20. David A. Leon et al., "Huge Variation in Russian Mortality Rates, 1984–1994: Artefact, Alcohol, or What?" *Lancet* 350 (1997): 383–388; Michael Specter, "Needing Taxes, Yeltsin Takes on a Religion of the Russians: Vodka," *NYT*, nat. ed., 21 January 1997, A1, A3; Robert B. Davis, "Drug and Alcohol Use in the Former Soviet Union: Selected Factors and Future Considerations," *IJA* 29 (1994): 303–323, "birthright" on p. 304.

21. United Nations, International Drug Control Programme, *The Social and Economic Impact of Drug Abuse and Control* (United Nations position paper, 1994), 40 (Pakistan); Salil Panchal, "Ragpickers—Biggest Drug Addicts' Group," *Times of India*, 20 August 1990, VF "India;" Yong Zhou and Xiaoming Li, "Demographic Characteristics and Illegal Drug Use Patterns among Attendees of Drug Cessation Programs in China," *SUM* 34 (1999): 907–920.

22. Allen Fields and James M. Walters, "Hustling: Supporting a Heroin Habit," in *Life with Heroin: Voices from the Inner City*, ed. Bill Hanson et al. (Lexington, Mass.: Lexington Books, 1985), 58 (IBM typewriter); Carl S. Taylor, *Dangerous Society* (East Lansing: Michigan State U. Press, 1990), 45 ("What's wrong?").

23. Peter Reuter, "Why Can't We Make Prohibition Work Better?" *Proceedings of the American Philosophical Society* 141 (1997): 264 (drug-war cost, prisoners) and Reuter, "The Mismeasurement of Illegal Drug Markets," in *Exploring the Underground Economy*, ed. Susan Pozo (Kalamazoo: W. E. Upjohn Institute, 1996), 63 (50 billion dollars). Michael Massing, *The Fix* (New York: Simon and Schuster, 1998), offers a concise account of the origins and politics of the drug war.

24. "Poll Shows Citizens of Vienna are in Favour of a Restrictive Drugs Policy," *http://mn.medstroms.se/cgi-bin/hassela/hpr-e.sh?p9701087.txt*, 30 July 1997.

25. Robert H. Bork, *The Tempting of America: The Political Seduction of the Law* (New York: Free Press, 1990), 123; Massing, *The Fix*, 11.

26. Joseph B. Treaster, "Some Think the War on Drugs Is Being Waged on the Wrong Front," *NYT*, nat. ed., 28 July 1992, A8 (Conyers); Desmond Manderson, *From Mr. Sin to Mr. Big: A History of Australian Drug Laws* (Melbourne: Oxford U. Press, 1993), 193; Christopher S. Wren, "$1 Million Gift for Needles Is a Lifesaver, Financier Says, Not a Ruse to Legalize Drugs," *NYT*, 17 August 1997, LN (Soros).

27. David Boyum, "The Distributive Politics of Drug Policy," *Drug Policy Analysis Bulletin*, no. 4 (February 1998): 3–4.

28. Robert L. DuPont, *The Selfish Brain: Learning from Addiction* (Washington, D.C.: American Psychiatric Press, 1997), ch. 12; Wayne Hall, "Appraisals of the Adverse Health Effects of Cannabis Use: Ideology and Evidence," *Drug Policy Analysis Bulletin*, no. 7 (June 1999): 1–2. Representative of the harm-reduction case is Don C. Des Jarlais, "Harm Reduction—A Framework for Incorporating Science into Drug Policy," *American J. of Public Health* 85 (1995): 10–12.

29. World Health Organization, "Report on the Global HIV/AIDS Epidemic, June 1998," *http://www.who.ch/emc-hiv/globalreport/rep_html/report5.html*, 31 July 1998; Robert Haemmig, "Harm Reduction in Bern: From Outreach to Heroin Maintenance," *Bulletin of the New York Academy of Medicine* 72 (1995): 371–379; and Robert MacCoun and Peter Reuter, "Drug Control," in *The Handbook of Crime and Punishment*, ed. Michael Tonry (New York: Oxford U. Press, 1998), 226.

30. Goodman, *Tobacco in History*, 243 (1.5 billion); "Tobacco Control Can Prevent Millions of Deaths Worldwide," *M2 Presswire*, 19 May 1999, LN (World Bank); "Nonsmoking Sections for Hostages," *NYT*, nat. ed., 6 January 1997, A3.

31. Ron Roizen, "How Does the Nation's 'Alcohol Problem' Change from Era to Era?" and John Slade, "Changes in the Clinical Perceptions of Tobacco Addiction since 1890," papers presented at the Conference on Historical Perspectives on Alcohol and Drug Use in American Society, College of Physicians of Philadelphia, May 1997 (AA founders); "Survey of Medical Opinion" (TS, 1955), box 111, folder 6, HP (pediatrician). Mark A. R. Kleiman, *Against Excess: Drug Policy for Results* (New York: Basic Books, 1992), is a leading example of the "convergence" school of drug policy.

32. Thomas C. Schelling, "Addictive Drugs: The Cigarette Experience," *Science* 255 (1992): 431.

33. David J. Pittman, "What Do We Know about Beneficial Consequences of Moderate Alcohol Consumption on Social and Physical Well-Being? A Critical Review of the Recent Literature," *Contemporary Drug Problems* 23 (1996): 389–406.

34. "Cigarette Smoking: Health Issues for Smokers," *http://www.philipmorris.com/tobacco_bus/tobacco_issues/health_issues.html*, 13 October 1999.
35. "High and Hooked," *The Economist* 327 (15 May 1993): 105 (three-quarters); Virginia Berridge, "Science and Policy: The Case of Postwar British Smoking Policy," in *AA*, 156.
36. Daniel Bell, *The Cultural Contradictions of Capitalism* (New York: Basic Books, 1976), 13–14.

Illustration Credits

page 12   KRF P14(a). Cf. R. J. Forbes, *Short History of the Art of Distillation* (Leiden: E. J. Brill, 1948), 93, 109. Brunschwig's name is spelled variously.

page 17   Fairfax Downey, *Lorillard and Tobacco* (n.c.: P. Lorillard, 1951), 8.

page 24   This copy of the *Tractatus* is from CPPL. The work, whose English title is *The Manner of Making Coffee, Tea, and Chocolate,* is attributed to Philippe Sylvestre Dufour and/or the French Protestant physician Jacques Spon. The latter is variously described as Dufour's assistant, translator, or the book's sole author. Cf. *The National Union Catalog: Pre-1956 Imprints,* vol. 150 (London: Mansell, 1971), 540–541, and R. Desgenettes, "Spon (Jacques)," *Dictionaire des Sciences Médicales: Biographie Médicale,* vol. 7 (Paris: C. L. F. Panckoucke, 1825), 248.

page 29   LC, British Cartoon Collection.

page 47   KRF P39(g): coca; promotional quotation from Mariani Collection, MTE.

page 49   KRF A2: Rusby.

page 63   LC, Prints and Photographs Division; quotation from Everard's *Panacea; or the Universal Medicine, Being a Discovery of the Wonderful Vertues of Tobacco . . .* (London: Simon Miller, 1659; first pub. in Latin in 1587), 17.

page 74   KRF P39(k) I: Proprietary; Boise from biographical scrapbook, vol. 7, KSHS.

page 76   *Harper's Weekly* 27 (15 September 1883): 592.

page 88   Quotation from J. M. Flagler, "Drugs and Mysticism: The Visions of 'Saint Tim,'" *Look* 31 (8 August 1967): 18; photograph by James Karales, used with permission and the following memory: "Those people were nuts."

Index